Recession, Crime and Punishment

Also by Steven Box

DEVIANCE, REALITY AND SOCIETY
POWER, CRIME AND MYSTIFICATION

Recession, Crime and Punishment

Steven Box

**MACMILLAN
EDUCATION**

First published 1987

Published by
MACMILLAN EDUCATION LTD
Houndmills, Basingstoke, Hampshire RG21 2XS
and London
Companies and representatives
throughout the world

Printed in Hong Kong

British Library Cataloguing in Publication Data
Box, Steven
Recession, crime and punishment.
1. Crime and criminals—Social aspects
I. Title
364. 2'56   HV6155
ISBN 0-333-43852-3 (hardcover)
ISBN 0-333-43853-1 (paperback)

For Patricia

Contents

Preface

If Weber didn't say 'sociology starts off disenchanting the world and ends up disenchanting its practitioners', he should have. For the longer one considers society, the more difficult it is to resist an invitingly cynical conclusion: it is a 'confidence trick'. Durkheim sensitised us to this when he pointed out that social order cannot be maintained by giving people what they want – that would be impossible – but by persuading them that what they have is just about all they deserve morally. And of course, in a society like ours, which pontificates about equality, freedom and human rights, even whilst encouraging enormous differences in the distribution of income and even more in wealth, the problem of persuading those who haven't got very much to regard it as 'just about right' poses a constant headache. Well, to be more accurate, it poses a headache for those trying to pull off this 'confidence trick', who, by pure coincidence, as Vonnegut would say, happen to be earning and owning a great deal and *naturally* don't want to be separated from it.

Fortunately for them, when the economy is expanding, most people's attention can be diverted from these enormous material inequalities by giving them a little of the enlarging cake. If a majority of people experience some improvement in their living standards, then the comfort of relative contentment seems to cloud their vision of those at the top and makes them indifferent to a small disreputable bunch beneath them – although it needs to be added that the media, including educational institutions, try to fill people's heads with 'fairy stories' about the rich deserving their wealth because of the energy, risk-taking, creativity and, above all, the sacrifice they made earlier in life to acquire qualifications. Those who object to this rosy self-serving story can be stigmatised easily as 'wicked', 'lazy', 'communists', 'nutters', 'criminals', 'jealous', 'anarchists' and 'envious', and dealt with accordingly. Since these 'outsiders' are only a minority, posing no serious threat to discipline or to law and order, controlling them raises few difficulties and the state need not reveal too much of its unacceptable coercive face. The rich can carry on accumulating wealth under the benign smiling face of consensus which brings a contented workforce to their places of employment and leaves a few at home to stew in their personal inadequacies.

It is indeed a wonderful racket. Well, almost. It tends to come unstuck, as it is currently, when the economy is in a prolonged recession. For over the last decade or so, workers were replaced by labour-saving machinery, the numbers unemployed and unemployable grew to an ugly size, the welfare system bled from a thousand cuts, wages failed to keep pace with inflation or were reduced, sometimes below legal minimum levels, and many full-time workers became part-time. One outcome was widening income inequalities: the poor simply got poorer. Under these conditions, it has been harder to sustain the 'myth' that capitalism is not only good at creating wealth, but it is also good at distributing it – particularly when those shouldering most of the recession's burdens were not doing that well before, while the wealthy continue almost untouched by what a Cabinet minister described conveniently as 'economic misfortunes no national government can control'.

This book considers one major response adopted by some of those suffering from the worst ravages of recession, namely resistance, including criminal activity. In particular, it considers reasons why the unemployed and economically marginalised might turn to property offences, and evaluates the evidence on this possibility. It also examines how governments deal with this potential resistance, particularly by allowing the social control system to expand both at the *hard* end (prisons) and the *soft* end ('community treatment'). It draws almost exclusively from the evidence in the UK and the USA but does consider the applicability of major arguments to other industrialised countries. Chapters 2, 4 and 5 are devoted to theoretical issues, such as 'why' recession leads to more crime, and 'why' the government and minor state officials produce more repression as the economy slumps. Chapters 3 and 6 contain evaluations of the relevant research. For the layreader, these two chapters may be too lengthy and tedious – maybe a quick glance with a longer stop over the conclusions would be in order. But for the serious student, there is no such quick and easy route to knowledge. As Lewis Carroll, on one of his off-days, might have put it very succinctly:

Don't Hunt in the Dark

The moment is due, the Criminologist knew,
As the view from his room was a mess.
So he set boldly forth, and studied in the North,
To uncover 'the truth', nothing less.

He beavered away, for a night and a day,
Reading journals, both ancient and new,
Till in the end, near 'round the bend',
He discovered a 'secret' or two.

'Should unemployment rise, to an enormous size,
And the poor get poorer too,
Then crime will increase, and harmony cease,
It's as clear as the sky is blue.'

'Build prisons', they say, 'to put them away,
Till their thieving is over and done'.
But he informed them thrice, although it's not nice,
'That's like burying your head in The Sun!'

He'll tell it all now, and then take a bow,
So listen! allow him to plead,
'No need for those walls, or disciplinary tools,
Its just fairer shares that you need.'

Now's an opportune time, to put this in rhyme,
And capture 'the truth' for a day.
'Don't hunt in the dark, not even for snark,
You'll never make progress that way.'

In preparing this book, I have been dogged by the usual round of domestic duties which seem, in an age of 'female liberation', to have expanded out of all proportion to my abilities. In addition to these intrusions, I have had my 'collar felt' by P. C. Edwards on more occasions than I care to remember. Hopefully, with her recent semi-transfer from a social control bureaucracy to a 'Seat of Learning', she may cease this arresting habit.

Chris Hale, with whom I have collaborated previously, would have been an enthusiastic and positive contributor to this project, but he cleared off to China in hot pursuit of the ancient Pot of Gold. A variety of 'friends' in the 'invisible college' of critical/radical/realistic criminology communicated their gratefulness for receiving a draft manuscript and then the lines went curiously dead. I've assumed it's something to do with the inefficiency of British Telecom under privatisation. On the positive side, it is nice to belong to a department of sociology on which the University Grants Committee pinned the equivalent of a Michelin three-star rosette, even if the methods of arriving at this decision were bizarre to say the least.

Finally, in addition to driving me round the vineyards of Burgundy, Michael Lane and Joan Busfield diligently ploughed their way through wine merchants' catalogues and located some delightful bargains. Without the sustenance derived from these strenuous efforts, this project could never have been completed. When your domestic life is chaotic, and your academic friends have not got time to whisper a word of advice in your ear, there's nothing like a bottle (or two) of Grand Cru Chablis to help you through the working day. It is more than a pity that a large section of the British and American population cannot afford their favourite tipple.

Rutherford College STEVEN BOX
University of Kent

1 The Lost World of the Sixties

Even without looking through the sanitary prism of nostalgia, it is easy to see that some things *really* were better twenty or so years ago. There was consensus that 'full employment' should be maintained, the principle of reducing income inequalities occupied a space on the political agenda, and the idea of reducing the prison population by encouraging alternatives in the community was taken seriously. Others may remember the Sixties differently, but it is hard to imagine that any person, sensitive to human suffering and hardship, could be indifferent to or not grieve over the disappearance of these modest liberal objectives.

Fewer people were unemployed

In 1965, the Beatles thought Strawberry Fields would last forever. The knowledge that only a handful of Britains were unemployed (328,000, or 1.4 per cent of the workforce) may have contributed to this sense of optimism. In the USA that year, while Bob Dylan revisited Highway 61, the total unemployed was 3.4 million (or 4.4 per cent of the labour force). Not only did these proportionately small numbers of unemployed persons have the joy of pleasant music, but they did not expect to be listening to it from 9 to 5 for long. In Britain, job vacancies more or less matched the number registered as unemployed. This high unemployment/vacancies ratio enabled people to lose one job and obtain another within a matter of weeks. Of those unemployed in the summer of 1965 one-quarter had only been without work for two weeks and a further quarter for less than two months. Over two-thirds could expect realistically to be back in work before Christmas that year.

1

The US unemployment rate may have been double the UK rate, but the average duration of unemployment was under twelve weeks. Nine out of every ten people made unemployed in June 1965 were working again before the New Year. In those halcyon days before monetarism mesmerised politicians, Keynes was not a dirty six-letter word. The Kennedy–Johnson administrations and the Wilson government were 'interventionalists', committed to managing the economy to maintain 'full employment'.

Alas, all that is no more. The recession since the mid-1970s has transformed this rosy landscape into a polluted dump. The British official unemployment figure by the end of 1985 reached 3.28 million, which was *ten times* higher than twenty years previous. However, even this frightening total is an undercount because Ministers of Employment since 1979 have altered the counting procedures to massage the figure gently downwards. The Unemployment Unit, which publishes data comparable to that produced by the previous counting procedures, calculated that the total stood at 3.72 million (or nearly 15 per cent – *one in seven* – of the labour force). Even this omits nearly 500,000 young people on various temporary 'training' schemes, such as Community Programmes and Youth Training Schemes. So by the beginning of 1986, the total unemployed in the UK pressed hard up against, or even spilled over, the 4 million barrier. Such a total out of work would have been unthinkable twenty years ago; then, there was a comforting and, as it turned out, naive conviction that any government allowing unemployment to race past that necessary to oil friction between parts of the economy would be swept from office by a morally outraged electorate. Yet the unimaginable happened, not only in the UK but also in the USA. By the end of 1983, there were nearly 11 million unemployed American citizens, or *one in ten* of the potential workforce. The difference, however, is that the American government, no doubt shocked by the ravaging effects of monetarism, reflated the economy and engineered the 'official' total unemployed down to around 8.5 million, although that still represents *one in fourteen* out of work by the end of 1985. However, some of this reduction is more illusion than real. There is more than a suspicion that the 'official' unemployment rate is manipulated downward, presumably for political reasons. For example, according to Cunniff (1983), an Associated Press business analyst:

The Bureau of Labor Statistics announced a decline in the jobless rate to 10.2 per cent in January from 10.8 per cent in December, creating confidence in and beyond the White House . . . however . . . the number of jobs didn't rise at all . . [and] . . . the number of jobless actually rose to 12,517,000 from 11,628,000.

A major proximate reason for these high levels of unemployment is that fewer jobs are available. Using UK Department of Employment estimates of the proportion of vacancies recorded by Jobcentres, it was possible for the Unemployment Unit to report that 'by the late 1985 the average number of vacancies in the U.K. economy in each month would be approximately 480,000, or *one for every seven unemployed claimants*' (*Statistical Supplement*, Nov. 1985).

The typical unemployed Briton therefore no longer expected re-employment within a matter of days or weeks at the most. Of those unemployed at the end of 1985, 40 per cent (or 1.5 million) had been so for more than one year and a further 20 per cent had been on the register for between six months to one year. Whereas the typical unemployed Briton in the mid-Sixties was between jobs, now that person is literally between being employed once (if at all) and being *unemployable*.

A similar, though less pronounced, pattern occurred in the USA. Between 1965 and 1983 the average duration of unemployment nearly doubled from eleven to twenty weeks, and the proportion unemployed for half a year increased from 10.4 to 23.9 per cent. Undoubtedly a major reason for this was the substantial drop in the number of vacant jobs. The US Employment Service received 724 new vacancies per month in 1965, but by 1983, when there were three times as many people unemployed, it received only 541, a drop of 25 per cent (US *Statistical Abstracts*, 1985, p. 409).

Not only were more and more unemployed Britons and Americans being transformed from 'temporary' to 'long term', but another significant change accentuated this shift. It would be out of place to talk of unemployment in the Sixties as a *burden* unevenly shared among the population. But it would be incongruous not to do so now. Unemployment is a long-term *burden* involving financial hardship, psychological trauma, marital tension and interpersonal disharmony, and it is a *burden* unevenly shared out. It is primarily experienced by youth, especially young ethnic minority males, and by semi-/un-skilled workers and inner-city dwellers. The rates of unemployment, and particularly long-term unemployment, experienced by these groups are grotesque. At the end of 1985, 1 in 4 British males and 1 in 5 females aged 18–24 were unemployed. Nearly one-quarter of the long-term unemployed were young males and just over one-third were young females. Both these rates are higher than would be expected if unemployment, temporary or long-term, occurred randomly throughout age cohorts.

A similar pattern exists in the USA. The unemployment rate in 1983 for white males aged 16–19 was *twice* that of white males aged 20–24 and *triple* that of older white males. These differences between age and unemployment are just as marked for American blacks and Hispanics (see Table 1.1).

Table 1.1   *Males unemployed in the labour force by race and age (rates)*

	Ages 16 to 19			Ages 20 to 24			Ages 25 and over		
	Whites	Hispanics	Blacks	Whites	Hispanics	Blacks	Whites	Hispanics	Blacks
1978	13.5	19.7	36.7	7.7	9.4	21.0	3.0	5.6	6.8
1979	13.9	17.5	34.2	7.5	9.2	18.7	2.9	5.0	7.2
1980	16.2	21.6	37.5	11.1	12.3	23.7	4.2	7.3	9.9
1981	17.9	24.3	40.7	11.6	14.2	26.4	4.5	7.5	10.6
1982	21.7	31.2	48.9	14.3	18.3	31.5	6.7	10.5	14.8
1983	20.2	28.7	48.8	13.8	17.1	31.4	6.9	11.1	15.2

Source: US Department of Labor.

Besides age, ethnic group membership is another major factor associated with unemployment. The unemployment rate for ethnic groups in Britain was estimated by the *Labour Force Survey* 1984 and reported in the *Employment Gazette* (Dec. 1985). According to this survey, 29 per cent of West Indians compared with 11.0 per cent of whites were unemployed in spring 1984. When ethnic origin is compounded with age, the disparities in unemployment are shocking, to say the least. As can be seen from Figure 1.1, the unemployment rate for West Indian males aged 16–24 was 42 per cent and for whites it was 19 per cent. For other age groups, the magnitude of these unemployment-rate differences among ethnic groups persists, although the absolute rate drops. The same pattern exists for females, although as can be seen from Figure 1.2, the differences are less marked: 17 per cent of white females are unemployed compared with 27 per cent of West Indian females. This economic marginalisation of young, males, and ethnic groups also occurs in the USA. As shown in Table 1.1, the total unemployment rate in 1978 was 6.5 per cent, but for black males aged 21–24 it was 21.0, and for 16–19-year-olds, it was 36.7. By 1983, when the national unemployment rate had risen to 9.6 per cent, the rates among teenage blacks stood at a staggering 48.8 and for young adult blacks at 31.4. These rates far exceed both the national average and that experienced by older persons and by whites of the same age (Austin and Krisberg, 1985, p. 27).

In addition to age and ethnic group, the level of occupational skills is related to unemployment rates. Thus those with semi- or un-skilled capacities are very vulnerable, particularly when, as has happened, the manufacturing, industrial and construction sectors which would employ proportionately more semi- and un-skilled workers, shed jobs at a much faster rate than the service sector. Thus although the semi- and un-skilled represented 20 per cent of the economically active population in the UK in 1985, they represented 40 per cent of the unemployed; in contrast, those with managerial and professional skills represented one-quarter of the economically active but only one-tenth of the unemployed.

By the end of 1983, nearly 20 per cent of US construction workers and miners were unemployed. These rates stand in stark contrast to the rates of 5.5 per cent for government employees and 4.3 per cent for those employed in finance, insurance and real estate.

Vast differences in economic sector unemployment rates are reflected in the wide differences per region of the UK. Top of the league are old industrial areas like Cleveland (22.2) and Merseyside (21.0). Close behind in the league of regional recession are other parts of the North East such as Tyne and Wear (19.9) and Durham (18.7), and parts of Wales, such as Gwynedd (19.3), Glamorgan (18.7) and Glwyd (18.5). At the other extreme are relatively sheltered areas where professionals and other high-status white-collar workers congregate, such as Cambridgeshire (9.6), Oxfordshire (7.7), Berkshire (7.2) and Hertfordshire (7.1). As the manufacturing and industrial infrastructure of the British

6

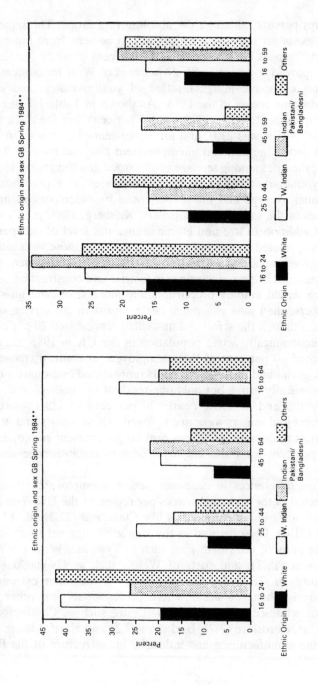

Figure 1.1 *Unemployment rates for males by age*

Figure 1.2 *Unemployment rates for female by age*

Source: *Employment Gazette* (UK Dept. Employment) 1985, p. 474.

economy collapsed so those areas that were traditionally its backbone found themselves redundant and experienced regional rates of employment exceeding one-fifth of the labour force. Furthermore, within these regions there is also considerable variation, particularly between inner-city areas and the rest. Thus although unemployment in the Metropolitan area of London was 10 per cent by the beginning of 1986, it was double this figure, or more, in those inner-city areas abandoned by entrepreneurs seeking havens elsewhere for capital accumulation.

Paul Harrison's (1983) evocative and haunting account of 'life under the cutting edge' in an inner-city borough of London reveals an isomorph description of these cross-national characteristics. According to him:

> unemployment became a vast engine for increasing the existing inequalities in British society – a welfare state in reverse gear. There was no question of equality of sacrifice in the fight against inflation. The belts of those who were thinnest had to be tightened hardest. The most disadvantaged areas and the most disadvantaged people were hit most brutally. The Hackney figures tell a sad tale, paralleling national developments. Unemployment hit manual workers harder than non-manual: between 1979 and 1980 14 per cent of jobs in the 'operative' category disappeared, but less than half of 1 per cent of office jobs. It hit women harder than men: between 1979 and 1981, female unemployment rose at twice the rate of male. Black unemployment rose twice as fast as white. Recession hit the younger harder than the old, the unskilled harder than the skilled, the disabled harder than the fit. (p. 113)

A similar variation in the geography of unemployment, reflecting the concentration of manufacturing and mining enterprises, occurred in the USA. Thus West Virginia had twice the national average, whilst the rate in suburban and urbane New Hampshire, home for many aspiring Booker or Pulitzer Prize novelists, was only half the national average.

So by the mid-1980s a future of endless possibilities that dominated the psychedelic mind of the Sixties turned out to be a present of immense suffering and hardship, particularly for those carrying the lion's share of unemployment and unemployability –

the young, the unqualified, inner-city dwellers, amongst whom ethnic minorities were over-represented. It has been a nightmare trip from a 'permissive' to a 'dismissive' society; those strutting down the corridors of power replaced compassion for the disadvantaged with a passion for market forces and were morally indifferent to the avoidable human suffering this produced.

Income inequalities widened

Not only did the recession result in grotesque numbers of people being made unemployed and unemployable, but the income differentials between the poorest and richest, already morally repugnant, actually *widened*. According to *Social Trends* (1986, p. 91) the distribution of final income (i.e. original income less direct and indirect taxes, plus benefits in kind, like National Health Service) between 1976 and 1983 revealed more inequality; the bottom one-fifth share dropped from 7.4 per cent to 6.9 per cent whilst the top one-fifth share rose from 37.9 per cent to 39.3 per cent.

In other words, during that seven-year period, the poorest fifth of the British population experienced nearly a 7 per cent drop in their share of the country's final income. This was of course not offset by any redistribution of wealth. Between these years the most wealthy 50 per cent slightly increased their share from 95 per cent to 96 per cent. In a society described as a 'property owning democracy', this did not leave much to be shared out among the poorest half of the population! This redistribution of income, in the direction of more *inequality*, affected groups of people already on the razor-edge of material existence, including the unemployed. In 1978 30 per cent of the unemployed received 'replacement incomes' (from various state benefits) that were less than half they had received while in work. Changes in the benefit system between then and the end of 1982 resulted in one-third more unemployed persons' 'replacement incomes' being less than equivalent to half their previous income. This redistribution also adversely affected manual workers. Male manual workers in all industries and services in 1979 managed to earn £93.0 per week, compared with £113.0 earned by non-manual workers. This can be expressed as a ratio: manual workers' weekly earnings were 18 per cent less than non-manual workers'. By 1985, six years later, this ratio had dropped: manual workers earned 27 per cent less than non-manual workers. A similar drop in relative earnings occurred for full-time female workers. In 1979 female manual workers earned 84 per cent compared with female non-manual workers; by 1985 this relative earnings had dropped to 74 per cent. So just as manual workers were most vulnerable to unemployment, those fortunate enough to remain at work experienced a considerable widening of income inequalities during these years. During the last decade, living standards of both the unemployed and most manual workers have deteriorated. According to Mack and Lansley (1985):

> There have been many government policies that have contributed to these trends, the most important being the changes in taxation and social security. Since 1979, the national level of taxes on incomes (income tax and national insurance contributions) has risen. However, while the low paid have had to hand over an increased proportion of their wages to the state, the burden of tax on those on the highest incomes has, by contrast, fallen. Overall, the well-off and the rich have gained about £2,600 million between 1979 and 1984 from tax concessions. At the same time, there have been several changes in social security that have made those dependent on benefits poorer. Earnings-related supplements for all short-term benefits – unemployment and sickness benefit, and maternity and widow's allowances – were abolished from April 1981. This hit, in particular, the rising number of people unemployed for less than six months, who were as a consequence forced on to the supplementary benefit. In addition, the statutory link between long-term benefits, such as pensions, and earnings was repealed and these benefits were increased in line with inflation only. Housing benefits has also been sharply cut. All in all, benefit cuts over the life of Mrs. Thatcher's first term in office amounted to some £1,600 million, most of which represented a cut in the incomes of the poorest sections of the community. (pp. 5–6)

A point worth stressing is that a stark contrast between the unemployed and those at work should be avoided, at least when discussing the poorest sections of Britain. As Harrison (1983) sees it:

in the inner city, and in recession, those in manual employment
are not too fortunate either: they find themselves with low and
declining real wages, unpleasant work conditions, and growing
work-load, reduced security, and weakened trade-union protection. And the growing reserve army of the unemployed is the
principle threat through which this position is maintained: the
destinies of the employed and the unemployed are inseparable.
(p. 108)

A similar widening of income inequalities occurred in the USA.
Thus between 1977 and 1983, the bottom fifth income-earners
share *dropped* from 5.2 to 4.7 per cent of total incomes. In other
words, the poorest fifth of the population became roughly 10 per
cent worse off during this six-year period. The top fifth, however,
experienced a 3 per cent *improvement* in the income they had
available to spend. Their share of national income increased from
41.5 to 42.7 per cent (US *Statistical Abstracts*, 1979, p. 452, and
1983, p. 448). The proportion of the population officially categor-
ised as 'poor' also increased from 12.3 in 1975 to 15.5 in 1983, an
increase of 26 per cent. The proportion of blacks officially recognised as 'poor' in 1983 was 35.1 compared with 31.5 in 1975, an
increase of just over 11 per cent.

These deteriorating living standards and widening income inequalities are a direct consequence of the Reagan Administration's attack on the Welfare State. According to Piven and Cloward
(1982) – who between them received the prestigious C. Wright
Mills Award for the Study of Social Problems and the Dennis
Carroll Award of the International Society of Criminology – in this
'New Class War' the first objective was to limit the bargaining
power of workers by driving down the level of income-
maintenance for the poor and unemployed. The effect of slashing
'energy assistance', 'housing assistance', 'public service jobs'
(CETA), 'job training and youth programmes', 'school feeding',
'aid to families with dependent children' (AFDC), 'food stamps',
and Medicaid, was to put pressure on the 'reserve army of labour' –
the unemployed – to seek jobs, thus bringing down manual workers'
wage levels. By intensifying competition between the poor, the
unemployed, and the slightly better-off employed, the government
brought about a widening of income inequalities by making the
poor poorer. At the other extreme, argue Piven and Cloward, the
government enabled the rich to get richer:

The Reagan administration also set out to save business and industry billions of dollars by undoing the apparatus through which government regulates business. The budgets and powers of agencies responsible for controlling the polluting effects of industry, enforcing health and safety standards in the workplace, overseeing guidelines for the hiring of women and minorities, prosecuting antitrust suits, and limiting the exploitation of mineral resources on federal lands, to mention a few, were all reduced or abolished. Directives were promulgated that explicitly relaxed enforcement standards and lowered the penalties for violations. The agencies were internally reorganised to remove stubborn bureaucrats from the scene of enforcement, and a new crop of officials was recruited, usually from the regulated industries. (pp. 7–8)

There can be no doubt that the recession blowing across America and Britain over the last decade has made some sections of the population worse off; within this relatively deprived population, the unemployed and ethnic minorities are over-represented. It is indeed a long way from the post-war hope of a fairer and more equal society; it is also a far cry from the 'Brave New World' implicit in Prime Minister Wilson's 'white hot technological revolution' or President Kennedy's vision of the 'Great Society'.

Fewer people were imprisoned

Another major change from the relatively pleasant days of the 1960s is that more and more people are now sentenced to imprisonment and the prison population has rapidly increased. In the USA in 1965, 87,505 persons, or 45.4 per 100,000 population, were received into state or federal prisons; by 1983, these figures had risen to 187,405, or 80.1 per 100,000. Nearly twice as many Americans were being imprisoned than two decades ago. Furthermore, because of higher average length of prison sentence, particularly following the widespread acceptance of the 'justice model' – i.e. return to punishment – in the late 1970s, the average daily prison population rapidly expanded during these years. Thus in December 1965 there were 210,895 prisoners (or 108 per 100,000), and by December 1983 this had risen to 438,830 (or 179 per 100,000). Furthermore, this increase occurred mainly in the

1980s; from 1970 to 1980 the prison population total only rose at a rate of 6 per cent per annum, or 4.3 per cent per annum controlled for population growth. But for the years 1980 through to 1983 this steady growth rapidly accelerated; the total prison size increased by 13.7 per cent per annum and 9.7 per cent per 100,000 population per annum. Over half the growth in the US state and federal prison population during the thirteen-year period after 1970 occurred in the last three (see Figure 1.3). This recent upward surge is not a freakish event – experts predict it will continue at an even greater pace. Austin and Krisberg (1985, p. 18) estimate that half a million will be in prison by 1986 and at the end of the decade it will stand at 566,170 (or 227 per 100,000). Furthermore, these estimates, both for Britain and the USA, have been too optimistic. For example, New York State's prison plan published in 1981 predicted the prison population would rise from 21,000 to 24,000 by April 1986. But by March 1985 it was already 35,000! Similarly the prison population for England and Wales was predicted to reach 48,000 by 1990, but it passed this total in 1985!

A similar pattern of prison population expansion has occurred in England and Wales (see Figure 1.3). Receptions of prisoners under sentence into prison department establishments was 56,000 in 1956 (or 117 per 100,000) and 93,000 in 1984 (or 187 per 100,000), an increase of 60 per cent. The average daily prison population increased from just over 30,000 (or 64 per 100,000) to about 42,000 (or 87 per 100,000) in 1984 and rose steadily throughout 1985 and reached an all-time high of 48,165, which was over 60 per cent higher than the 1965 figure.

Not only have the total numbers and percentage of the population being sent to prison increased, but within this group the economically disadvantaged figure prominently. Unfortunately there is little information on the previous employment status of prisoners, but a survey of the US jail population (excluding state and federal prisons) in 1978 revealed that 43 per cent of the inmates had been unemployed at the time of arrest compared with a national average that year of 6.5 per cent (US *Statistical Abstracts*, 1985, p. 183). A slightly later study of federal and state prison inmates in 1979 shows that 30 per cent of them were unemployed a month before being arrested (US Department of Justice, 1982). This was more than *four* times larger than would be expected from the national unemployment rate.

Figure 1.3   *Prison population USA and England and Wales (1965–86)*

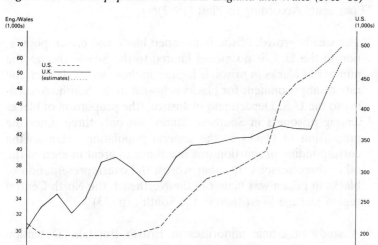

There are few other worthwhile details about the previous employment status of prisoners. However, there exist many more details about their ethnic origins, which, because of the relationship between youth, race and unemployment, also reflect the extent to which the prison population consists of economically marginalised persons. Christenson (1981) analysed US state prisons for the period 1973–9 and found that the number of black prisoners increased from 83,000 to about 132,000 and that the black share of the state prison population rose from 46.4 per cent to 47.8 per cent, which is amazing considering that American blacks constitute only 11.5 per cent of the total population. But even these figures conceal huge differences in the incarceration rates between whites and blacks. Thus in 1973 the incarceration rate per 100,000 population was 368 for blacks and only 46.3 for whites; the chances of a black American being imprisoned in the early 1970s were between 7 to 8 times greater than for a white American. By 1979 the respective incarceration rates had increased to 544.1 and 65.1; thus by the end of the 1970s blacks had an even greater chance of being sent to prison. Furthermore, in many states the proportion of prisoners who are black is much higher than the national average; in Delaware it is 60 per cent, in New Jersey 62 per cent, in Mississippi 64 per cent, in Louisiana 71 per cent, in Maryland 77 per cent, and in the District of Columbia 97 per cent. According to Platt (1982):

> The steady growth of the imprisoned black and brown population in the U.S. is no means limited to the South, though the number of blacks in prison is highest in those states. In fact, the rate of imprisonment for blacks is lowest in the South. According to the U.S. Department of Justice, 'the proportion of blacks among prisoners in Southern States was only three times the proportion of blacks in the general population, whereas the corresponding proportion was five times as great in each of the other three regions. In other words, the overrepresentation of blacks in prison was higher in the Northeast, the North Central region and the West than in the South'. (p. 33)

A study of ethnic minorities in British Borstals, Detention Centres and Young Persons Prisons by Fludger (1981) shows that the West Indians constituted 3 per cent of the prison population but were only 0.7 per cent of the 15–19 age group. Their presence was more than *four* times larger than chance. This difference is very surprising because the survey related to 1971, before the mugging panic that finally forged the black=crime equation (Hall *et al.*, 1978), and at a time when the police:

> in their evidence to the House of Commons Select Committee on Race Relations and Immigration denied that black crime rates were any different from those of any other sections of the population. (Lea and Young, 1984, p. 136)

A recent and comprehensive survey (Home Office, 1986) shows that the race-differentials revealed in Fludger have widened. Data collected between June 1984 and March 1985 show that although males of West Indian or African origin constitute about 1 per cent of the general population, they constitute 8 per cent of the prison population; the respective percentages for females are 2 and 12. In other words, the chances of a black British male being imprisoned are *eight* greater than chance, and for a black female they are *six* times greater. These differences certainly have something to do with the criminal justice system. The rates of arrest for young blacks are much higher than those for young whites (Stevens and

Willis, 1979), and these cannot be accounted for entirely by differences in criminal activity. Furthermore, black British youths tend to be charged for offences easy to 'prove' and appear before 'tough-minded' magistrates (Cain and Sadigh, 1982). These disparities are bound to percolate through and produce a blacker prison population.

Prisoners are overwhelmingly male and disproportionately young. In England and Wales, males outnumber females by nearly twenty to one; in the USA there is a similar ratio, the actual figures in 1983 being 419,811 male prisoners compared with 19,019 female. However, the male:female ratio is changing. In England and Wales between 1974 and 1984, males received into prison under sentence increased by 70 per cent compared with a 125 per cent increase in receptions for females under sentence. During the same period, the average daily population for females increased by 45 per cent while the male population only went up by 10 per cent. The prisoner sex-differential in the USA has also narrowed slightly. In 1970 females represented 2.87 per cent of the prisoner population. By 1983 this had grown to 4.33 per cent. Put another way, during this thirteen-year period, the female proportion of the total state and federal prison population increased by 66 per cent. Whatever the reasons for this narrowing of the sex-differential, it is worth pointing out that increased unemployment and deteriorating living standards affect many women, particularly single-women household-heads dependent on the welfare state, and young and ethnic minority women. As the economic marginalisation of these female groups increased so their risk of imprisonment also went up.

Young people in prison are also over-represented. Over a quarter of the prison population are under 21, whereas the 15–20-year-olds constitute only 10 per cent of the total British population. Furthermore prisons have become younger in their age profile. In 1955 only 19 per cent were under 21 (Baldock, 1980) whereas by 1984 under-21s constituted 28 per of the prison population.

A clear pattern of those materially disadvantaged and imprisoned is emerging. Those social groups most at risk of being unemployed and unemployable and of experiencing lower living standards are virtually identical to those with higher risks of imprisonment.

Are unemployment and inequality linked with imprisonment?

The fact that these changes have been happening simultaneously, and the coincidence that the same types of people are being made unemployed, experiencing comparative reductions in living standards, and being imprisoned, have resulted in an intriguing question reappearing on the criminological agenda. Are unemployment and inequality linked with imprisonment?

To some conservative commentators, this question is easily dismissed. These changes are not linked at all. They may have occurred simultaneously, but their causes are separate and unrelated. Increased unemployment arose because trade unions priced their members out of jobs by forcing up wage settlements too high to make the UK or the US manufacturing industries competitive with those of newly industrialising countries. And as for imprisonment, that increased simply because the number of crimes increased, and this upsurge in criminal activity had nothing to do with unemployment or income inequality in particular or economic conditions in general. The causes of crime are to be located in 'wicked' people who will 'seek it out even if we do everything to reform them', and in the way we respond to crime, for there are many people 'neither wicked or innocent, but watchful, dissembling and calculating of their opportunities, who ponder our reaction to wickedness as a cue to what they might profitably do' (Wilson, 1975, p. 209).

To other, more liberal commentators, there is a link. People's material circumstances have an influence on their behaviour, and so increased unemployment and widening income inequalities would be expected to push up the crime rate. In turn, more crime would lead to more convictions and this would automatically push up the number of people imprisoned. In this formulation, criminal activity becomes the simple mechanical bridge over which the economically marginalised cross to enter penitentiaries erected by our wise and virtuous Victorian or Quaker ancestors for the redemption of lost Christian souls.

While there is some plausibility in this 'work-load' thesis, there are a number of problems which limit its claim to be a totally satisfactory explanation. First, the link between unemployment/inequality and crime is nowhere near as simple or proven as is

Figure 1.4 *Recorded crime per 100,000 population, UK (1963–84) and USA (1965–83)*

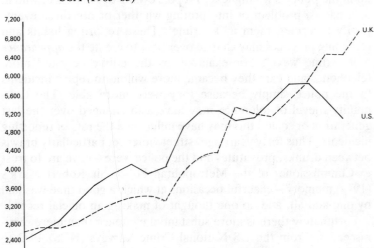

commonly assumed. Chapters 2 and 3 deal with these issues fully and so there is no need to rehearse them here. However, what does need to be considered now is just how much the crime rate is going up and whether this increase is sufficient to explain adequately the growing prison population.

The basic, and frequently the *only* evidence for the alleged 'crime wave' is derived from the Home Office annual publication, *Criminal Statistics, England and Wales*, or, for the USA, from the FBI's *Uniform Crime Reports*. Among much other data, these contain information on the number of serious offences recorded by the police, usually as a result of the public reporting them in the first place. It is certainly true, as can be seen from Figure 1.4 that these recorded crimes, even controlling for increased population size, have gone up 'alarmingly'. This is particularly 'true' for the 5-year period ending 1984, when in England and Wales, for example, robbery increased by 67 per cent, burglary by 43 per cent, fraud and forgery by 19 per cent, theft and handling by 18 per cent, and violence against the person (excluding sexual assaults) by 14 per cent (*Criminal Statistics*, 1984, p. 33). But what does all this mean?

Many critics have pointed out that these data are dependent upon the public's willingness to report events to the police, who in turn have a problem of interpreting whether or not these events justify recording them as a 'crime'. These reporting habits and recording practices may change over time to create the *appearance* of a 'crime wave'. For example, as the public acquired more telephones and cars they became more willing to report incidents to the police simply because they were more able. The community's level of tolerance may have also changed over the last generation or so and this may have influenced the rate of reporting incidents. Thus forty years ago, street violence, particularly brawls between drunks, prostitutes and the police were – if we are to trust ex-Commissioner of the Metropolitan Police Sir Robert Mark's (1979) memory – cheerful occasions at which a good time was had by one and all, and no one thought of making an official record.

Fortunately there is more substantial evidence than mere reminiscences. From the US National Crime Surveys (NCS) 1973 to 1982 it is easy to document an upward trend in the willingness of victims to report to the police those offences which are alleged to constitute the major crime problem. Thus in 1973, 48.9 per cent of rape victims indicated that they reported this incident to the police. By 1982, this reporting rate increased by one-twelfth to 52.8 per cent. Similar increases occurred for reporting robbery, assault, burglary, and particularly theft (US *Statistical Abstracts*, 1985, p. 409). These increases are less than the total rise in the levels of 'crimes known to the police'. Increased 'public willingness' to report crimes to the police can therefore only be a partial explanation for rises in this 'official' measurement of crime levels.

In addition to changing public practices and attitudes, police ability to record and process allegations has rapidly increased with the invention of technological means of recording, storing and recalling data. Whereas in the past a sudden gust of wind through an open window could have scattered papers to all corners of the police station, everything is now stored safely on computers. The easier it was to record crimes, the more likely it was that the number of recorded crimes would increase.

Finally, changes in the definition of serious crime artificially alter the contours of our crime problem. Pearson (1983) illustrates this nicely. He writes:

the case of vandalism – a favourite hunting ground for 'law and order' critics – is particularly interesting in that recent changes in record-keeping have produced an altogether dizzying statistical effect on the crime figures. Until 1977 a distinction had been made between 'major' and 'minor' damage, whereby only those cases which resulted in damage above an arbitrarily agreed sum of £20 (itself vulnerable to the ravages of inflation) were entered in the official statistics. From 1977 this distinction was abandoned, and all criminal damage incidents were recorded as 'known crimes'. In a single year, this simple administrative change produced the statistical illusion that vandalism had more than doubled, adding at a single stroke *a sixth of a million* indictable offences to the criminal record. (p. 217)

An obvious objection could be raised to these arguments: they don't *prove* that 'crimes recorded by the police' fail to reflect accurately changes in the rates of serious crime, they merely *speculate* that this is a possibility. Why believe in speculation? Let's not; instead consider some evidence based on criminal victimisation surveys.

O'Brien (1985) reports on victimisation survey data in the USA for the years 1973–81. These show that victim reports of rape per 100,000 population only rose by 4 per cent, from 177 to 183. During that same period, aggravated assault fell by 3.5 per cent, from 1,007 to 964, and so did motor-vehicle theft, from 818 to 772. Messner (1984), analysing the same data-set, concluded that:

regardless of the weighting system, the average annual increase in the National Crime Survey index is less than 1 per cent. The indexes based on *Uniform Crime Reports* data reveal much more appreciable increases in crime between 1973–1981 – from 3.5 to 5.0 per cent. (p. 44)

These are global indicators of a slightly increasing crime rate. However, this may conceal significant changes *within* it. For example, the 'crime problem' is perceived to be fundamentally a problem of delinquent youth in inner cities. This may well be increasing, but its effect is masked by decreasing adult 'conventional' crime. However, the available evidence does not seem to support this either.

Laub (1983) analysed victimisation data on personal crimes of rape, robbery, assault and personal larceny (pocket-picking and purse-snatching) – crimes which figure prominently in both the 'crime problem' and the 'fear of crime' – derived from the annual US NCS for the years 1973–9. Being aware that the 'crime problem' is alleged to be associated with large cities and their inner areas, he analysed the data for these possibilities. He also converted the data into age-specific categories so that he could examine the allegation that the 'crime problem' is primarily caused by ungovernable youth. On the basis of his results, he came to the following conclusion:

[there are] generally steady or declining patterns in the rate of juvenile offending in personal crimes by year for the U.S. as a whole, as well as in urban areas and places with a million or more residents [p. 497] . . . Thus to the extent that recent legislative and policy changes are premised on the assumption that juvenile involvement in personal crimes has increased substantially, or on the assumption that juveniles constitute an increasing proportion of those committing personal offences, particularly violent offences, the data . . . simply do not support such changes. (p. 499)

This conclusion is strengthened by data from self-reported delinquency studies. The Office of Juvenile Justice and Delinquency Prevention (1980) surveyed national self-reported delinquency trends and concluded that:

the level of delinquency behaviour has remained about the same over the past decade (1967–1977). This finding contradicts the popular misconception that juvenile delinquency has been increasing over this period. (p. 13)

Even if US evidence indicates that youthful crime is not increasing as fast as the media argue, that does not prove it is not happening in Britain. It is difficult to respond to this because no similar time-series victimisation studies for Britain exist. Victimisation data in the 1982 and 1984 British Crime Surveys, which show that burglary, robbery, theft and vandalism increased by 10 per cent compared with a 12 per cent increase in the number of crimes recorded by the police, are not an adequate base to detect trends over time. However, there is one piece of evidence that certainly proves that 'crimes recorded by the police' in England and Wales over the decade can be highly misleading. The General Household Survey recorded householders' experiences of being burglary victims for the years 1972, 1973, 1979 and 1980, and the British Crime Surveys for 1982 and 1984 continued this. If the results of these surveys are compared with burglaries recorded by the police and appearing in *Criminal Statistics*, the results are very interesting, particularly because burglary is a major contributor to both the 'crime problem' and the 'fear of crime'. What this evidence shows (see Figure 1.5) is that in 1972 there were 370,000 cases of burglary of which only 164,000 were reported to the police. However, by 1983 the total number of burglaries had gone up to 435,000 (an increase of only 18 per cent, or just over 1.5 per cent per annum), whereas the total recorded by the police went up to 342,000 (an increase of 109 per cent or 10 per cent per annum). Since it is the recorded burglary data that politicians, police and the media pick up, it means that the public have been fed the idea that burglaries have gone on rising at an annual rate that is *six* times larger than that reported by burglary victims. In other words, this particular part of the crime problem is not as alarming as it appears from *Criminal Statistics*, or as politicians and their allies would have us believe. What has happened is that more householders have insured their premises, and because claims cannot be made until the police have been notified, victims have increasingly reported them.

Thus although both measures of criminal activity indicate an underlying upward trend, the National Crime Survey and the British Crime Survey/General Household Survey, which are probably more accurate than 'crimes recorded by the police', show that this is nowhere near as high as 'law and order' campaigners claim, and is certainly not large enough to require a massive expansion of the prison estates and more offenders being imprisoned.

However, it may not be the 'crime rate' that pushes up the prison population directly, but the numbers of persons arrested/ convicted. This latter population are the courts' real 'work-load', whereas the 'crime' rate is merely an abstract proxy for it. The number of arrests and convictions in the USA and UK have *doubled* during the two decades beginning 1965. This is slightly

Figure 1.5 *Recorded and unrecorded burglaries involving loss, 1972–83*

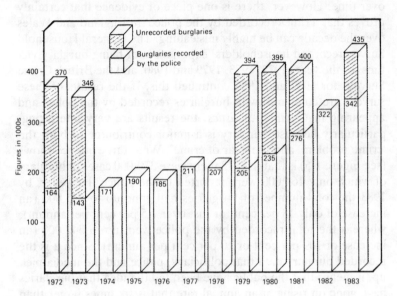

Notes:
1. Figures for unrecorded burglaries (hatched) are derived from the GHS for 1972, '73, '79 and '80, and from the BCS for '81 and '83. The BCS figures have been calculated to be comparable to the GHS figures.

2. The unhatched part of the columns are burglaries involving loss recorded by the police (i.e. residential burglaries minus nil-value cases).

3. GHS respondents were asked about their experiences 'during the last 12 months', a period which usually began before the relevant calendar year shown in the figure:

Source: Hough and Mayhew (1985, p. 17).

greater than the increased rates of prison receptions or prison population. Although this means that a considerable amount of the increases in prison receptions and population can be accounted for by a simple 'work-load' model, there are other considerations.

First, some of the increases in arrest/conviction have been in crimes which do not attract a high incarceration rate, such as minor thefts and non-aggravated assault. Increases in arrest/ conviction would therefore not necessarily lead to more prison receptions or population.

Second, the number of convictions has gone up, but this cannot be entirely explained by increasing crime activity. The fact is, the police now are able to arrest more people, and hence prosecute them successfully, because the public have become increasingly more willing, and/or able, over the last two or three decades, to report 'crimes'. This expanded information base, as much as any increase in 'crime', percolates through to the number of convictions. This is not consistent with the 'work-load' model which specifies that increased convictions are merely a mirror of increased crime levels. Furthermore this model remains silent about the fact that, and the reasons why, the public have become more willing to report crimes to the police.

Finally, and most important, sentencing practices have not remained static. In the USA with its desertion of 'rehabilitation' and its advocacy of the 'justice model', and in the UK with its tough-minded 'law and order' government and judiciary, there has been a tendency to increase the *incarceration rate*. For example, during the period 1977–84, the incarceration rate for all offenders convicted for an indictable offence in England and Wales went up by 27 per cent (from 12.9 to 16.5 per cent); this increase occurred mainly in motoring offences, such as driving under the influence of alcohol, driving without tax, insurance or licence (200 per cent), theft and handling (23 per cent), burglary (27 per cent) and robbery (10 per cent). *Had the judiciary maintained the same rate of incarceration in 1984 as in 1977, they would have sent nearly 14,000 fewer offenders to prison. Put another way, there would have been 16 per cent fewer offenders received into prison in 1984; instead of it being over 92,810 it would have been just under 77,934.*

Thus while the numbers convicted pushes up the prison population, the changing propensity of judges/magistrates to imprison offenders pushes up the population even further. This increasing propensity to incarcerate is not part of the 'work-load' thesis and cannot be explained by it.

The thesis to be developed in this book opposes the first conservative view above and complements the second, more liberal, view. Unemployment and income inequalities are linked to imprisonment, but not in a mechanistic way. They are linked because they are part of an overall process. The causes of unemployment and widening income inequalities are to be found not in excessive wage levels but in the need, as seen through the eyes and interests of finance capitalism, to radically restructure the labour force. The situation confronting both British and American governments, and beyond them, financial interests, is that their respective economy is suffering from 'import penetration', low 'profit margins', flight of investment capital, and an inability to compete effectively with others, mainly industrialising countries, because of excessive prices and costs. The 'logic' of this situation leads, at least to those with a particular point of view, to an obvious solution. Trade unions have to be weakened by criminalising practices associated with strikes and picketing and by encouraging the police to prioritise defending the 'right to work' (in a country with 4 million unemployed!) over the 'right to strike'. Health and safety standards have to be dismantled or not enforced by underfunding regulatory agencies and encouraging 'self-regulation' or persuasion over prosecution. Fair wage agreements have to be nullified, partly by expanding the proportion of part-time, especially female, workers, and by 'contracting out' government work to private contractors not party to such agreements. Wage Councils, responsible for enforcing legal minimum wages, have to be weakened or abolished. The surplus labour force – the unemployed and unemployables – has to be allowed to grow so that wage levels can be frightened down and trade-union membership reduced.

High levels of unemployment are not a mechanical market response to comparatively high labour costs. They are a direct result of governments, in the USA and the UK, deciding, under present material conditions, to restructure their labour force in order to make national economic enterprises attractive havens for international capital investment. This 'South-Koreanisation' of the labour force has repercussions on those experiencing its harsher edges. Some may well turn to criminal activity as a response and some may turn inwards towards forms of psychological and mental disturbance. But a prudent government pursuing a policy of 'South-Koreanisation' cannot afford to wait for events or resistance to happen. Those experiencing reduced living standards and higher rates of unemployment, and witnessing the sterilisation of their strongest collective asset – trade unions – cannot *all* be expected to take it lying down. Some will be moved to resist, either individually or collectively. Any government, mindful of these possibilities, needs to nip any potential disorder and 'lawlessness' in the bud. To this end, British and American governments recently have pursued 'law and order' campaigns that have directly and indirectly facilitated the increased use of prisons: directly, by providing more resources and power to criminal justice personnel; indirectly, by ideological communication, in which ideas of tough sentencing, more deterrence, more punishment, more police efficiency, and more social defence against 'the enemy within', are presented as top of the menu.

These arguments are spelt out in Chapter 4 to 6 and so no further details are required at this point. However, it is important to clarify whether politicians' intentions and motives ('idealism') are the driving force behind the 'South-Koreanisation' of the labour force, with its mass unemployment, declining living standards and greater use of prison, or whether these intentions and motives are better viewed as being determined by contradictions within not only the national economy but the international economy ('materialism').

It is not part of this thesis that political motives and intentions develop in a vacuum. Although intentions and motives guide action, they are themselves reflections of underlying structural conditions, particularly contradictions produced by economic crisis. The current crisis in both the UK and the USA is fundamentally a reflection of the deteriorating position of these countries within the world economy. Their ability to compete with industrialising countries, which have been so attractive to international capital investment over the last decade or so, has created a domestic contradiction. Goods produced at home are simply 'outpriced' by imported goods. This vulnerability to 'import penetration', plus the relative unattractiveness to international capital investment, plus a passion for 'free-trade', created a massive problem for political leaders in the UK and USA. Like everybody else, they too make decisions, guided no doubt by their intentions and motives, but under conditions forced on them. Of course these conditions do not automatically compel one solution. But given the cultural socialisation of politicians and the social groups from which they emanate, given the instilled cultural beliefs about capitalism, free-enterprise, and the sacred right of property, the 'solutions' to this contradiction are more or less predetermined. Restructuring the labour force, by fundamentally altering workers' rights, and by expanding the control and discipline of those not in work, as a means of reducing the average labour costs to make domestic industry more competitive, is predictable given the 'logic' of capital accumulation. Governments, while not being exactly 'pawns in the game', are none the less steered by the 'invisible hand' of history.

For the most part, people's actions, including those of elites and political leaders, are guided by routinisation and habituation. Their motives and intentions may be shrouded in dense layers of thoughtlessness and ideological mystification. They will not necessarily be aware of, or think about, the consequences that flow from their actions; nor think about altering their actions to bring about novel consequences. But during times of crisis, particularly when material interests are threatened, either because the distribution system becomes too grotesquely unfair, or the ideological justifications for it wear threadbare, elites wake from the drowsiness of habit and remember some pertinent lessons of Machiavelli. At these crisis moments, political leaders become more cunning; plans to protect and preserve the material interests of elite groups are formulated. These plans do not need to be put directly into full-frontal action; neither do they need to be finely drawn. They need only be skeletal. The flesh is put on them by unwitting, unreflexive minor state officials who, acting in the 'logic' of their situation, bring about consequences acceptable to the government. Thus Chapters 5 and 6 will indicate how the behaviour of police, probation officers and magistrates/judges brings about the imprisonment of more unemployed and economically marginalised people not because the government demand it, but because each of these groups has its own rationale for regarding the unemployed with more suspicion and caution. The government merely needs to give these tendencies an occasional nudge in the Right direction to bring about the realisation of its plans. It need only communicate its growing anxieties about the 'crime problem', about the 'right to work' being threatened by strikers, about the 'right to manage' being threatened by trade unions, about 'human rights' being threatened by 'lawless criminal elements', about the fabric of civilisation being threatened by 'alien' cultures, 'scroungers', 'thugs', 'hooligans', 'anarchists', 'malingerers', and 'wicked people', and these anxieties will be picked up and incorporated into routinised everyday decisions of officials in the criminal justice system. Thus even when the financial elite and the government become more conscious and organise a 'radical reform' of the economy, it is still those marching to the hidden tune of material conditions who realise this plan in action.

Thus the thesis developed in this book falls squarely on the 'materialist' as opposed to the 'idealist' side of contemporary radical criminology (Reiman, 1982; Young, 1979). In order to complement the 'liberal' attempt to link unemployment/inequality with crime, it first considers the theoretical reasons why recession might lead to more crime and sifts the evidence relevant to testing hypotheses derived from this theorising. It then considers in some detail the changing contours of the criminal justice systems in the USA and UK in which 'more imprisonment' is a major feature. Government explanations for these changes are assessed and discounted. A 'materialist' explanation is then proposed and examined in the light of relevant research evidence.

2 Why Should Recession Cause Crime to Increase?

As this chapter was being drafted, there were 'riots' in Handsworth, Birmingham, and Brixton, London, leaving a smoky trail of smouldering property and ramshackle looted shops. The inner-city face, already pock-marked by inadequate houses, crumbling schools, closed hospitals, unrepaired roads, boarded-up shops, dilapidated public services and graffiti-covered walls, was further scarred by the effects of robbery, burglary, arson and other serious crimes. But what has all this to do with the question, Why should recession cause crime to increase? If we listen to our astute politicians, the answer is simple – Nothing!

Margaret Thatcher, in a rare compassionate insight, saw the unemployed as good honest British citizens doing their best to gain employment (although she failed to add that it was despite her government's endeavours to make this practicably impossible). To imply, she continued, that these people commit 'riotous crimes' is an insult which only increases the hurdles they have to overcome to earn a decent living. Gone from Mrs Thatcher's mind was the *really* 'insulting' idea, so vividly present till then, that the unemployed are 'scroungers' on whom her government has unleashed an extra couple of thousand Department of Health and Social Security inspectors to deter 'dishonest' citizens from making fraudulent claims.

Home Secretary Douglas Hurd regarded these events in Handsworth and Brixton as nothing but *crimes* committed by 'criminal elements'. They were not, in his opinion, social phenomena to be pawed over by sociologists and used as ammunition against the

28

government and its economic policies; they were matters for the police, and beyond them, the courts.

Conservative Party Chairman Norman Tebbit, like a demonic Witchfinder General, caught a frightening glimpse of the British urban landscape being cursed by carefully orchestrated outbreaks of 'wickedness'. In the riot areas 'agitators' were sighted, 'extremists elements' were present, 'Trotskyites' and 'anarchists' were reported, 'aliens' and 'outsiders' were stirring things up, and 'drug barons' were defending their illegal business interests by fermenting anti-police sentiments. This motley ragbag of excuses rolled off the tongue with calculated ease. Anything would do, it seemed, if it obscured the social causes of crime, including the government's own contribution via its economic policies.

These views were echoed by others across the political spectrum, all anxious to avoid giving the impression that they or their party condoned outrageous riotous behaviour. There was a political chorus innocently singing in unison: unemployment is neither an excuse nor a justification.

Of course, not even a sociologist, like me, would claim otherwise. Acts of violence and property destruction are wilful crimes deserving punishment commensurate with their seriousness. It is inconceivable that unemployment is such a mitigating circumstance that the offender should be regarded as absolutely blameless and without responsibility. But a demand for justice must go beyond retribution for the offence and reparation for the victim. It has to include a demand for *understanding* the offender. It needs this not in the hope that the offender will then be excused, condoned or justified. Nor does understanding the offender necessarily shift the blame to the victim. The demand for understanding is necessary because *although people choose to act, sometimes criminally, they do not do so under conditions of their own choosing.* Their choice makes them responsible, but the conditions make the choice comprehensible. These conditions, social and economic, contribute to crime because they constrain, limit or narrow the choices available. Many of us, in similar circumstances, might choose the same course of action. Furthermore, if we understand the intimate relationship between economic and social circumstances and criminal behaviour, then we might be in a better position to intervene effectively and humanely to reduce the incidence of crime.

Of course, some commentators claim we need not bother. For them, social or economic circumstances are either unrelated to behaviour or too complex and subtle ever to be captured by the sociological imagination. In their eloquent *Honest Politician's Guide to Crime Control*, Morris and Hawkins (1969, p. 45) stated bluntly that:

the search for the cause of criminality . . . is generally thought to be an illusionary quest, not unlike the 18th Century chemists' search for the elusive hypothetical substance, phlogistic.

More specifically, James Q. Wilson (1982), the doyen of American 'policy-oriented' criminology, which argues that crimes can be prevented best by designing out the *opportunities* for their commission, claims that:

overall unemployment seems to bear little or no relationship to crime . . . there's no basis for a prediction that a deepening or continuing of the recession will lead to increases in the crime rate.

Against these sceptical views are others detecting a relationship between economic conditions in general, and unemployment in particular, and criminal behaviour. Thus the Select Committee of the House of Lords on Unemployment, 1982, stated its belief that unemployment was:

among the causes of ill-health, mortality, crime or civil disorder. Although this is an area where irrefutable proof is virtually impossible, we find the evidence highly indicative and we are satisfied that the link is sufficiently probable to allow the drawing of certain conclusions. We regard the connection as more than plausible. (p. 59)

Lord Scarman (1982) in providing the social background to the Brixton disorders on 10–12 April 1981, was at pains to point out that deprivations do not 'justify' attacks on the police, or 'excuse' such disorders. But at no stage did he deny that these conditions are part of the 'explanation'. Indeed, among the many deprivations he listed, unemployment figured prominently. It stood at 13 per cent in Brixton in early 1981 and 'for black people, the percentage is estimated to be higher (around 25 per cent)'. Furthermore, young blacks were even more affected, for 'unemployment among black males under 19 has been estimated at 55 per cent' (ibid, p. 27).

Clearly there is not only disagreement on whether recession in general and unemployment in particular lead to crime, but there is also confusion over the issue of 'causation' and 'excuse'. Unemployment and widening income inequality might not be an excuse recognisable in law, but that does not mean that these two features of recession do not affect the level of crime. Whether or not a 'cause' of crime is regarded as an 'excuse' is a political decision; to declare it unacceptable as an excuse is not simultaneously to effectively deny its possible contribution to the causes. Politicians like to slide over this distinction because stating that 'unemployment is no excuse' conceals the possibility that it could be a circumstance which narrows options and shapes choices to such an extent that crime becomes an attractive, maybe compelling, possibility.

So the issue of whether 'unemployment is no excuse' can be set aside while the issue of causation – Why should recession lead to more crimes? – is considered. After that trip through the tangled forest of sociological theorising, we can turn to the bewildering array of evidence relevant to assessing whether recession is linked to crime. However, before that particular fleet-footed exercise is undertaken, some issues cluttering the path have to be cleared.

In nearly all the literature on recession and crime, it is the *powerless* rather than the powerful who are portrayed as the offenders. Of course there are plausible reasons for thinking that a recession, causing widening income inequality and increasing unemployment, might result in the powerless committing more conventional crimes. But the *powerful* will also experience more temptation to commit crimes as the struggle for scarce resources intensifies and group or class tensions mount. This latter possibility seems to have been virtually ignored. Yet Bonger (1916) pointed out that, in promoting 'egoism', capitalism not only brutalises the poor, it demoralises all those caught up in the struggle and competition to survive or succeed, and makes those exploiting others particularly insensitive to the misery this produces. Echoing this point nearly sixty years later, an American criminologist David Gordon (1971) wrote:

> Capitalist societies depend . . . on basically competitive forms of social and economic interaction and upon substantial inequalities in the allocation of social resources. Without inequalities, it would be much more difficult to induce workers to work in alienating environments. Without competition and a competitive ideology, workers might not be inclined to struggle to improve their relative income and status in society by working harder. Finally, although rights of property are protected, capitalist societies do not guarantee economic security to most of its individual members. Individuals must fend for themselves, finding the best available opportunities to provide for themselves and their families. At the same time, history bequeaths a corpus of laws and statutes to any social epoch which may or may not correspond to the social morality of that epoch. Inevitably, at any point in time, many of the 'best' opportunities for economic survival open to different citizens will violate some of those historically-determined laws. Driven by the fear of economic insecurity and by a competitive desire to gain some of the goods unequally distributed throughout the society, many individuals will eventually become 'criminals' . . . nearly all crime in capitalist societies represent perfectly *rational* responses to the structure of institutions upon which capitalist societies are based. Crimes of many different varieties constitute functionally similar responses to the organisation of capitalist institutions, for those crimes help provide a means of survival in a society within which survival is never assured. (p. 58)

By concentrating on competition and struggle and the ethics these generate *throughout* society, it becomes easier to see that the working class have not secured a monopoly on criminal activity. Crime is endemic throughout the class structure, but this is obscured by differential law-enforcement and law-makers who prefer to regulate the powerful's worst excesses by administrative or civil law and rely on criminal law only as the final resort.

Second, the link between recession and crime seems to have concentrated on property offences, such as robbery, burglary and theft. The result is a neglect of violent crimes, such as homicide, rape, wife-battering and assault, and 'crimes of domination and repression' (Quinney, 1977, pp. 31–62) committed by the *powerful*.

This concentration on property crimes of the powerless reflects simplistic views about who gets adversely affected by recession, and what types of crimes they might commit. Although property offences appear a 'rational' response to unemployment, deteriorating living standards and widening income inequalities, the psychological effects of these experiences and how they can be transferred into 'irrational' outbursts of violence, cannot be ignored. Indeed, many feminists over the last decade have argued for there being a causal connection between inequalities and rape. Some men who experience their disadvantage as unfair or who consider themselves failures in competition with other men, may, out of frustration and anger, assault women, a vulnerable and easy target (unless they have attended self-defence classes). This is 'irrational' because sexual assaults fail to address the cause of men's oppression and, at the same time, contribute to the oppression of women. As Klein (1981) sees it:

male physical power over women, or the illusion of power, is none the less a minimal compensation for the lack of power over the rest of one's life. Some men resort to rape and other personal violence against the only target accessible, the only one with even less autonomy. Thus sexual warfare often becomes a stand-in for class and racial conflict by transforming these resentments into misogyny. (p.72)

A similar frustration-aggression misplaced onto an accessible and vulnerable target underlies Coser's (1963) account of murder. He argues that inequalities perceived as unjust may lead to frustration, this in turn might lead to aggression which might be directed against the self but also might be directed against others, and that the rates of violence, including homicide, will be particularly high for categories of persons who experience disproportionately 'structurally induced frustrations' and for those in strata where 'internalised social controls are not strong enough to prevent . . . homicidal aggression'.

Not only might recession lead to more crimes of violence, but it obviously affects more than the economically marginalised. The two major motivations behind crime examined below – thwarted ambition and relative deprivation – are not confined to the powerless. The powerful too have problems during a recession, and these problems can and do lead to such 'crimes of domination' as corporate violations of administrative, civil and criminal law, including price-fixing, pollution, selling unsafe and untested products, ignoring health and safety regulations, and bribery. They also lead to 'crimes of repression' committed by state social control agencies, such as the police, when they brutally assault and sometimes unjustifiably kill civilians (Box, 1983; Jacobs and Britt, 1979) and commit illegal violence against strikers and sympathisers (Coulter *et al.*, 1984; Fine and Millar, 1985; Scraton, 1985), or the prison service, when prisoners are murdered or maimed (Coggan and Walker, 1982) or their legal rights violated (Cohen and Taylor, 1976; Thomas and Pooley, 1980).

Finally, there is a point, obvious once made, but which is hardly ever heard in the recession–crime debate: irrespective of the economic cycle, most crimes are committed by people *at* work! Some of these – corporate and police crimes – are discussed below, but others deserve a brief mention.

'Retrieving' a portion of one's surplus value from the employer is a fairly traditional response among employees (Ditton, 1977; Henry, 1978; Hollinger and Clark, 1983). Fiddling customers is also a way many service workers enhance their earnings, and this is not confined to those two obvious bogeymen, watch and car repairers (Mars, 1983). Nor is this 'crime at work' confined to the 'lower orders'. Embezzlement, computer fraud, professional malpractice, and government corruption are but a few of the illegalities engaged in by managers, technicians, solicitors, doctors, architects, engineers, civil servants and other 'top people' in the USA (Bequai, 1978; Douglas and Johnson, 1977; Geis and Meier, 1977; Johnson and Douglas, 1978) and the UK (Doig, 1984; Leigh, 1982; Levi, 1981). Furthermore, inflation, another feature of contemporary recession, but one which makes the middle and upper classes relatively worse off, pushes people into higher tax bands and reduces the buying power of their remaining income. Some, experiencing reduced standards of living, and not being prepared to put up with it, might turn to tax evasion, embezzlement and fraud as means of supplementing their dwindling incomes.

These crimes 'at work' have a number of characteristics: they are not frequently reported to the police since employers prefer to administer 'private justice' rather than spend time, money and energy pursuing employees through the courts (Robin, 1970); they are not feared much by the public, probably because people are less aware of such crimes; they are not part of the 'folk devil' and 'moral panic' scenario embraced by the media and politicians (Cohen, 1972; Hall *et al.*, 1978; Pearson, 1983); the police do not deploy many personnel or devote large resources to prevent, solve or prosecute these types of crime.

The outcome is that most of these 'occupationally related' crimes do not appear in the Home Office's *Criminal Statistics* or the FBI's *Uniform Crime Reports* and do not therefore penetrate the recession–crime debate. Yet not only are they widespread and committed frequently, but their monetary value far outstrips 'conventional crimes' of burglary, robbery and theft. As Ramsay Clark (1970), one time Attorney General of the USA, saw it:

> Illicit gains from white-collar crime far exceed those of all other crime combined . . . One corporate price-fixing conspiracy criminally converted more money each year it continued than all of the hundreds of thousands of burglaries, larcenies, or thefts in the entire nation during those same years. Reported embezzlements cost ten times more than bank robberies each year. (p. 38)

Clark's is not a lone voice crying out in the wilderness. Many other writers since then have estimated the physical, economic and social costs of corporate crime and have all agreed that these far outstrip comparable costs of 'conventional crimes' (Box, 1983, pp. 25–34).

Since it is 'conventional' crimes of the powerless that prey on the public consciousness and are the central focus of attention in the recession–crime debate, it is clear that many other serious crimes, crimes which undoubtedly would not fit easily into this tight, neat framework, are dismissed, ignored or forgotten. But this amnesia has to be avoided. Whatever the outcome of both theorising about and locating evidence for the recession–crime debate on 'conventional crimes', we have to remind ourselves constantly that many other crimes are being committed by people at work, often in high-status and respectable positions, and, objectively, these are more damaging to people, property and our political system.

Recession and the 'conventional' crimes of the powerless

There are numerous sociological reasons for linking recession with crime. Nearly every major sociological theory can be construed in such a way that it predicts more crime when unemployment increases and income inequalities widen. Although no one of these is totally satisfactory, it is possible to integrate them into a plausible and parsimonious theory which makes sense of a relationship between recession and crime. But first, what contributions does each major theory make to an overall integrated account?

(i)   Strain theory

In strain theory, people are viewed as being essentially good and would conform were it not for stresses and contradictions in their lives. Individuals cannot ignore the problems these strains produce. In attempting to resolve or reduce them, individuals occasionally drift into deviance and crime. Two criminological strain theories – anomie, which can lead to 'thwarted ambition', and material inequalities, which can lead to 'relative deprivation' – lend themselves to the argument that recession and crime are causally linked. Both of them address the fundamental issue of motivation: Why would anyone want to commit a crime? Neither theory claims that the motive itself is a sufficient condition for crime to occur, but both claim that it is a necessary condition. Thus, blocked opportunities of work/education which might lead to 'thwarted ambition', or material inequalities which might lead to 'relative deprivation' make crime possible, but neither make it mandatory or utterly compelling. But what is important is that both these approaches stress social structure – blocked opportunities or material inequalities – as the key to understanding crime. The subjective elements which form the motivation to commit crime are merely the mediating factors between structure and behaviour. This process may be absolute – 'Am I worse off than I expected or had been led to believe?' – or comparative – 'Am I worse off than others like me?'. But either way, it is triggered by external circumstances. This is not to argue that subjective elements are irrelevant; human beings are capable of attributing a variety of meanings to structural factors, such as income inequalities widening or being made unemployed. None the less, those external factors exert a 'facticity' upon the minds of most people and constrain the meanings they can attribute to them.

(a)   Anomie theory. Anomie theorists argue that the motivation to commit crimes will increase whenever legitimate opportunities to achieve culturally defined success, particularly material success, are narrowed or closed off (Merton, 1957; Cohen, 1955; Cloward and Ohlin, 1960). Since in a 'meritocratic' society the major avenue for realising material success is the occupational one, it follows that during a recession when unemployment rises and levels of inequality widen, more people will experience a failure to achieve culturally defined goals of success.

In itself this 'failure' is not necessarily 'solved' by deviance or crime. Other solutions are possible. For example, some people could modify their aspirational 'fantasies' and align them to outrageous reality. What counts as 'success' could be scaled down even to the point of withdrawing from the competition altogether. But this escape route is difficult to achieve when the media, particularly TV, which ironically is a form of entertainment affordable by poorer people, pumps out 'the good life for you' every hour of the day, creating in those who haven't got it a sense of disillusionment and deprivation. Turning one's back on the competition game, 'Occupational Success', requires an effort of will, and, of course, feasible alternatives, beyond the reach of many.

Some people whose legitimate avenues to success are blocked by being unemployed or unemployable will blame themselves. They see in their inability to secure or retain the 'good job' nothing less than a flawed personality. For these self-incriminatory people, a period of anxiety and maybe depression, illness, drug addiction or suicide could be expected. Exacerbating these possibilities are other social psychological effects of unemployment: the loss of structure to one's daily life, the disruption to one's routine patterns of relating which often require more money than is now available, the growing sense of purposelessness, the loss of identity, and a deterioration in physical health (Fagin and Little, 1984; Hakim, 1982; Jahoda, 1982). And for many of those managing to avoid these extremely debilitating consequences, there is only a weary resignation and apathetic acquiescence, particularly among older unemployed persons.

So, an important conclusion for the recession–crime hypothesis is that only a minority experiencing unemployment and hence material failure will be candidates for predatory property and violent crimes. Whether they do offend depends partly on how *intensely* they feel their 'failure'.

In modern Anglo-American society, during a recession, there are many who 'fail' to achieve the cultural goal of success, but only a minority who feel so *intensely* about it that they decide to commit crimes. Thus, a sense of thwarted ambition will be exacerbated and experienced acutely by those who feel they are excluded from the avenues of success by the operation of unfair and discriminatory criterion. Intense indignation is likely to develop, given the rigged nature of competition in meritocratic capitalist societies. As Lea and Young see it, this competition takes place on a very strange racetrack:

> In reality some people seem to start half-way along the track (the rich) while others are forced to race with a millstone around their necks (for example, women with both domestic and non-domestic employment) while others are not even allowed onto the track at all (the unemployed, the members of the most deprived ethnic groups). (1984, p. 95)

Pointing out the costs of these inequalities, Blau and Blau (1982, p. 118) argue that:

> inequalities for which individuals themselves can be considered responsible, even though differential advantage makes this a fiction, are held to be legitimate, whereas inborn inequalities that distribute political rights and economic opportunities on the basis of the group into which a person is born are feudal survivals condemned as illegitimate in a democracy. Such inborn inequalities exist . . . if membership in ascriptive groups, such as race, is strongly related to socioeconomic position . . . Ascriptive socioeconomic inequalities undermine the social integration of a community by creating multiple parallel social differences which widen the separations between ethnic groups and between social classes, and it creates a situation characterized by much social disorganization and prevalent latent animosities. Pronounced ethnic inequality in resources implies that there are great riches within view but not within reach of many people destined to live in poverty.

Thus, a sense of injustice, discontent, and distrust generated by the apparent contradiction between proclaimed values and norms and social experiences becomes, among certain groups, too deeply irritating and too constantly whipped up by the media to be easily shrugged off.

So the apparent relationship between recession – widening inequalities and increased unemployment/unemployability – and crime becomes compounded by a subjective element. What inequalities and unemployment *mean* becomes crucially important. Not only might this *meaning* vary between racial groups, but it might well vary between gender, age-cohorts and over time.

To the extent that individuals accept culturally defined gender roles, then men would tend to feel more discontent when unemployed because occupational success is supposed to fulfil men whereas women are argued to be more fulfilled by marital/domestic success. However, with the rise of female employment during the 1960s and 1970s, and the increasing number of female-dominated single parent families, it is *family status* – i.e. who occupies the bread-winner role – that will affect the *meaning* of unemployment. It is increasingly naive to assume that sex determines gender and therefore biological men fulfil 'male' social roles. To the extent that more women head households and need to work, then being made unemployed, particularly if it is believed to result from sexist beliefs – 'a woman's place is in the home with her children' – may lead to a sense of injustice. From this well of discontent might spring more crime, but its volume would be muted by female socialisation which praises passivity and recommends that suffering should be endured (Cloward and Piven, 1979). So although both unemployed male and female household heads may be motivated to commit crimes, it is likely that proportionately more men, socialised to be competitive, aggressive and domineering, will actually offend.

Similarly the young when compared with middle-aged or older persons might feel more 'putout' by unemployment because it would be more difficult for them to view this as a premature, and even welcome, release from the rigours of unfulfilling tedious work. By middle-age, most outrage and resistance will have been replaced by accommodation, displacement and passivity; the idea of crime, as a means of coping with unfulfilled ambitions long since deadened by the realities of work and domestic obligations, will simply hold little appeal. For the young, however, not yet brutalised by the harsh realities of economic and domestic life, resistance, protest and active indignation will come much easier, and with it, a preparedness to commit crimes.

Thus even in a society where the gap between culturally proscribed goals and legitimate avenues for their realisation is increasing, this might only provide a motivation for deviance/crime among small but identifiable groups of people. Others, despite a failure to achieve culturally defined success, might adopt different criteria for success, flop into a pool of self-flagellation, or adjust in the myriad ways that humans cope with the 'slings and arrows of outrageous fortune'. Although many factors shape these various responses, one in particular – *the duration of employment* – is expected to lead to criminal behaviour. The long-term unemployed, especially the young long-term unemployed who see no future before them, clearly have greater problems than those who merely slip onto and off the unemployment register because of minor friction in the labour market.

Strain theory therefore predicts more crime during a recession. Higher crime rates are the price a 'meritocratic' society pays for blocked opportunities and thwarted ambitions which increase when recession bites and are compounded by the intensified operation of ascriptive criteria, such as race, gender and age, in the allocation of employment and unemployment. These ingredients are likely to create more alienation, despair and conflict, and out of this cauldron creeps more conventional crime. But – and this is *the* point of this analysis – any relationship between recession and 'conventional' crime would only be expected to appear in particular populations: younger males more than older ones; economically independent rather than dependent women; racial minorities, particularly those with Afro-Caribbean backgrounds; working class rather than middle class. These relationships would be expected to be more pronounced in inner-city areas. Even then, other social factors might mute or encourage a criminal response. One of these – political marginalisation – will be considered in the next section, although it could equally affect the unemployed, just as the operation of ascriptive criterion in the allocation of income could lead to a sense of injustice.

(b)   Relative deprivation.   Closely related, and often confused with anomie theory, particularly of the Mertonian variety, is

relative deprivation theory. This theory, first formulated into a rigorous body of argument by Runciman (1966), has now been adopted by a host of radical criminologists. According to Runciman:

A is relatively deprived of X when (i) he does not have X, (ii) he sees some other person or persons, which may include himself at some previous or expected time, as having X (whether or not this is or will be in fact the case), (iii) he wants X, and (iv) he sees it as feasible that he should have X. . . . Given the presence of all four conditions, relative deprivation produces feelings of envy and injustice. (p. 10)

Although Runciman never applied this concept to the study of crime, others have done so. Thus Stack (1984, p. 231) argues that relative deprivation will occur to the extent that:

1 people lack an average income (the greater the size of this group, the greater the frequency of relative deprivation);
2 they are aware that others in a comparative reference group have incomes equal to or greater than the average (the greater this perceived gap between groups, the greater the magnitude of relative deprivation);
3 they are desirous of a higher income (this desire should increase the intensity of relative deprivation); and
4 it is historically feasible for such income redistribution to take place.

Stack believes that although relative deprivation leads to a sense of injustice it will not necessarily produce more crime. For this to occur, other conditions have to 'whip up the feelings of animosity' generated by wide and widening levels of income distribution. Essentially it all turns on whether persons experiencing relative deprivation believe the system can and will be drastically improved. To the extent that there exist free and strong trade unions and a political party committed to income redistribution, and the relatively deprived are involved in these reforming institutions and perceive the chances of success to be realistic, then crime will not necessarily increase even when income inequalities widen. However, if individuals and groups feel they are marginalised from the political process and trade-union movement, *as do many of the*

young unemployed and ethnic minorities, then the relative deprivation they experience will inevitably be transformed into deviant
behaviour. This is not to suggest that most property crime is an
extra-legal method of achieving income redistribution. Far from it.
The evidence from numerous victimisation surveys is unanimous:
the vast majority of victims of these crimes are themselves poor or
badly off. For example, the US National Crime Survey 1975
showed that the rate of victimisation for larceny, assault, robbery
and rape, per 1,000 persons, was 93 for those earning less than
$3,000, and this dropped steadily as incomes increased, to a rate of
56 for those earning more than $25,000. One conclusion is obvi-
ous: increasing property crimes are not inspired by the Robin
Hood principle of robbing the rich to feed the poor; instead they
result in income being redistributed amongst the poor.

Relative deprivation, at least in its more radical versions, differs
from 'thwarted ambition' of anomie theory, despite the fact that
both make similar, although not identical, predictions about a
recession–crime relationship. Relative deprivation theory implies
that only a redistribution of income brought about by progressive
tax reforms, high minimum legal wages and full-employment
policies can bring about humanely a reduction in the crime rate.
Anomie theory, on the other hand, argues for the opening-up of
blocked opportunities by more education, vocational courses, job
training and counselling. The former thus argues for a more
socialist society, where income differences are narrowed, the latter
for a truly meritocratic society, where the cream justifiably rises to
the top. Both, however, predict a relationship between recession
and crime, because:

1 they predict that similar groups of people – lower class, young
  males, ethnic minorities – will either experience the strain of
  thwarted ambition as unemployment rises or relative deprivation as income differences widen; and,
2 these groups are likely to blame 'the system' for their unemployment, feel resentful about ascriptive practices excluding them,
  and be less involved in reformist organisation like trade unions
  and socialist political parties.

This is not to suggest that other groups are entirely immune
from these experiences. For example, conventional crimes com-

mitted by females have increased considerably over the last decade both in the UK and USA. The most plausible reason for this is that more women have become economically marginalised during the recession. As Box and Hale (1984) argue:

> although some upper-middle-class women have made inroads into formerly male professions, the vast bulk of women have become increasingly economically marginalized – that is, they are more likely to be unemployed or unemployable or, if employed, more likely to be in insecure, lower paid, unskilled part-time jobs in which career prospects are minimal. This marginalization, particularly in a consumer-oriented and status-conscious community that is continuously conditioned by aggressive mass media advertising, is . . . an important cause of increases in female crime rates . . . Furthermore, anxieties concerning their ability to adequately fulfill the social roles of mother, wife, and consumer have been heightened during the late 1970s and early 80s because the British welfare state, on which proportionately more women than men depend, had tightened its definition of who deserves financial assistance and, at the same time, has become increasingly unable to index-link these payments to inflation. (p. 477)

Relative deprivation, particularly in an egalitarian society, is likely to increase as income differentials widen during a recession. Those who make unfavourable comparisons with others like them, or who regard their past as more rewarding economically, will have a higher rate of criminality, particularly if they do not see on the horizon any serious structural change in the allocation of rewards being attainable.

(ii)   Control theory

Although strands of control theory existed before 1969, it was Hirschi's formulation that year which became the orthodox version that now straddles American mainstream criminology. The reasons for its current pre-eminence are not hard to fathom. In the first place, it is a theory which lends itself to empirical research. Indeed, over the last fifteen years it has become *the* most tested crime causation theory. But more important than that, the results have nearly all been favourable. The most that critics of its empirical adequacy have been able to come up with are minor reformulations of the relationships between social bonds. It is therefore a theory which enjoys a rare fruit in sociology: it is very well supported empirically (see LaGrange and White, 1985 and Box, 1981, ch. 5 for references). Second, it is a theory which avoids 'implicating' social structure and is therefore appealling to the established 'right' in American politics and culture. This makes it eminently attractive for research funds, and for that reason alone many scholars gravitate towards it. Control theory is therefore the dominant explanation of delinquency and 'street crime' in mainstream American criminology and therefore it has to be considered for inclusion into an 'integrated theory'.

American control theorists such as Hirschi (1969, pp. 66–75) and Johnson (1979, p. 100) do not give much credence to a strong unemployment–crime link. However, it is not at all clear that their research demonstrates no relationship. In both cases the research subjects were school-children whose social class was measured by taking the father's occupation! This is inappropriate, for it is the class of *destination*, as perceived or anticipated by the school-children, which affects their present behaviour.

When these weak tests are put aside and the theoretical arguments of control theory re-examined, it is contended that they do provide a bridge between the motivational element supplied by strain theorists and eventual criminal activity.

In control theory, individuals low in *attachment* to others, lacking a strong *commitment* to the future, and not holding the right *beliefs*, are predicted to be comparatively more likely to commit crimes. In other words, the level of offending will be higher among those lacking a strong emotional attachment to others, particularly family members, who do not see their future offering good prospects for achieving social or material success, and who do not subscribe to the moral principle that rules ought to be obeyed regardless of detection.

There are plausible grounds for believing that recession leads to a weakening of these social bonds and hence facilitates the commission of more crime and therefore a higher crime rate. First, it affects *attachment* because it threatens to weaken, and in some cases destroy, family relationships. The increased tension, resentment and bitterness which accompanies higher levels of unemployment and widening economic inequalities is often displaced onto the family, resulting in more wife-battering, child-abuse (Straus *et al.*, 1980) and divorce (Thornes and Collard, 1979; Colledge and Bartholomew, 1980). In turn, these fracture the love and attachment between family members who then feel freer to deviate because they care less about what other family members think of them.

Second, it affects *commitment* because unemployment casts a long shadow over those institutions formally supposed to prepare people for a job. The absence of future employment prospects delegitimises schools and results in many pupils becoming cynical, bored and rebellious. Through jaundiced eyes, the hidden purpose of school becomes redundant. Teaching kids the virtues of obedience, punctuality and ability to perform repetitive alienating tasks, becomes patently absurd if there isn't even a dull, boring, alienating job at the end of it. The new marginal youth do not have much to lose, so they become strong candidates for criminal activity, particularly when after leaving school they actually experience strain in the form of unacceptable unemployment or unemployability.

Third, recession affects individual *beliefs* in the legitimacy of conformity to conventional rules and norms because having undermined the stability of the family and the relevance of schools, both major institutions for socialisation, it damages the ability of one generation to imprint its values on the next.

Thus not only does recession produce more individuals who have a motive to deviate, but it also creates within this population a group who feel free to deviate because they do not have loved ones to whom they are sensitive, they do not view the future as sufficiently rosy to justify making a 'stake in conformity' now, and they do not believe that all law-breaking is intrinsically wrong. This does not mean that lower-class children have weak or non-existent social bonds. In all the research on control theory, the link between bonds and class has not been established empirically, and theoretically it is not predicted. However, there are a proportion of lower-class children (and middle-class children too) whose social bonds are weak. The *combination* of weak social bonds with a motive to deviate is predicted to produce higher rates of criminal activity than either the motive or weak social bonds separately. This combination is likely to be more prevalent in lower-class children not because their bonds are necessarily weaker, but because their motivation to deviate is stronger.

(iii)   Societal reaction and conflict theory

Following the publication of Becker's *Outsiders* (1963), societal reaction or labelling theory became fashionable, particularly among the rising and expanding generation of young 'radical' academics, partly because it promised to explore the innovative proposition that 'social control leads to crime' whereas the mundane orthodox view was the reverse of this. However, despite its potential, labelling theory failed to incorporate structural or macro factors and there was a growing disenchantment which came with the realisation that the primary focus of attention was micro-processes of interaction, particularly between state officials and putative deviants. This tendency was further exaggerated by the incorporation of phenomenologically inspired research towards the end of the 1960s (Cicourel, 1968), which seemed to disappear up the entrails of endless analyses of half-minute video-recordings of ordinary conversations. Conflict theory developed partly in reaction to this tendency and sought to strengthen societal reaction theory by anchoring it firmly to social structure; it sought particularly to place it within the context of the establishing and maintaining power relationships through coercive means, including criminalisation (Chambliss, 1969; Chambliss and Seidman, 1971; Quinney, 1974, 1977; Turk, 1969, 1976).

As a detailed summary of social labelling and conflict theory can be found elsewhere (Box, 1981; Downes and Rock, 1982; Taylor, Walton and Young, 1973), there is no need to cover the same ground. However, there are two major arguments within labelling conflict theory which are directly relevant to the issue of recession and crime.

The first is that these are particular groups who more than others are selected for criminalisation. Those groups who fit criminal 'stereotypes' or who can cause the least trouble for those administering the criminal justice system, are more likely to be apprehended, arrested, prosecuted and severely sanctioned (Box, 1981; Chambliss, 1969; Turk, 1969). The dominant imagery of persons committing such conventional crimes as robbery, bur-

'working-class' males, living in urban areas, and more likely than not to be unemployed and/or a member of an ethnic minority. Those fitting these stereotypes are more likely to be viewed with suspicion and subjected to higher rates of criminalisation. The police adopt deployment policies and methods of routine suspicion that result in the surveillance and apprehension of 'suspicious' persons – i.e. those resembling stereotypes. To the police, these policies look justified because, according to the evidence from victimisation surveys, those fitting criminal stereotypes do commit more 'conventional', mainly 'street' crimes (Hindelang, 1978, 1981). But the population under surveillance views this differently. 'Justified suspicion and warranted apprehensions', including stop and search, entry and seizure, are perceived by those on the receiving end as pure harassment and, to some, racial discrimination and prejudice. This leads a community to think of itself as 'under occupation'. It leads to the police being viewed with extreme suspicion and hostility. It inflames discontent already generated by thwarted ambition or relative deprivation. It creates an atmosphere where the unemployed and ethnic minorities feel that the forces of law and order are merely there to oppose them and therefore shore up a system of social injustice. These processes get caught up in a vicious amplification system as a deepening recession gives the civilian casualties more reason to deviate and the police and authorities more reason to be suspicious.

The second relevant feature of societal reaction theory follows from the first. Those subjected to higher rates of apprehension, arrest, prosecution and conviction are also likely to suffer from a sense of criminal injustice. This provides an additional push into further deviant acts, particularly by those who, when released from prison, find themselves so disadvantaged and discriminated against that they are unable to secure employment. This is a likely prospect even during affluent boom periods (Boshier, 1974; Buikhuisen and Dijsterhuis, 1971; Schwartz and Skolnick, 1964; Stebbins, 1971). It becomes a 'racing certainty' during recession when the levels of unemployment soar to 10 or 15 per cent of the labour force. Furthermore, stigma attached to the ex-prisoner status also creates acute problems of homelessness (Davies, 1974), and this interacts reciprocally with unemployment to create a massive push into recidivism. This in turn complicates the monocausal relationship between unemployment and crime because it is quite feasible to argue that unemployment leads to crime, but crime leads to imprisonment, imprisonment leads to unemployment (homelessness), and unemployment leads to more crime. After a while this circle obscures the original cause and the only sensible approach is to regard it as a fully interactive relationship (Thornberry and Christenson, 1984).

(iv)   Theory integration

These arguments can now be summarised. During a recession, when unemployment soars and income inequalities widen, crime is predicted to rise among those experiencing 'thwarted ambition' or 'relative deprivation'. Within these groups, those not tied to the conventional order by informal bonds, or marginalised from the institutionalised organisations for social change, or alienated from the forces of law and order, are likely to have the largest and the fastest-growing rate of committing conventional crimes; those suffering *in addition* from ascriptive discrimination are predicted to commit even more conventional crimes.

Finally, these objective strains with their accompanying subjective stresses, low social controls, particularly the lack of a 'stake in conformity', and militaristic-style policing, tend to coalesce in inner-city areas. These areas, deserted by industrialists and manufacturers who find capital accumulation easier elsewhere (Wallace and Humphries, 1980), scarred by a thousand cuts in public services and amenities where alternative jobs and entertainment could have been provided (Piven and Cloward, 1982), blemished by crumbling, insanitary, overcrowded houses and high-rise flats jerry-built in the flush of post-war short-sightedness (Harrison, 1983), and polluted by the sickly smell of failure, are where the relationship between recession and crime should be most marked. It is in these areas, deserted by the professional middle class and skilled working class who find suburbs more amenable, and by governments who believe in public expenditure restraint, that the cutting edge of recession is sharpest.

The above arguments are presented in diagrammatic form in Figure 2.1.

Any attempt to integrate a number of strands from different theoretical traditions is bound to run into opposition. There are those like Hirschi (1979) who argue in favour of 'separate and

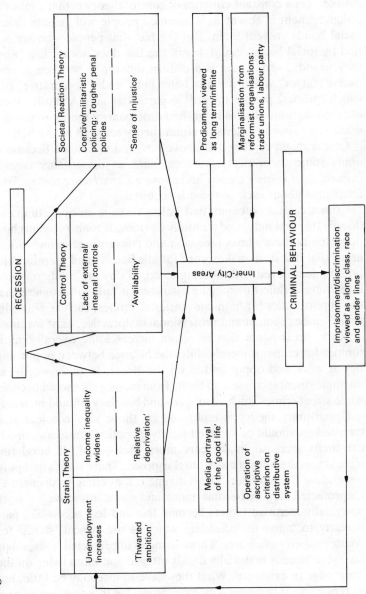

Figure 2.1 *Causal links between recession and crime*

unequal'. For him, strain and control theories are simply incompatible. Yet a constant criticism of control theory is that a motivational element is absent; it is assumed people will deviate unless social bonds prevent them. But the fact that people who are not tied by social bonds 'could' break the law does not explain 'why' they would do so. There is a distinct difference between a 'conducive' factor, which permits behaviour, and a 'generative' one which 'pushes' people towards a particular act. A motivational element therefore has to be grafted onto control theory to make it work. The above variants of strain theory seem to fit the bill.

Others might criticise the above integration scheme because it omits some theoretical traditions, such as *opportunity theory, cultural transmission theory,* and above all, *deterrence theory.* So a few words about each of these is required.

Crimes cannot be committed unless there is an opportunity to do so – this is plainly, and painfully obvious. It is also obvious how opportunity theory links recession and conventional crime. Some argue that 'the devil makes work for idle hands', and therefore the bored unemployed with nothing to do all day are easily tempted into crime. While this may be plausible, it fails to recognise that the opportunities for 'non-conventional' crimes, such as pilfering, fraud, embezzlement and professional malpractice, exist for those *at* work. So it is not that recession increases the overall opportunities for crime; it merely shifts the balance between opportunities at work and opportunities on the street. In other words, as unemployment increases, so thefts from employers should decline, while street crimes, such as robbery and burglary, should increase.

Opportunity theory is embraced by those who consider that criminology should be directed purely by policy considerations. If car thefts increase, make cars more theft-proof. If burglaries increase, make houses more burglar-proof. There is *no* attempt to *understand* the offender. The outcome is that crime is 'displaced'. Unprotected targets become more and more attractive as more potentially lucrative targets become less and less accessible, particularly to 'amateur' offenders which is the typical 'status' for young property offenders. Those living in unprotected houses/flats are those already materially disadvantaged and often living on the razor edge of existence. What they have to lose may be little, but its replacement becomes a major problem for those on low income or supplementary benefits. Thus the 'solution' to some people's fear of crime creates conditions that feed others' fear and give them another anxiety in addition to those caused by lack of material resources. Opportunity theory is therefore doomed to sterility because essentially it recommends sticking one's finger in the crack appearing in a giant dam. Only by understanding the pressures behind these cracks can there be a chance of preventing a disastrous flood. And only in this way can the 'displacement of crime' onto those least able to cope with it be avoided.

Cultural transmission theory has not been mentioned directly in the above integrated model. However, it may well be that different cultural and subcultural heritages lead to different *meanings* being attributed to unemployment and income inequalities. Some groups may be socialised into viewing inequalities as natural and desirable – so that the brightest and fittest can be motivated to fill the most important jobs – while others have been historically conditioned to see inequalities as unnatural and undesirable – merely being expressions of greed among those who already have plenty. However, such systematic variations in meanings have already been built into the above integrated theoretical scheme, and although there is a need to trace the origin of these meanings, that particular exercise is extraneous to the present task of considering why recession should lead to more crimes.

Finally, a brief mention of deterrence theory. The idea that criminals can be deterred by increasing both the certainty of being apprehended and the severity of punishment mesmerizes even those far removed from the 'Law and Order' brigade. Yet this compelling 'common sense' view overlooks a crucial distinction between 'objective' factors, such as the number and efficiency of the police, or the proportion of convicted persons sentenced to imprisonment, and 'subjective' factors, such as the *perceived* chances of not getting caught or not being severely punished even if caught (Erickson *et al.*, 1977; Jensen *et al.*, 1978; Waldo and Chiricos, 1972).

Given the cloak of magical immunity with which many contemplating crime shroud themselves, it is not likely that the 'objective' and 'subjective' views of deterrence will overlap considerably. Thus, even if the police were to become more efficient and increase the clear-up rate, many potential criminals would either not know this fact, or consider themselves sufficiently clever and smart to avoid the longer arm of even a more efficient police force. Similarly, even if the imprisonment rate of convicted burglars increased from 30 to 40 per cent, it is unlikely that many potential burglars would be familiar with this fact, or even if they were, they would not necessarily think it altered *their* chances. Maybe there is a category mistake here. Maybe these 'objective' factors, briefly mentioned above and developed at greater length in Chapters 4 and 5, should not be located within the deterrence debate at all. It could be that they are more suitably located within conflict theory where they become clues to the increasing tensions between groups and social classes and reflect the growing anxiety of those with the power to shape penal policy and police efficiency. In other words, maybe increased rates of arrest, conviction and imprisonment should be seen as indicators of state coercion rather than factors taken into account by people contemplating crime.

This leaves the 'subjective' version of deterrence theory. There are those (Tittle, 1977, 1980) who argue that the perception of legal sanctions only has a deterrent effect if accompanied by the perception of non-legal sanctions, such as parental or peer disapproval. In the absence of the latter, the former may have little constraint on behaviour. There are others (Minor and Harry, 1982; Saltzman *et al.*, 1982; Paternoster *et al.*, 1983) whose research results were not consistent with the deterrence model. But the most sophisticated test of both formal and informal sanctions as well as normative constraints – borrowed from control theory – concluded that although these three factors interacted to produce an overall level of deterrence, it was the acceptance of conventional norms which shaped the perception of risks. In other words, an element from control theory – beliefs – was the major determinant, and the perception of legal and non-legal sanctions were variables intervening between this and criminal behaviour (Bishop, 1984). This means that weakened social bonds are likely to be accompanied by a perception that crime can be committed without incurring high prohibitive costs. Consequently, the 'subjective' version of deterrence theory is already included in the above integrated theory and does not deserve a separate entry.

Evidence in support of this integrated theory is presented in Chapter 3. But before moving onto the plane of 'facts', there is a further strand to this theoretical excursion.

Recession and the 'unconventional' crimes of the powerful

Of all the crimes committed by the powerful, two stand out as being particularly linked with recession. The first is corporate crime, a 'crime of economic domination', which includes bribery, corruption, espionage, arson, price-fixing, tax-evasion, fraud, false labelling and misleading advertising, paying less than legal minimum wage or not complying with health and safety regulations, pollution and environmental destruction. The second is police crime, a 'crime of repression', which includes brutality, violation of citizens' civil and legal rights such as illegal phone-tapping and surveillance, strike-breaking, false arrest and evidence-fabrication, perjury and conspiracy to pervert the course of justice.

(i) Strain theory, recession and corporate crime

Despite the pioneering work of Sutherland (1940, 1945, 1949), the study of corporate and organisational crime has only become a central criminological issue over the last decade (Braithwaite, 1984; Box, 1983; Clinard and Yeager, 1981; Conklin, 1977; Ermann and Lundman, 1982; Geis and Stotland, 1980; Hochstedler, 1984; Simon and Eitzen, 1982). This body of work, which includes such pertinent titles as *Dying For a Living* (Tataryn, 1979), *Assault on the Worker* (Reasons *et al.*, 1981), *Death on the Job* (Berman, 1978), *Unsafe at Any Speed* (Nader, 1965), *Screwing the Average Man* (Hapgood, 1974), *Massive, Hidden Agony of Industrial Slaughter* (Scott, 1974) 'Silent Killers at Work' (Swartz, 1975), and *Eating May Be Dangerous to Your Health* (Carper, 1975), documents the widespread nature of corporate and organisational crime, the seriousness of these crimes in terms of the bodies killed, maimed and injured, and the billions of pounds illegally obtained. In addition, it has developed a theoretical framework which not only seeks to explain these crimes, but also provides a basis for predicting that they will increase during a recession.

Corporations and organisations are goal-seeking entities operating in an unpredictable and contradictory environment full of competitors struggling over scarce resources. Consequently, their executives frequently find themselves in a situation where strict adherence to regulations governing their activities would not be a rational course of action to pursue. It would result in their corpor-

ation or organisation failing to achieve its goal (or goals) and
maybe even going out of existence. In these dire circumstances,
executives investigate alternative means, including law avoidance,
evasion and violation and pursue them if they are evaluated as
more likely to lead to goals being achieved. In addition, corporations form powerful and, with the right government, persuasive
pressure groups to change regulations and laws originally designed
to limit corporate behaviour so that employees, consumers and the
general public would be better protected.

Two particular environmental uncertainties are important in the
context of discussing recession and corporate crimes. First, employees organised in trade unions become an increasing problem.
They attempt to restrict the numbers made redundant. They
struggle to prevent cuts in workers' real earnings. They fight for
the maintenance and improvement in general employment conditions, particularly health and safety standards. All these threaten
to maintain the unit costs of production at a level higher than that
desired by corporate officials feeling the cold wind of recession on
their backs. To solve this problem executives and managers consider ways of reducing the power of trade unions and regulatory
agencies, such as the Health and Safety Executive in the UK, and
the Occupational Health and Safety Administration in the USA,
whom they perceive to be the worker's ally.

Second, competing organisations become a greater nuisance.
Recession not only increases the numbers unemployed but these in
turn lead to lower aggregate demand and therefore a shrunken
market. In order for profit margins to be maintained, other competitors have to be controlled or eliminated to prevent prices
falling as a consequence of market forces. The outcome could be
illegal price-fixing or a conspiracy to drive competitors out of
business. The collapse of Laker Airways in 1982 as a result of
American and British airways corporations conspiring to fix prices,
and which led to a $40 million settlement out of court, is a recent
and dramatic illustration of this type of corporate crime.

As these two environmental uncertainties multiply during a
recession, so the strain towards corporate illegalities increases.
However, corporate crime need not occur. Corporations have two
tactics not available to those tempted to commit conventional
crimes.

In the first place, some corporations, particularly multinationals, can engage in *law evasion*. That is, they may choose, for example, to export manufacturing plants emitting too much illegal pollution. Thus a multinational asbestos corporation found that new pollution laws passed in Australia in the 1970s interfered with its production routines and raised its costs, so they closed down the plant and relocated in Indonesia – 'a country not noted for the stringency with which it enforces safety regulation to protect workers' (Braithwaite, 1980). Similarly, multinational pharmaceutical corporations might decide to flood the Third World market with drugs banned in the industrialised world. For example, the drug entero-vioform was banned in many Western countries after it was discovered that any dose above the minimum could cause a devastating syndrome of paralysis, blindness and sometimes death. Yet this drug is now being sold on the open market in many Third World countries, without warning of adverse side-effects on the labels (Bodenheimer, 1984; Braithwaite, 1984, pp. 245–78). In other words, multinationals dump some of their products, plants and practices, illegal in industrialised countries, onto undeveloped and under-developed countries. This dumping is possible because these countries are more dependent upon multinational capital investment for their modernisation and Westernisation plans, they have fewer resources to check manufacturers' claims or police corporate activities, and their government officials are more susceptible to the 'folded lie' – bribery and corruption (Braithwaite, 1984, pp. 11–50; Reisman, 1979). Given these lucrative opportunities, corporations facing contraction in industrialised countries are able to avoid breaking the law by acting immorally and exporting their 'illegal' behaviour to where it is legal. By the expedient of catching a jet, a would-be burglar would not be afforded the opportunity to carry out his plans and still remain within the law. A multinational corporate executive is more fortunate!

A second strategy available to would-be corporate offenders, but not would-be conventional offenders, is that they often have sufficient economic and political clout to get law-enforcement minimised or even repealed. The history of the Occupational Safety and Health legislation in the USA is a good illustration of this.

By a conservative estimate, there were in 1980 13,000 workers killed and 2.2 million suffering from disabling injuries received at the workplace. Workers' increasing sensitivity to these annual colossal numbers of victims of avoidable suffering, plus a favourable political atmosphere, paved the way for the Occupational Safety and Health Act of 1970 (Donnelly, 1982). However, from its very inception, industrial leaders sought to limit the implementation and enforcement of this legislation. In 1971, according to Szasz (1984):

> Large firms and business trade associations sent their lobbyists to advise that management be given advance notice of inspections, that management be allowed to refuse entry to OSHA (Occupational Safety and Health Administration) inspectors, that management be allowed to limit inspections in the name of protecting trade secrets, and that inspection results be kept secret by OSHA. Industry asked for rules limiting the access of OSHA inspectors to company health data and establishing the right of management to legal counsel during inspections. Lobbyists also demanded that enforcement be applied to employees as well as management, so that employees would be equally liable for health practices and would be penalized for false complaints to OSHA. And industry continued to emphasize due process safeguards in both enforcement and standard-setting. (p. 107)

These manoeuvres were only partially successful and so during the 1971–4 period, when the number of inspections and cited violations rapidly grew, industrial leaders sought to contain the damage being committed on 'good honest business' by OSHA. Small businesses, lacking large managerial structures, powerful Washington law firms and wealthy trade associations, lobbied their Congressional representatives and pursued relief through the federal court system. The latter course was more successful, for the Supreme Court finally ruled in favour of significant limits to the enforcement powers of OSHA. Large corporations, who were not being inspected with the same vigour that OSHA applied to small businesses, were primarily alarmed at the prospect of workers demanding the rights to accompany inspectors, to request inspection and to abandon potentially hazardous sites. They were also very worried about the possible imposition of stringent health standards, particularly those related to 'coke-oven emissions, noise, heat stress, cotton dust, lead, pesticides and arsenic' (Szasz, 1984, p. 109).

To prevent new health standards being formulated and enforced, large businesses practised information concealment, and when that was not entirely successful, they insisted on 'participation', which meant in practice that they would urge caution, demand more stringent scientific evidence and generally cause as much delay as possible in the hope that the political climate would change. It did, when the recession beginning 1974–5:

> cast a pall over the latter half of the decade and altered the political balance of forces in the debate over occupational safety and health. The Gross National Product fell in 1974 and 1975, the unemployment rate rose to 8.5 per cent in 1974, up from 4.9 in 1973, and the rate of inflation reached 9.1 per cent in 1975. The recession and the growing national economic crisis weakened organised labour and compromised public concern over environmental issues. (Szasz, 1984, p. 111)

Under these new circumstances large-business leaders turned from containment of OSHA to counter-attack. Ironically, under the Carter Administration, OSHA increased its inspections, average fines went up, and new more stringent health standards and workers' rights were formulated. But, by then, big business felt able to challenge all these in courts and won a major victory in 1980 when it opposed the new benzene standard. In this case, the Supreme Court declared that OSHA had to take economic factors into consideration when adopting standards and that there had to be a reasonable relationship between costs and benefits. The health and safety of workers had to be balanced against the costs to employers of supplying it. This spelt the end of any serious attempt to regulate industry. In its place, the recession succeeded an 'ideology of deregulation', which grew steadily stronger through the 1970s (Weidenbaum, 1979) and found a receptive American audience worried more about economic performance than workers' health and safety.

Finally, there was the Reagan denouement. He appointed a new head of OSHA who immediately declared that 'cooperation' should replace 'punishment'. New health standards were dropped, existing ones weakened, OSHA lost 20 per cent of its inspectors,

and enforcement declined and workers' rights were shelved (Calavita, 1983).

A similar deregulatory stance followed the arrival of the Conservative government in the UK in 1979. There is no need to spell
this out in too much detail, but the emasculation of agencies
establishing, monitoring and enforcing health and safety standards, such as the Health and Safety Commission/Executive,
whose umbrella covers the Factories, Mines and Quarries, Alkali
and Clean Air, Agriculture, Explosives, and Nuclear Installations
Inspectorates, and the 'reform' of Wages Councils provides sufficient indicators of the government's determination to ease conditions for employers.

Just before Mrs Thatcher's first victory, Her Majesty's Factory
Inspectorate had already indicated that its resources were not
sufficient to perform effectively. In the *Manufacturing and Service
Industry Report, 1978*, the Inspectorate wrote:

> The Factory Inspectorate . . . works against a background of
> increasing commitments and slender resources. There is a limit
> to what a force of some 900 inspectors in the field (700 general
> inspectors and 200 specialists) can do in practice. The Inspecto-
> rate is responsible for some 18,000,000 people at work scattered
> through some 500,000 or 600,000 different workplaces . . . It is
> obvious that an Inspectorate of its present size in relation to its
> responsibility cannot hope to achieve either all it would like or
> all the public would like it to do. (Health and Safety Executive
> 1980, pp. vi–vii)

Yet despite this, the Conservative government, almost immediately after taking office, required the Health and Safety Commission to *reduce* its budget for the year 1982/3 by 6 per cent
compared with the 1979/80 level. The Commission's response to
this loss of vital and essential resources was immediate and blunt.
It replied that 'cuts of that size in our budget cannot be achieved
without a reduction in our programmes directly concerning the
health and safety both for workers and general public' (Health and
Safety Commission Report 1980/1, 1981, p. 1). This warning, too,
fell on ears only receptive to a different ideological message.
Industry had to be freed from excessive regulation; market forces
should be allowed to prevail. So in addition to the proposed 6 per

cent cut, the government also required a further budget reduction equivalent to the loss of 150 posts. At the same time, the Commission was squeezed financially by central pay settlements exceeding the sum allowed for them in 'cash limits', a device imposed by a government concerned to reduce public expenditure – except for 'law and order.' One pertinent outcome of these funding cuts has been a dramatic loss of employees, which stands in marked and significant contrast to the expansion of both the police and prison services during the 1980s. Thus from being established in 1974, following the Health and Safety Act that year, the Executive's total staff in post rose steadily to 4,168 by April 1979, and, of these, 1,424 were field inspectors responsible for ensuring that standards and regulations were being obeyed. However, by 1984, the Executive's staff has been slashed by *one-seventh* to 3,563 and the total number of inspectors in the field dropped to 1,242. Furthermore, the projections are for more cuts. By 1986, the total inspectors in the field were expected to be around 1,200 which is the equivalent to 85 per cent of the 1979 total.

Armed with knowledge of the government's intentions and projected cuts, the Commission's plan of Work 1983/4 made gloomy reading for those concerned with health and safety at work. The Commission wrote:

> Most recently, recession, scarce resources, and rising unemployment have brought a changed focus and a new pressure to our work, raising questions about whether our activities, and those of the Health and Safety Executive are going to enhance manufacturing activity, and influencing the priority given by some groups of employers and workpeople to improving working conditions, as one objective alongside their wider objective of economic survival . . . The changing nature of economic activity and the acute problems of recession have raised fundamental questions about our activities and, more generally, the role of interventionist policies for health and safety at work. (Health and Safety Commission, 1983, pp. 1–2)

Soon after this, the Commission's director, Bill Simpson, who had been the General Secretary (Foundry Section) Amalgamated Union of Engineering Workers (1967–75) and a member of the Labour Party's National Executive Committee, was replaced by

John Cullen, who had been a director of ICI (1958–67) and Rohm and Haas (1967–83). It is noticeable that the last two annual reports have not made similar complaints about resources or questioned the ability of the Health and Safety Executive to do its job.

The latest stage in deregulation of health and safety standards has been for the government to permit the Commission to 'contract out' inspection to the industries concerned. This 'self-regulation' sounds fine in principle and makes some sense when the resources of Health and Safety agencies cannot inspect a substantial proportion of establishments under its jurisdiction. But imagine the response to the suggestion that young unemployed males should monitor their own behaviour and report themselves to the police whenever they discover they have broken the law!

In addition to facilitating a reduction in production costs by weakening the effectiveness of the Health and Safety Executive and its Inspectorates, the government has directly affected wage levels by abolition of the Fair Wages Resolution in 1983 and by threatening the Wage Councils with 'reform' and abolition. The Fair Wages Resolution provided that government contractors should observe such terms and conditions for their employees as had been generally established for the trade or industry in which they operated. The argument behind this abolition was that 'fair wages' inhibited employment. However, the result, according to the Civil Service Union and the Contract Cleaning and Maintenance Association has been that both wages *and employment levels* have fallen, and they have been accompanied by a worsening in other conditions of employment.

Wages Councils, of which there are 26 covering nearly 2.75 million low-paid workers, have the power to set legally enforceable minima for wages, holidays and other conditions of employment. The government has 'reformed' these by budgetary cuts which have resulted in the number of inspectors being cut by *one-quarter* from 166 in 1979 to 120 in 1985. In a year, this handful of inspectors is only capable of inspecting 10 per cent of the 400,000 establishments under Wage Council jurisdiction. It's effectiveness, never that remarkable, has now been further reduced, and, with the threat of abolition, morale is very low. Joining the government in its desire to release market forces on the already low paid and poorly unionised, and at the same time release corporations from previously legal obligations, are the Institute of Directors, the National Federation of Self-Employed and Small Businesses, and slightly less vigorously, the Confederation of British Industries.

It would all be very different if would-be burglars urged the government to exclude supermarket stores from the category of property that could technically be burgled on the economic grounds that 'times are hard' and breaking into and taking from such stores is a rational way of making ends meet. Similarly the plea that the police should be de-established or at least dissuaded by the Home Secretary from pursuing burglars would also drop on deaf ears. But, then, would-be burglars are not respectable executives whose corporations have economic and political clout.

So, as recession deepens, the prediction that corporate crime increases has to be formulated cautiously. Large multinationals will spend more energy exporting 'crimes' to Third World countries and whittling away laws and enforcement agencies so that behaviour previously banned will now be permitted. Only in that section of industry where these two options are not so readily available will the temptation to cut corners and operate illegal practices be pronounced. Small and middle sized national companies are therefore expected to be the locus of crimes in a recession; although it has to be stressed that much avoidable suffering resulting from large multinational 'immoral' behaviour will also increase, but this will not be technically illegal.

Changing economic conditions compounding environmental contradictions and uncertainties are not the sole cause of corporate crime. There are many other factors which complete the explanation, involving personnel who are 'ambitious, shrewd and possessed of a non-demanding moral code' (Gross, 1978, p. 71), a 'subculture of structural immoralities' (Mills, 1956, p. 138) which sanitizes crimes by elevating them to a higher moral plane, a cloak of corporate respectability that shields corporations and their officials from damaging self-images and minimising negative social reaction (Benson, 1984), and an awareness that 'corporate crime pays' (Box, 1983, pp. 44–53). However, with the exception of the last factor, these remain fairly constant throughout the business cycle. During a recession, however, environmental uncertainties increase and the costs of corporate crimes decrease because enforcement agencies are systematically weakened by government

policies and the judiciary adopts a more sympathetic stance towards businessmen 'in trouble'. In these circumstances an invitation to break the law will be eagerly accepted by those for whom
law evasion is not a real alternative. Corporate crime committed
by small to middle-sized companies should therefore increase as a
recession deepens. Evidence from research on corporate crime
and its relation to changing economic conditions is reviewed in
Chapter 3.

(ii)   Conflict theory, recession and crimes of repression

Conflict theorists suggest a link between recession and such crimes
of repression as police killing of civilians and brutality. As
Chambliss and Seidman (1971) argue:

> The more economically stratified a society becomes the more it
> becomes necessary for dominant groups to enforce through
> coercion the norms of conduct that guarantee their supremacy.
> (p. 33)

What they imply is that although governing elites have always had
a respectable fear of hooligans (Pearson, 1983) and the 'dangerous
classes', this anxiety oscillates with economic cycles. As unemployment rises, so the surplus labour force becomes a body viewed
more suspiciously by the governing elite, not because it actually
does become disruptive and rebellious, but because it *might*. Any
widening of economic inequalities increases these fears, because
the potential insubordination of the unemployed and marginalised
might be actualised through militant, maybe revolutionary, organisations springing up to defend and raise the consciousness of
the swelling army of the underprivileged. Under such circumstances, conflict theorists predict more state coercion.

This state coercion takes many forms. Of more relevance to
criminologists is the likelihood that the state will increase the
number of police and extend their powers, extend the sentencing
powers of courts and encourage longer sentences for particular
types of offenders, build more prisons to accommodate greater
numbers being processed by a more efficient police and court
system, and introduce more laws to criminalise behaviour which is

seen, by some, to threaten particular economic interests, such as industrial disputes and strikes. At the same time, the state would focus these greater powers against those committing 'conventional' crimes rather than against those committing 'crimes of the powerful'.

However, all these attempts to allay respectable fears by 'sterilising' the potential ability of the subordinate surplus population to give birth to an uncontrollable rebellious movement are relatively more costly than one other simple possibility: the authorities could become more indifferent to such police crimes as unjustified arrest, evidence fabrication, brutality and even killing, particularly when the victims of these crimes are just those persons perceived to be potentially dangerous and possible recruits for political resistance.

This is not to argue that the state *directs* the police to engage in these crimes more often, or that there is a *conspiracy* to pervert the course of justice in this way. That argument would be too crude and unnecessary. The logic of the situation leads to this scenario without any cigar-filled back-room meetings being necessary. As Jacobs and Britt (1979) point out:

> For inequality to lead to more lethal violence by the police it is *not* necessary to assume that elites make direct demands for harsh methods. All that is required is that elites be more willing to overlook the violent short cuts taken by the 'dirty workers' in the interests of order. Of course this interpretation fits with Hughes' (1963) argument that a willingness to remain conveniently ignorant is a fundamental explanation for much official brutality. (p. 406)

Although conflict theory provides an account of increasing police crime during a recession – the state is more willing to turn a blind eye to illegalities – this has to be supplemented by a consideration of why the police themselves would want or have a motive to commit more crimes. To understand this, the changing nature of police work during a recession needs to be examined. From the officers' perspective, police work is dangerous, socially isolating, and contains problems of authority which not only undermine efficiency, but frequently poison police–public encounters. The police regard themselves as front-line troops against certain types of violent criminals, terrorists, militant dissenters and industrial agitators.

During the last decade or so, when class tensions increased and the 'fear of crime' became a growing social problem, these police perceptions of their job and their 'symbolic assailants' sharpened. Not only were criminals viewed as becoming more desperate, as the increased use of firearms testifies, but the growing militancy of certain social groups threatened to undermine social order, the very reason for having a police force. Responding to the public fear of crime became the 'end' by which the 'means' of bending the rules were justified.

From the police's point of view, this serious situation of rising crime and public fear had to be met with equal determination. In the mounting war on crime and dissent, the police, fortified with support from the 'respectable' public, increasingly granted themselves a licence to break the law when it came to the disreputable elements. In this way the law was broken but order maintained.

This slip towards police crime, particularly brutality, was given a further nudge by deteriorating relationships between the police and that narrow section of the public on whom they concentrate most of their powers of surveillance, arrest and prosecution. When the police came to be viewed by this section of the public as an 'army of occupation', and when accounts of police brutality fanned the flames of discontent and resentment among many inner-city dwellers, then the situation was ripe for the police to feel threatened. Naturally, despite their professional training, they protected themselves as best they could, sometimes with a 'protective first strike' or by 'fitting-up' a suspect when they 'knew' the public would be better protected if he were behind bars. When politicians and some sections of the public responded by stating that 'the police are doing a wonderful job', and anyone who criticised them was very suspect indeed, then no wonder the police took this encouragement as an invitation to continue. Furthermore, the absence of an effective complaints procedure, ridiculously low levels of prosecution and conviction, even for assault (Box, 1983, pp. 98–111; Stevens and Willis, 1981) – they wobbled between 1 and 2 per cent during the 1970s – and the growing awareness among senior police officers that they are not accountable to publicly elected local government officials (Hewitt, 1982; Spencer, 1985), simply reinforced this invitation.

Given the encouragement, and the government's willingness to turn a blind eye to irregularities if they achieve the object of defeating the 'enemy within', as Mrs Thatcher calls them, it is understandable why police crimes against civilians might increase during a recession. These ideas are presented diagrammatically here (see Figure 2.2) and evidence relevant to assessing their accuracy is presented in the next chapter.

Concluding thoughts

In this chapter there has been developed an account of why people might be motivated to break the law and how other conducive factors might transform this motive into action. But to render action comprehensible is not to 'excuse' it. It may well be that the motivation to crime is a purely 'rational' response to the pressures, strains, stresses and contradictions people face. None the less, this does not make their *response* rational. Indeed, much crime is so horrendous in its victimisation, so imbued with racist and sexist overtones, and hits hardest those already on the razor edge of desperation, that it does not deserve to be excused. Legal competition and struggle under present economic conditions is bad enough, but capitalism with its clothes off is frequently beyond any human response other than condemnation.

If crimes evoke such outrage, and they clearly do, then their reduction ought to be prioritised. The 'no excuse' position is simply an impoverished response. Only when the motivation behind them, and the structural conditions, particularly inequality and competitiveness, behind the motivation are analysed can there be an appropriate point of intervention to bring about a reduction in the level of criminal activity.

Just before this chapter was finished, there were riots in Toxteth, Liverpool, and Tottenham, London. The same old tired 'folk devils' were conjured up. There was the same old refusal to admit that social causes could play a significant part in the outburst of social protest and criminal behaviour. It was the same old myopic debate that followed the riots of 1981, but with one significant

Figure 2.2 *Recession and crimes of the powerful*

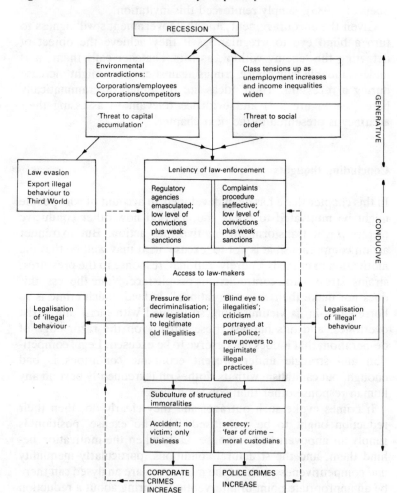

difference. This time the UK government refused to set up a judicial inquiry. Clearly it did not want to receive the unpleasant news again from Lord Scarman, or someone like him, that conditions in inner-city areas were criminogenic. In place of understanding there was now only a demand for more and better tools to 'do the job' properly. Metropolitan Commissioner Newman warned the capital that next time he would not hesitate to use CS gas and plastic bullets, and water cannons were in their final testing trials. The Home Secretary promised the police a new arrestable offence of 'disturbing behaviour'. This wide discretionary power could in principle be used to protect the Asian community from racist insults, but will in practice probably be used to intensify the policing of marginalised populations. Maybe it is a sad indictment of politicians who choose not to see the legacies of their economic policies, or, if they do, refuse to admit it. Hopefully, this chapter has pointed out some of the observations or admissions politicians would make if they were more sensitive or honest. But maybe they too only make choices – to appear naive or dishonest – under circumstances not of their own choosing. If, as was hinted in the previous chapter, these circumstances are nothing less than the 'South-Koreanisation' of the British labour force, itself brought about by the logic of international capitalism, then what politician would want to make this public? Better to take refuge is stupidity than to admit to such a policy.

Having hacked a path through the tangled forest of sociological theorising, there is now an even more daunting task – to assess the evidence relevant to testing hypotheses derived from this arduous journey into theorising.

3 Does Recession Lead to More Crime?

Demonstrating that a theory of crime causation is supported empirically is 'easier said than done'. This aphorism is even more apt when, as in this instance, most of the research studies on unemployment, inequality and crime had already been completed before the formulation of the theory in Chapter 2. A review of 'relevant' research literature therefore necessarily has to contain much that addresses itself marginally to that theory or even a ghost within it. Only a minority of existing research projects comes close to fitting the requirements for testing the above theory – although, as will become clear later, the picture is not absolutely bleak.

This review will examine, first, *time-series* and *cross-sectional* studies which have 'manipulated' aggregate data, e.g. rates of behaviour, to discover whether there is an empirical relationship between unemployment and crime, or income inequality and crime. It will then turn to *longitudinal* research which has examined the first of these possibilities by considering individual experiences. This involved interviewing people to ascertain whether they committed more crime *after* becoming unemployed. As these three research strategies are examined, methodological issues which plague each type will have to be raised in order to evaluate more precisely whether or not 'the case is proven'. Finally, there has to be a limit on how far back the net should be cast to trawl research studies on unemployment, income inequality and crime: this particular review is limited to research reported after 1950 and is mainly confined to North American and British research.

Recession and 'conventional' crimes

Time-series studies on unemployment and crime

Eighteen time-series studies which examined the relationship between unemployment/labour-force participation rates and criminal activity have been located. Of these, thirteen report a positive relationship, i.e. as unemployment increases so does crime, and five were unable to locate any such relationship (see Table 3.1 for references). That result 13–5 – looks overwhelming, a bit like the half-time score in a friendly football match between Manchester United and Thanington Without (in this case without too much defence). But appearances can be, and in this instance are, deceptive. So a precautionary investigation, backstage as it were, is required.

An early study by Glaser and Rice (1959) examined unemployment and arrest rates for property crimes and offences of violence against the person, in Boston, Cincinnati and Chicago for the period 1936–56. They concluded that:

> despite large deficiencies of available data, we have presented evidence which suggests . . . constant support . . . for the hypothesis that adult crime rates vary directly with unemployment, particularly rates of property offences by persons of 20 to 45 years of age. (p. 168)

A major problem with this type of research is that arrest data are a long way removed from actual criminal behaviour. Not only do cases that are cleared up and therefore potentially leading to an arrest, constitute a minority of all crimes, but there is no guarantee that they are representative. Given the evidence on discriminatory policing, the inclination to stereotype certain social groups as potential delinquents, and selective deployment in 'criminal areas' (Box, 1981, pp. 167–76), the arrested population is more likely to contain lower-class males among whom ethnic minorities will also be overrepresented. The outcome is that arrestees, as a sample of all those committing crimes, will contain disproportionately more unemployed persons, thus creating the appearance of unemployment and crime being linked when it is just as likely, as is shown in Chapter 6, that unemployment is linked to arrest.

70

Table 3.1 *Time-series and cross-sectional studies on unemployment and crime*

Positive relationship	Time-series	Cross-sectional
Yes	Box and Hale, 1985 Brenner, 1978 Cook and Zarkin, 1985 Ehrlich, 1975 Fleisher, 1963 Glaser and Rice, 1959 Land and Felson, 1976 Leveson, 1976 Phillips *et al.*, 1972 Phillips, 1981 Singell, 1967 Votey, 1979 Wolpin, 1978	Allison, 1972 Bechdolt, 1975 Block, 1979 Booth *et al.*, 1977 Brown *et al.*, 1972 Carroll and Jackson, 1983 Chapman, 1976 Cohen and Land, 1984 Danziger, 1976 DeFronzo, 1983 Hakim, 1982 (reanalysis of Carr-Hill and Stern, 1979) Hemley and McPheters, 1974 Hoch, 1974 Kvalseth, 1977 Pyle, 1982 Sampson *et al.*, 1981 Schmid, 1960 Sjoquist, 1973 Zedlewski, 1983
No	Danziger and Wheeler, 1975 Danser and Laub, 1981 Fox, 1978 Orsagh, 1981 Vandaele, 1978	Avio and Clark, 1976 Bartel, 1979 Danziger and Wheeler, 1975 Forst, 1976 Gylys, 1970 Pogue, 1975 Schuessler and Slatin, 1964 Singell, 1967 Spector, 1975 Stevens and Willis, 1979 Swimmer, 1974 Wadycki and Balkin, 1979 Williams and Drake, 1980

Fleisher (1963) reanalysed the Glaser and Rice data, paying special attention to the 17–24-year-olds. He believed that:

an examination of delinquency rates and other variables by age and through time suggests that the effect of unemployment on juvenile delinquency is positive and significant . . . [However] . . . many factors which affect delinquency have not been considered and one cannot assert that unemployment is more important than those factors left out of account. (p. 555).

Thus, to the weakness of arrest data he added the need not to lay too much weight on research containing few variables, particularly as both unemployment and crime might be caused by a third factor. As it turned out, Weicher (1971) showed the absence of other variables in Fleisher's research, such as education and type of neighbourhood, to be a crucial weakness and their inclusion reduced the relationship between economic conditions and crime below a statistically significant level.

A slightly later study by Singell (1967) examined males under twenty-one years old who had been in contact with the Detroit Police Bureau over the period 1950–61. He warned that although caution must be exercised in interpreting the statistical estimations, none the less,

the data suggests that at current levels of youth unemployment, a cut in the rate of unemployment by 1 per cent would lead to a cut in delinquency rates from one-fourth to one-sixth of 1 per cent. The results seem significant enough to excite honest hopes for corrective action. (p. 386)

To this must be added a further caution: contacts with the police bureau, like arrests, are not always, as any streetwise Afro-Caribbean youth will tell you, in connection with criminal behaviour.

There are three studies by Phillips and various collaborators which are very relevant to the issue of age/race, unemployment and crime, although, like the above studies, their measure of criminal behaviour – arrests – is not very valid. The first study (Phillips, Votey and Maxwell, 1972) was limited to a manageable short time-span, 1952–67, during which youth unemployment for whites rose from 7 per cent and peaked at 17 per cent in 1958 and the rate for young blacks rose from 10 per cent to peak at 27 per cent in 1959. Because it both explored age-specific relationships and examined regression coefficients for whites and non-whites separately, this research is particularly pertinent to the 'strain-control' features of the theory in Chapter 2.

Phillips and his colleagues considered arrest rates for property offences and calculated these along with unemployment data on an age-specific basis. Their conclusions, which were reasserted eight years later in a slightly extended analysis (Phillips and Votey, 1981), were that:

> fluctuations in unemployment apparently have less impact for whites than non-whites . . . nonetheless . . . the changing labour market opportunities are sufficient to explain increasing crime rates for youth . . . and . . . our findings indicate that a successful attack on rising crime rates must consider the employment problems facing young people. (p. 170)

Votey (1979) extended the model in Phillips, Votey and Maxwell, to examine whether the policy of detaining heroin addicts had an appreciable effect on the rates of property offences. As part of this research, he was also concerned to assess the impact on unemployment over and above the 'voluntary unemployment' taken by most addicts. In addition, he argued that any effect of unemployment would appear some time after being made unemployed and therefore it was important to make allowance for lagged effects. To test these arguments, Votey used monthly crime data from the Santa Barbara Police Department for the period January 1970 to December 1974. He reported that the results were 'substantially improved by the distributed lags, thus tending to support the hypothesised lagged-response pattern for loss of employment' (p. 596).

Although these results support the argument that the effects of unemployment on crime rates will only appear some time afterwards, when other alternatives have been explored and found unsuitable, it should be noted that the effects of detention for heroin addicts on property offending rates had a far greater effect than did unemployment.

Finally, Phillips (1981) brought the analysis more up to date by examining the years 1964–77, and considering 16–17-year-old males. However, his results are only weakly consistent with the unemployment-causes-crime hypothesis. He wrote:

increases in the fraction of sixteen-and-seventeen-year-olds not working increase the arrest rates for property crimes for males less than eighteen for both blacks and whites. The results are not statistically significant, but there are only fourteen observations for each group. Because the parameter estimates were similar for blacks and whites, the observations were pooled . . . The positive impact of the fraction not working on arrest rates is significantly different from zero at the 10 per cent level. Changes in the fraction not working explain only about 9 per cent of the variance in changes in arrest rates. (pp. 187–8)

To these six American studies, ought to be added two British studies because they measured criminal activity by conviction rates, which is an even more deficient indicator than arrests. Wolpin (1978) considered males convicted of indictable offences over the period 1894–1967 in England and Wales and concluded that:

the unemployment rate is positively related to the overall crime rate and, specifically, to non-violent property crime, consistent with an economic model in which alternative opportunities enter the decision calculus. (p. 828)

Box and Hale (1984) considered females convicted of indictable offences over the period 1951–80 and reported that increases in the rate of female unemployment were significantly related to increases in the *rate of conviction* for violent crime (assault, and wounding), theft, handling stolen goods, and fraud.

Since conviction data is even further removed from criminal behaviour than is arrest data, these two British studies are probably weaker than the six American studies already discussed. If these eight researches are put in brackets on the grounds that their measure of criminal behaviour is too distant from the 'real thing' to be valid, then the score for studies finding a positive relationship between unemployment and crime and those finding none, is even: five to five.

Nine of these remaining studies used 'crimes known to the

police' as their measure of criminal behaviour. Of course this measure too is removed from actual behaviour, notably by the public's willingness to report crimes, and variations in police decisions to record events as criminal. Since the late 1950s in the USA numerous self-reported crime and criminal victimisation surveys have revealed a considerable gap in the actual number of crimes committed and those known to the police. This finding seemed to doom the claim, widely accepted in criminological circles, that 'crimes known to the police' are a relatively valid guide to criminal activity. However, recent reassessments (Elliott and Ageton, 1980; Hindelang, 1978; Savitz, 1978; Skogan, 1974) have concluded that despite numerous shortcomings in these data, they none the less provide robust estimates of relative changes in crime rates over time. But maybe this should be qualified: the longer the time-span under consideration, the less valid 'crimes known to the police'. This is because over time there is a greater chance of disturbances in the data being caused by changes in the public's willingness to report crime, the police's recording practices and, of course, the legislators' definitions of crimes.

Having established that these nine studies have a more valid measure of crime rates, and can therefore provide a more accurate estimate of the relationship between unemployment and crime, what do they conclude?

Ehrlich (1975) analysed rates of homicide, robbery and burglary annually published in the FBI *Uniform Crime Reports (UCR)* for the period 1933–69. He believed that:

> regression results . . . corroborate the specific theoretical predictions regarding the effects of . . . unemployment and labour force participation [p. 409] . . . and . . . preliminary time-series regressions shows that the elasticities of robbery and burglary rates with respect to the unemployment rate are even larger in magnitude than the corresponding elasticities of the murder rate. (p. 411)

Land and Felson (1976) limited their analysis to property offences in the USA for the period 1947–72, but they also built in some age-specific calculations. They concluded:

> the unemployment rate exhibits a coefficient with a theoretically expected sign that is statistically significant . . . Taken together

(with findings on age) . . . the results accord well with sociological theory, on the basis of which one would expect an increase in unemployment rate to have the greatest impact on the job opportunities structure of young males. (p. 592)

This supports nicely the hypothesised relationships between sex–age, unemployment and property crime. However, neither Ehrlich nor Land and Felson argue that unemployment is the major cause of increased crime rates. Indeed, both have quite different theoretical priorities. Ehrlich is much more concerned with the effects of deterrence, and Cohen, Felson and Land (1980) argue that as unemployment goes up there are reasons for thinking that crime rates will drop! The unemployed will be at home more and therefore burglaries will not be committed as frequently. Similarly, since the unemployed do not have to travel to work, there will be fewer opportunities for them to be robbed or mugged on the streets. Whatever one makes of these possibilities – and they were not supported in the 1982 *British Crime Survey* (Gottfredson, 1984, p. 8) – neither Land nor Ehrlich have continued to argue that unemployment is a major cause of crime.

Stronger support comes from another US study. Leveson (1976) analysed unemployment and crime from 1950 to 1972 and reported that there was a significant statistical relationship for young males but not adults. These results are consistent with the hypothesis that the effect of unemployment on crime differs between gender and age groups.

There is only one study on Britain which has to be mentioned here. Brenner (1978) correlated recorded crime rates and unemployment in England and Wales for the period 1900–70 and reported a significant relationship even when other economic factors were controlled. Indeed, from this and other evidence Brenner felt able to make a strongly worded submission to the US Joint Economic Committee. He claimed that:

a sustained 1 percent rise in unemployment will be followed by an increase in the homicide rate over that year and the subsequent five years. Thus, the effect is cumulative. Moreover, the increase in homicide is comparable to 5.7 percent of the homicides which occur in the fifth year following the sustained rise in unemployment. This increase is based on 34-year data from 1940–1973. (p. 6)

However, Brenner's assessment had been criticised by Orsagh (1980, p. 182), who argues that different, even contradictory, results could be achieved by making very minor adjustments in the technical procedures for analysing the data.

Finally, the most recent contribution to the unemployment-causes-crime debate comes from two American economists, Cook and Zarkin (1985), who analysed time-series data from 1933 through to 1980. They were primarily concerned to determine whether or not the business cycle and four crimes – murder, robbery, burglary and auto-theft – were statistically related. Their two indicators of the business cycle were (i) the civilian unemployment rate, and (ii) the employment–population ratio. They reported that during the post-war period 1947–81 the unemployment rate correlated with robbery (0.56), burglary (0.60), and auto-theft (0.46). Similarly high correlation were reported for these crimes and the employment ratio. After further regression analysis, they illustrated a hidden social cost of recession in the following dramatic presentation:

> Robbery and burglary rates are sensitive to fluctuations in economic conditions. Recessions appear to cause increase in these two crimes . . . *The magnitudes involved are not insubstantial. An increase in the unemployment rate from, say, 7 percent to 8 percent will result in a 2.3 percent increase in the robbery rate and a 1.6 percent increase in the burglary rate.* (p. 126)

On auto-theft, the other property offence they analysed, there was slight evidence that this went up as unemployment went down.

Against these five studies have to be weighed four which did not report similar findings. Orsagh (1981) used UCR data, numbers arrested and charged, and the unemployment rate for the age-group 14–21 over the years 1951–77. He concluded that although 'the unemployment rate may be related to the crime rate . . . the magnitude of its effects must be small' (p. 184). This is not exactly a damning conclusion. Danziger and Wheeler (1975) analysed US rates for aggravated assault, burglary and robbery for the years 1949–70 and concluded that 'the male unemployment rate does not seem to be systematically related to the crimes in question' (p. 124). However, their findings from a cross-sectional study (reported below) point to a different conclusion!

After examining data on auto-theft in the USA for the 35-years span 1935–69, Vandaele (1978) decided that 'unemployment rate . . . and labour force participation rate . . . have an insignificant impact on the supply of stolen cars' (p. 345). This is, however, a very weak study because it limited its analysis to only one serious offence, and one which is closely linked to the number of cars available. Fox (1978) analysed US data for the period 1950–74 and could find no positive relationship between unemployment and crime. However, in most of his analysis, he drops the unemployment variable and substitutes Consumer Price Index data. This has been described as 'conceptually bizarre' (Decker and Kohfeld, 1982) and 'technically unpersuasive' (Brenner, 1978).

The only remaining study, Danser and Laub (1981), is more or less unique because it used 'victimisation' survey data rather than 'crimes recorded by the police', and it cannot be as easily criticised as the above four studies. These authors analysed quarterly fluctuations in age–race–sex specific unemployment rates and comparable age–race–sex specific rates of offending – the base for the latter being derived from information supplied by victim respondents to the National Crime Surveys 1973 through to 1978. They found that unemployment was not related 'to the total rate of offending, i.e. for simple and aggravated assault and robbery, for juvenile, youthful and adult offenders for both black and white' (p. 35). However, they had to qualify this blanket conclusions because when then examined particular types of crime, that found that:

> robbery has a weak relationship with unemployment, although the results are inconsistent across offender age groups. For juvenile white males aged 12–17, and adult white males, aged 21 or older, unemployment rates explain a significant ($p < .10$) proportion of the variance in the robbery rate of offending. (p. 40)

These results are therefore slightly contradictory. At best they offer partial support for the theory in Chapter 2, but on the whole this study is a headache for those supporting the view that unemployment and crime are invariably linked irrespective of the offence. However, a cross-sectional anaylsis based on the same victimisation data reported results much more favourable to the unemployment–crime hypothesis (see Sampson *et al.*, 1981).

On balance, and considering the weaknesses in the research,

*existing time-series studies provide some support for the idea that
unemployment and crime, particularly for younger males, are causally linked.* This preliminary evaluation echoes Freeman's (1983),
who reviewed ten of the above studies for the Institute of Contemporary Studies in San Francisco – a right-wing think-tank – and
concluded that:

> despite differences and weaknesses among the studies, a general
> finding emerges: namely that rises in unemployment and/or
> declines in labour participation rate are connected with rises in
> the crime rate, but the effect tends to be modest and insufficient
> to explain the general upward trend of crime in the period
> studied. The labour participation rate is, moreover, often found
> to have a closer link to crime than does unemployment, sug-
> gesting that those who actually leave the labour force are the
> most crime prone. (p. 96)

However, it would be premature to come to a firm conclusion until
other methods of unravelling a connection between unemployment and crime have been examined.

Cross-sectional studies on unemployment and crime

Cross-sectional studies take 'photographs' of the social structure at
any one time. They then examine these to see if patterns of
similarity can be detected. For example, if 'photographs' of the
social structure of, say, Manchester, Bristol, Birmingham and
other major British cities were taken and examined, it might
become apparent that in those cities with higher unemployment
rates there were also higher rates of crime. If that were the case, a
causal relationships could be inferred. It cannot really be put
stronger than that because ideally unemployment would have to
be measured at time *t* and crime at some later time *t* + 1.
Cross-sectional studies often lack a true temporal dimension and
are therefore suggestive rather than conclusive. However, where a
temporal sequence is included, then a stronger conclusion than
mere inference is possible.

A total of thirty-two cross-sectional studies on unemployment
and crime have been located (see Table 3.1). Of these, nineteen

report evidence supporting a relationship and thirteen were unable to do so. However, those using arrest data (Bartel, 1979; Sjoquist, 1973; Stevens and Willis, 1979), contact with the police (Singell, 1967) and conviction rates (Brown *et al.*, 1972) can be bracketed off on the grounds that their measure of crime is suspect. That leaves a score of fifteen to ten in favour of a positive relationship.

Considering the positive studies, only two (Hakim, 1982; Pyle, 1982) refer to England and Wales. Pyle examined age-specific groups, unemployment and recorded property offences for the year 1975. The results, he believed, 'support the view that increases in unemployment are likely to significantly increase recorded property crime rates (most notably robberies)' (p. 15). Hakim (1982) took the unusual step of reanalysing the data of Carr-Hill and Stern (1979) who are usually quoted as providing strong evidence that unemployment and crime are *not* related. However, Hakim argues:

> a careful reading of this study shows that the authors never carried out the test in question . . . but instead test the contribution of unemployment to explaining the number of police per capita in each area. In effect the authors reject the hypothesis about unemployment contributing to crime on the theoretical (or subjective) grounds, but they imply that they tested it fully. However, they are unable to sidestep the results that show that areas with a high proportion of young men aged 15–24 years and a high proportion of working class have a significantly higher crime rates – and both these groups have the highest levels of unemployment experiences.(p. 452)

Hakim presents reanalysed data from the Carr-Hill and Stern research and shows for the three years examined (1961, 1966 and 1971) that 'the results . . . confirm the association between crime and unemployment, and suggest it has been increasing over time' (p. 453).

Thirteen of the remaining positive studies are all US based and can be divided into two groups: first, four which used Standard Metropolitan Statistical Areas (SMSAs) as their basic unit of analysis, and second, nine which analysed major cities. This is a relevant distinction because the hypothesised relationships would be expected to be more consistently supportive in cities than in SMSAs which extend beyond cities and include suburban and rural communities.

DeFronzo (1983) studied 39 SMSAs for 1970 and reported that 'unemployment rates had statistically significant positive effects on rape, burglary and larceny' (p. 128). Danziger (1976) had a larger sample consisting of 222 SMSAs for the same year and concluded that 'for both the robbery and the burglary regressions, the signs for the income level, income inequality, and the *male unemployment* rate are positive (as predicted)' (p. 293). Hoch (1974) examined two years, 1960 and 1970, for which he based his analysis on 136 and 137 SMSAs respectively. His results led him to declare that 'increased unemployment is associated with increased rates for burglary and assault in both periods, and for larceny and robbery in 1970. The *t*-ratio for burglary in 1970 is one of the highest attained in all the analyses' (p. 204). Finally Hemley and McPheters (1974) took the same two years but limited their analyses to 32 states. They concluded that 'urban unemployment had a pronounced positive effect on the rates of burglary and larceny, but did not significantly effect robbery rates' (p. 83).

For those studies concentrating on cities the results were just as pronounced. Allison (1972) examined Chicago for 1960 and concluded that 'the analysis indicates a strong relationship between the rate of crime and the rate of unemployment' (p. 195). Bechdolt (1975) considered Los Angeles in 1960 and Chicago in 1970 and decided that 'unemployment is a significant and important determinant of property crime rate . . . and . . . the violent crime rate is explained best by the unemployment rate . . . These analyses . . . suggest that property and violent crime rates could be reduced in the short term through policies and programmes to reduce unemployment' (p. 136). Block (1979) examined rates of homicide, robbery and aggravated assault in Chicago 1974/5. His results showed strong positive correlations between each of these and the percentage of males aged 16–21 unemployed. However, the proximity of poor neighbourhoods to rich ones was a stronger statistical factor, suggesting that sense of a relative deprivation was greater where those materially better off are highly visible. Carroll and Jackson (1983) studied 93 non-southern cities of 50,000-plus population for the year 1970. Their findings are 'partially consistent with . . . [the view that] . . . the effects are more likely for property crime and more likely to be found by the more recent research . . . in that unemployment is found to have its strongest effect on burglary. It also . . . is found to have a moderately positive effect on the rate of personal crime but virtually no effect on the rate of robbery' (p. 191). Chapman (1976) aggregated data from 147 Californian cities ranging from 20,000 to over 100,000 in 1960 and 1970, and examined the influences of numerous factors on crime as measured by crimes known to the California State Bureau of Criminal Statistics. He came to a strong conclusion:

> the most important variable in terms of elasticity is the employment variable which indicates that for a one percent increase in the percent labour force employed full time, there is a 1.8 percent drop in the crime rate. (p. 59)

Kvalseth (1977) considered Atlanta, Georgia, and although he cautioned that the evidence was not entirely conclusive or consistent, none the less wrote:

> the total urban unemployment rate has a positive influence on the rates of burglary and larceny; the male unemployment rate exerts a positive influence on the robbery rate; and both male and female unemployment rates have a positive effect on the rate of rape. (p. 109)

Schmid (1960) analysed pooled data for 93 census tracts in Seattle for the years 1949–51 and reported a relationship between larceny and unemployment, but not for auto-theft.

Finally, four studies deserve to be held back till last because, unlike those above, they included crime rates derived from *victimisation* surveys. Although it has its critics, this measure is generally thought to be a more valid indicator of the actual amount of 'conventional' one-to-one crime in the community. It is therefore probably the best 'rate of criminal activity' against which to test the unemployment-causes-crime hypothesis.

Cohen and Land's (1984) data is derived from the 1970 census and 1972/3 National Crime Survey in 26 of the largest US cities. Their results show that unemployment makes a significant contribution to the victimisation rates for rape, robbery and vehicle theft, and a slighter, although still statistically significant, contribution to burglary, aggravated assault and larceny-theft. But it has to be stressed that other social structural variables, such as age and racial composition, population size, density and mobility, are at least as important.

Booth *et al.* (1977) studied the same 26 cities as Cohen and Land, and in addition to unemployment, took into account the possible effects of population density, household crowding, racial composition, marital instability, proportion under eighteen years, residential mobility, size of community and resources allocated to public safety. They discovered that irrespective of whichever crime measure were used – UCR or victimisation survey data – unemployment was strongly related to burglary, slightly related to robbery, and did not affect the rate of auto-theft. Rape, homicide, assault and larceny were not analysed. However, the main purpose of their study was to see if the correlations between social factors (other than unemployment) and crime, and therefore the explanation of crime, remained the same irrespective of whether the crime rate was measured by 'crimes known to the police' or by victimisation survey data. It is depressing to read that 'quite different conclusions would be reached' depending upon which of these two measures the researcher(s) choose to use, and therefore 'neither is a satisfactory index of crime for purposes of explaining the causes of crime' (p. 196).

Fortunately, for the business of criminological research, this damaging conclusion is not consistent with other attempts to see if these two measures tap the same behaviour (Hindelang, 1978; Savitz, 1978; Skogan, 1974, 1976). It would be prudent therefore to remain agnostic on this issue until further research on these two measures produces some agreement on their relative merits for the purposes of testing hypotheses on the causes of crime rates. But it is worth noting that Zedlewski (1983), who analysed 137 SMSAs in 1977, examined both NCS and UCR data for burglaries, larcenies and property crimes, and found that 'both series indicate a strong positive association between labour-force participation rates and crime rates' (p. 270).

The fourth, and final study (Sampson *et al.* 1981), attempted to assess the impact of neighbourhood unemployment rates on criminal activity by using the NCS data from 1973–8 and matching these against Census data on the neighbourhoods covered in these surveys. First they considered the evidence on whether or not most 'conventional crime' is committed within neighbourhoods and concluded that 'the available evidence indicates that a sizeable proportion of all crimes, especially juvenile crime, is "ecologically bound"' (p. 32). Second, they analysed the effect of neighbourhood unemployment on crime and concluded that:

> The relationship between neighbourhood unemployment and victimisation was moderate and positive for juvenile and adult victimisation, but weak and inconsistent for 18–20 year old victimisations. The relationship was stronger for theft than violent victimisations, especially among blacks. The extent of urbanisation difference were also revealed with victimisation rates in urban areas being more strongly related to neighbourhood unemployment than victimisation rates in rural areas. (p. 2)

All the above cross-sectional studies show some support for the idea that unemployment is linked to crime, but there are others, fewer in number, which came to a different conclusion.

Forst (1976) studied 51 US States in 1970 and concluded that 'unemployment was unimportant'. However, Wadycki and Balkin (1979) reported that Forst's data were blemished with some errors and therefore his results were unreliable. They replicated his analysis with the data set corrected, but were still unable to discover any relationship between unemployment and the total numbers of index crimes recorded by the FBI. Spector (1975) considered 103 SMSAs in 1970, but only for violent offences, and concluded that 'there is no significant relationship between unemployment and violence in the American city . . . at best . . . unemployment is a minor contributor to the high rate of violent crime' (p. 401). Swimmer (1974) analysed all cities with over 100,000 population in 1960 and concluded that in comparison with other variables 'the unemployment rate [has] the least explanatory power' (p. 305). Gylys (1970) could find no relationship between unemployment and rates for numerous crimes in 50 large central city areas for the years 1960 and 1968. Danziger and Wheeler (1975) analysed 57 large SMSAs for 1960 and came to the same conclusion. So did Schuessler and Slatin (1964) who surveyed 101 US cities in 1950; however, for 1960, when they examined 137 cities, they did report a positive correlation between unemployment rates and robbery and auto-theft. Pogue (1975) had a sample of 163 SMSAs for the years 1962 and 1967. His results support 'the hypotheses that crime rates are directly related to income, percent poor, percent young, and city size . . . and that . . . the most stable and relationship appears to be that between crime rates and percent poor . . . but none the less . . . unemployment rates appear to have little systematic impact on crime rates' (p. 33). Avio and Clark (1976) analysed property offences in Canada by pooling provincial data. They were unable to locate significant relationships between these and unemployment.

This leaves one final study to muddy the waters even further. Williams and Drake (1980) carried out a bivariate correlation on unemployment and crime, but took two different measures of the latter, namely UCR and victimisation data. Whilst they found statistically significant correlations between unemployment and UCR for rape and burglary, these results were not replicated on the victimisation data, which failed to reveal any significant relationships. Since this research is very similar to Booth *et al.* (1977) its results are indeed curious, not to mention different! Maybe one city provides the clue to this paradox, for Williams and Drake analysed 25 cities, while Booth *et al.* analysed 26!

Yet Another (British) Study

England and Wales is divided up into 43 police areas. The crime rates (specified crimes recorded by the police per 100,000 population) vary considerably. Thus serious crimes recorded in 1983 were as low as 3,117 in Dyfed-Powys compared with 9,692 in Greater Manchester. It is possible to match these police areas to administrative regional areas where, based on registered claimants as at December 1982, unemployment rates varied from the lowest 6.5 per cent in Surrey to 19.9 per cent in Cleveland. By correlating these against 1983 'crimes recorded by the police' per 100,000 population, it is possible to allow for a lagged effect in a cross-sectional analysis. However, four areas were excluded. Nottinghamshire, persistently having the highest rates of crime, has always been considered maverick in its recording practices, and so was omitted on these grounds. London (including both the City and Metropolitan police forces), being an enormous conglomerate, requires separate analysis at the Borough level because it contains such a heterogeneous social mix within its boundaries. Finally Warwickshire is counted by the Employment Department as a 'travel-to-work' area and so no data on unemployment are provided.

The results from the remaining 39 regional areas certainly support predicted statistical relationships between levels of unemployment and subsequent crime rates. It can be seen from Table 3.2 that the relationship is very strong for buglary, criminal damage (vandalism), burglary, theft and handling. Indeed, using a simple linear regression, over 30 per cent of the variance in these recorded crimes is accounted for statistically by unemployment. For two other crimes – robbery, fraud and forgery – the relationship is also strong, accounting for between 20 and 30 per cent of the variance. Only for sexual offences is unemployment a poor predictor. Since these results are lagged, i.e. measuring unemployment at the end of the year preceding the one in which these crimes were recorded, there is a temporal sequence built into the analysis, and this supports the view that unemployment is causally linked to crime levels.

Table 3.2 *Correlations between unemployment rate and serious crimes recorded by the police, England and Wales 1982–3, 39 police force areas*

Offence	Correlation
Burglary	0.572++
Violence against person	0.529++
Criminal damage	0.494++
Theft and handling	0.423++
Robbery	0.342+
Fraud and forgery	0.338+
Sexual offences	0.158

++ $p < 0.01$
  + $p < 0.05$

On balance, the evidence from cross-sectional studies favours the hypothesis that unemployment and crime are related, although as would be expected from studies concentrating on the total population as opposed to a theoretically relevant one, such as young males, this relationship is not consistently strong. This conclusion can be strengthened further by quoting Long and Witte (1981) who also reviewed most of the above studies. They decided that:

> there is a positive, although generally insignificant relationship between the level of unemployment and criminal activity . . . as would be expected . . . the relationship tends to be most strongly supported with respect to property crimes. (p. 126)

In order to complete this survey of the relevant literature, it is necessary to turn now to those studies which have concentrated on manipulating aggregated data to consider whether income inequality and criminal activity are related.

Income Inequality and Crime

Although there are many ways to interpret 'income inequality', in the following research literature the standard measure is known as the *Gini coefficient*. This variable is computed only for heads of households that are families. It is based on the combined incomes of all family members from any source and does not exclude taxes. The Gini index is derived by plotting, say, the top 5 per cent income recipients against their proportion of the community's total income. Under conditions of total equality, this plotted line would be a straight diagonal. The actual line deviates from this because incomes are concentrated in small groups of the population, and the gap between the equality line and the actual line is expressed statistically as the Gini coefficient. The assumption is that this 'objective' measure of income inequality has a 'subjective' counterpart – relative deprivation – particularly in cultures where formal equality is stressed and individuals are socialised to aspire for material success. This subjective discomfort provides the motivational element required for criminal activity.

As can be observed from Table 3.3, there are fewer studies testing the relationship between income inequality and crime than that between unemployment and crime, and only one of these, Danziger and Wheeler (1975), was based on time-series data. These authors considered burglary, robbery and aggravated assault known to the FBI for the years 1949–70, and concluded that:

Table 3.3 *Time-series and cross-sectional studies on income inequality and crime*

Positive relationship	Time-series	Cross-sectional
Yes	Danziger and Wheeler, 1975	Avio and Clark, 1976 Blau and Blau, 1982 Braithwaite, 1979 Carroll and Jackson, 1983 Cohen and Land, 1984 Danziger and Wheeler, 1975 DeFronzo, 1983 Jacobs, 1981 Smith and Bennett, 1985 Stack and Kanavy, 1983 Williams and Drake, 1980
No		Bailey, 1984 Loftin and Hill, 1974 Messner, 1982 Smith and Parker, 1980 Williams, 1984

the distributional impact of economic growth should not be neglected; increases in income which result from economic growth with a constant distribution lead to higher crimes rates. (p. 125)

Of the sixteen cross-sectional studies, eleven report that income inequality is causally related to crime and five do not. However, this gives a very misleading summary since the five negative studies all relate to only one crime, namely homicide (Bailey, 1984; Loftin and Hill, 1974; Messner, 1982; Smith and Parker, 1980; Williams, 1984). In other words, *every study to date on income inequality and property offences or non-fatal violence shows there is a statistical, maybe even a causal relationship.* This stands in sharp contrast to the ambiguous results of research on unemployment and crime, and the implications of this difference will be spelt out later.

Jacobs (1981) examined burglary, larceny and robbery in 195 SMSAs in 1970. He concluded:

the[se] results are consistent with an assertion that contrasts in economic privilege give rise to property crimes. The strong relationships between economic inequality and burglary and grand larceny rates when other factors are controlled supports theorists [who have argued] that pronounced differences in the allocation of resources cause less fortunate men to compare their life choices with others and decide that legitimate avenues to material reward must be supplemented by property crime. (p. 23)

Carroll and Jackson (1983) focused on 93 non-southern US cities of 50,000-plus for the year 1970 and discovered that:

inequality has strong causal effects on crime rates . . . [although] . . . the effect of inequality on crimes against the person was not as pronounced as the effect on burglary. (p. 186)

Blau and Blau (1982) analysed murder, rape, robbery and aggravated assault in 125 of the largest SMSAs for 1970 and argued that:

income inequality in a metropolis substantially raises its rate of criminal violence . . . and . . . socioeconomic inequality between blacks and whites has a positive direct effect on criminal violence. (p. 126)

Although Blau and Blau could find only an ambiguous relationship between income inequality and rape, this result was not replicated in either Stack and Kanavy (1983) or the more sensitive research of Smith and Benneth (1985). The former studied 50 US states for 1971 and found:

strong support . . . for an economic theory of crime based on unemployment as well as income inequality. Both variables exert a positive, independent effect on rape. The beta coefficient for income inequality is especially large, placing it in the top four determinants of rape. (p. 72)

However, with a more sophisticated research design, Smith and Bennett came to a less emphatic conclusion. They contrasted 44 SMSAs with a very high rate of rape, with 44 SMSAs with a very low rate of rape, and based their analysis on aggregated pooled data for the years 1979–83. They ask and answer the following question:

Do 'measures of economic deprivation (poverty, inequality) serve as predictors of rape rates'? the answer is a qualified 'yes'. Other variables, of which the divorce rate is one, are more predictive. (p. 334)

Braithwaite's study (1979) is important because he claimed that 'no previous study had tested the effects of a variety of indices of inequality while systematically controlling for key predictors of city crime rates' (p. 211). Braithwaite pooled annual crime data from 1967 to 1973 for 193 SMSAs, and decided that:

there is strong and consistent support for the hypothesis that cities in which there is a wide income gap between poor and average-income families have high rates for all types of crime. (p. 216)

Three studies with smaller data sets should be briefly mentioned. DeFronzo (1983) whose research covered 38 SMSAs in 1970 found 'income inequality statistically related to burglary and larceny . . . but not the other five Index crimes' (p. 130). Danziger and Wheeler (1975), with a slightly larger sample for the year 1960, concluded that:

crime rates are strongly affected by interpersonal welfare comparisons. Levels of criminal activity are responsive to changes in the distribution of income. . . . A one percent reduction in either dimensions of inequality was shown to reduce crime rates to a larger extent than a one percent increase in deterrence. (pp. 126–7)

Avio and Clark (1976) pooled data from Canadian provinces and found that it was a good predictor of rates for theft, fraud, breaking and entering.

Finally, there is the research of Williams and Drake (1980) in which income inequality was correlated with victimisation data in 25 SMSAs collected in 1971–4. They report that although there was a relationship between this social fact and rape, burglary, auto-theft and aggravated assault, it was only significant for the last offence. What is very interesting and will be discussed at length in Chapter 5, is that the correlation between *arrest* data and all these crimes was significant, for this raises the issue, Is arrest data a measure of criminal activity, or is it a measure of the state's activity, i.e. its propensity to criminalise?

It is clear from this review that income inequality and crime, with the possible exception of homicide, are strongly related. When inequalities widened, *as they did during the current recession*, so the crime rate went up. That it probably did not rise at the rate suggested by 'crimes recorded by the police' does not mean that crime has not increased over the last decade or so. This relationship between inequality and crime has important implications for policies designed to reduce crime and these are discussed at length in Chapter 7.

A cautionary note

Before the provisional conclusion on either unemployment and crime or income inequality and crime is taken too seriously, it would be wise to make a few critical comments on the use and limitations of aggregated data.

Sociological theorising is always more attractive, and rewarding, than getting down to the dirty work of research or research evaluation. None the less, flights of fancy have to be pinned down or they will soar recklessly, only to nosedive into that already overfull graveyard of mistaken ideas. Pinning down the integrated theory in Chapter 2 has not so far been a major success largely because much of the research on unemployment, inequality and crime was concerned only with the 'strain' component, and ignored the 'control-reaction' components, and it was of variable quality. On the issue of quality, three problems stand out:

1 Different measures of the *dependent variable*, the crime rate, make many of the results either invalid or non-comparable. Thus the above evaluation has taken exception to those researchers who employed very distant measures of crime, such as conviction, arrests or contact with the police. The reason for this

exception is that these are more properly viewed as measures of organisational behaviour – they tell us more about the police and courts than about offenders. Even with studies which have used 'crimes recorded by the police', there is still a lively debate over their validity, a debate certainly not silenced by Booth *et al.* (1977) and Williams and Drake (1980) who reported that different kinds of explanation could be supported or refuted simply by the expedient of choosing 'crimes known to the police' or criminal victimisation crime data.

An important part of this measurement problem is that researchers have to settle for second-best information, namely aggregated data. They do this because it is cheaper and available in huge quantities. But as Orsagh (1979) argues, 'those who settle for aggregated data almost always settle for an inferior statistical design and produce inferior statistical results' (p. 294). Ideally, of course, theorists concerned with explaining individual behaviour, for example 'all things being equal, the young male unemployed will commit more crime than others', should test this against separate data on individuals collected specifically for this purpose. Unfortunately, as will be discussed below, there is simply insufficient of that research, and what there is seems to be seriously flawed.

2 A second major problem is that researchers like to create the appearance of scientific objectivity by parading the most up-to-date sophisticated econometric/statistical procedure/design. But behind this appearance lurks a different reality: the problem of which *intervening variables* to select. When researchers explore the relationship between x and y they do so (or should) by controlling for other 'relevant' factors. In considering these other 'relevant' factors, they allowed their subjective judgement to creep in. As Orsagh (1979) puts it, 'empirical research . . . creates the semblance of scientific objectivity that masks the extraordinary extent to which empirical results are artifacts of discretionary research activity' (p. 294). Most of the above research, and particularly that on unemployment and crime, was conducted by non-sociologists who not only included different economic variables, but usually failed to include intervening variables usually considered by sociologists to have an influence on the crime rate. The outcome is that much research fails to be

cumulative, although this is not a criticism confined to social science. What is particularly problematic, however, is that it is difficult to say which of the various research designs contains the 'correct' collection of intervening variables, and therefore which of the above studies – and its results – ought to be embraced as 'the best there is'.

3 The third, and final, problem is that of measuring the *independent variable*. Take unemployment: should one use the percentage of the population employed, the percentage of the population not employed, the aggregate male unemployment rate, or the age-specific unemployment rate? Not surprisingly, different results have been obtained from using different measures. However, no sociological theory I know would recommend the first two measures of unemployment for explaining crime rates. Instead, a combination of the last two would be commended because these relate to theoretically relevant social groups – males, and youth. Unfortunately, most of the research, having been conducted by economists, has employed one of the first two measures, thus making their results, in many cases, marginally relevant to the type of sociological theorising in Chapter 2.

Of course, this would not arise with individual-based research, for then the only crucial question would be whether or not that person is unemployed, although this too is complicated by consideration of 'how long' and 'how does it feel'.

In making these simple criticisms of most of the research on unemployment, inequality and crime, it is not being recommended that the baby is thrown out with the bathwater. I am merely arguing that the research results we have so far must be treated cautiously, and that future research will have to be better guided than by the 'economic man' who chooses between legitimate or illegitimate activities in terms of the ratio between perceived costs and expected rewards. Furthermore, future research would need to dispense with 'crimes known to the police' and instead concentrate on self-reported crime data and would need to be individual-based rather than used aggregated data. Doubtless one would need the artful skills of Machiavelli to obtain funds for this!

Having made these critical points about research based on aggregated data, we can now turn to the final type of research strategy, namely *longitudinal* studies.

Longitudinal studies

One of the most sophisticated, and the only relevant, longitudinal analyses of unemployment and crime was conducted by two University of Georgia criminologists, Thornberry and Christenson (1984). They examined a 10 per cent sample of 10,000 members of the famous Philadelphia cohort study of boys born in 1945 that has reported on them at various stages of growing-up (Wolfgang *et al.*, 1972; Wolfgang *et al.*, 1985). Each person interviewed gave their employment history since leaving high school. For each year, both the number of times and the proportion of time the subject was employed were calculated. Data on criminal activity were calculated by taking the number of times the person was arrested at each age. This measure had been subject to much criticism because it could easily reflect police selectivity as much as actual criminal behaviour. None the less the authors defended it on the grounds that they discovered a high degree of agreement between arrest and self-reported activity which is, of course, free of any police selectivity (Thornberry and Farnworth, 1982). By having these biographical details, Thornberry and Christenson were able to measure unemployment at one time, and see if it affected criminal activity at a later time. Clearly this is a great advantage over cross-sectional research where associations can be measured but causality is difficult, if not impossible, to prove.

They reported that, overall, unemployment has an instantaneous effect on criminal involvement, and this relationship gets stronger with age, as the young men moved from their early to mid 20s. Even more interesting, because it fits directly into the theorising in Chapter 2, is that Thornberry and Christenson repeated their analysis for particular social groups – whites versus nonwhites, working class versus middle class. They concluded:

> The fit of the model is much better for the less socially advantaged groups – delinquents, blacks and subjects from blue-collar backgrounds – than it is for more-advantaged groups – nondelinquents, whites and subjects from white collar backgrounds. (p. 405)

Furthermore, they accounted for the better fit among the disadvantaged by arguing that in control theory it is assumed that for middle-class people all social bonds are sufficiently strong so that if one is weakened, say commitment (because of being made unemployed), the other two – attachment and beliefs – would compensate. For working-class kids they considered that the relative weakness of social bonds would not be sufficient to compensate if, say, commitment declined because the future employment looked distinctly bleak.

In a slightly later paper (Thornberry, Moore and Christenson, 1985), this analysis was extended further. The authors wanted to see if school drop-out, a measure of weakened or non-existent *commitment*, resulted in unemployment which in turn led to criminal activity. Their results, admittedly based on the same data as the above study, shows for each age from 21 to 24 that there is indeed a positive and significant correlation between unemployment and crime for school drop-outs.

There is, however, a problem with their analysis, and curiously it comes from their earlier paper (Thornberry and Farnworth, 1982) reporting research on job-instability and arrests. In an attempt to explore the social correlates of criminal activity, they considered job-instability – defined as 'the total number of periods of unemployment over the ten year span of the follow-up interview' – as a measure of social status. They had two measures of criminal activity, namely self-reported data and arrest data, having made certain that items on the self-reported crime schedule were similar to those included in the uniform crime reports.

If unemployment is that strongly related to criminal behaviour, as is suggested in their 1984 paper, then it ought to be the case that this relationship was reported in the earlier paper. However, on inspection, it turns out that neither self-reported 'serious' (index) offences nor violent crimes were related to job-instability. This was true for both whites and blacks. But when the authors examined data on arrests for index offences, they found that this was strongly related to job-instability, particularly for adults and blacks. There is here an apparent contradiction. Why should the relationship hold for arrests but not for self-reported serious offences? One possible explanation stands out: social status, of which job-instability is one dimension, affects the likelihood of being arrested, even when other relevant factors, such as an offence having occurred, are controlled. One implication of this argument is that arrest data are not a valid measure of criminal behaviour and therefore the results reported in the 1984 paper have to be treated cautiously.

This criticism would have no substance to it had self-reported offending been related to job-instability. But since it is not, it is plausible to argue that job-instability has only a slight relationship with criminal behaviour, although it strongly affects the decision of the police to arrest a suspect.

Consequently, the results reported by Thornberry and his research colleagues should be interpreted carefully. If self-reported crime is a more valid measure of criminal behaviour than is arrest – which I maintain in the case – then their results do not appear to support the 'unemployment causes crime among certain social groups' theory as strongly as they suggest.

However, there is one other consideration in their favour. Their research was based on a 10 per cent sample of the 9,945 males involved in the original survey. Of these, only 567 (62 per cent) were finally interviewed. Within those not interviewed, blacks and official offenders were over-represented. The absence of these two groups possibly resulted in Thornberry and Farnworth discovering a weaker relationship between job-instability and self-reported crime than they would have had their sample not suffered from this high rate of attrition. It should be stressed, though, that this is not a defence made by these American authors, nor one they would necessarily accept.

The only relevant longitudinal study therefore leaves us a little wiser. Unemployment is instantaneously related to subsequent arrests. This is best located within conflict theory, in which it is argued that the state, including police, becomes more coercive during a recession, and as part of this move towards a more 'authoritarian state', more arrests, particularly of the unemployed, are made. This leaves a different, more valid measure of criminal activity – self-reported crime – and this appears not to be related to unemployment.

Conclusion on recession and 'conventional' crimes

This survey of the literature has concerned itself primarily with examining research which has focused on the two major structural variables in the integrated theory, namely unemployment and income inequality. Before stating two main conclusions from this survey, a brief mention on other parts of the 'integrated theory', particularly 'control theory' and 'societal reaction' theory, is required.

Control theory has been mentioned in this survey wherever the researchers themselves brought it in. The extensive literature which tests this theory independently of motivating structural factors has been ignored. The reason for this is simple. There is only *one* conclusion to draw from this research: it all shows that weakened or absent social bonds predict much delinquency (see LaGrange and White, 1985, p. 19 for list of research supporting this view). There is therefore no need to review it. However, since it provides no motivation for delinquency, it does not in itself offer a totally satisfactory explanation. For that reason, strain theorists, with their emphasis on the structural origins of motivation have been *the* object of attention. To the extent that structural factors do motivate, control theory, if grafted on, would simply enhance the predictive powers because the research has universally found evidence consistent with it.

Societal reaction/conflict theory, although part of the integrated theory in Chapter 2, fits more conveniently into subsequent chapters on state coercion where they will be discussed at great length. Their relevance to this theory will then be considered.

Bearing in mind the cautionary points on aggregated data and the paucity of longitudinal studies, the research to date seems to support the following statements:

1 Income inequality is strongly related to criminal activity – with the exception of homicide. It should be emphasised that no existing research has produced results which contradict this. Any crime control policy which fails to recognise this finding clearly fails to get to grips with a major underlying structural factor which generates a strong motive to commit crime.

2 The relationship between overall unemployment and crime is inconsistent, even when victimisation survey data are used as the measure of crime. The earlier quoted evaluations of Freeman, and Long and Witte are as near as one can get to a balanced view. To repeat, on balance the weight of existing research supports there being a weak but none the less significant causal relationship. However, properly targeted research

on young males, particularly those from disadvantaged ethnic groups, which considers both the *meaning* and *duration* of unemployment, as well as measuring crime through self-reported techniques, and relating this to those periods *after* being made unemployed, is the only way of settling this issue. *That research has yet to be done.*

Much of the research evaluation above is post-1978. Braithwaite (1979), who carried out a similar extensive review of pre-1979 research, came, reassuringly, to a very similar conclusion. He wrote:

> while the evidence tends to favour the conclusion that cities or states with a high degree of economic inequality and/or unemployment have high crime rates, there have been a number of dissident findings refuting this conclusion. In particular, there are a substantial minority of studies that have failed to show a positive association between crime and unemployment rates, or crime and proportion of people below the poverty line. Significantly though, *the literature shows fairly uniform support for a positive association between inequality and crime among those studies which . . . use a global index of income dispersion such as the Gini coefficient.* (p. 211)

At the end of the harvest, there is usually a moment of moral licence, when release from the restrictions of status and social roles is permitted. After the strenuous effort of gathering nearly fifty research projects, maybe a certain latitude is deserved. It is certainly needed, if only to release some of the frustration that even a labour of love like this can produce. Throughout this survey runs a theme alien to the minds of some contemporary criminologists, of both right and left wing persuasions, and politicians, particularly Conservatives. Criminal activity, it says, can be altered by paying attention to the social and economic conditions which contribute to it. This is not to 'excuse' the behaviour or 'condone' the offender. Indeed, its primary object of attention is not the past but the future. What can be done to reduce the tidal wave of crime and the terrible suffering it leaves in its wake? This survey leaves the answer in no doubt. The uneven distribution of income and the unfair burden of unemployment should be points of intervention in any 'honest politician's guide to crime control'. The problem, unfortunately, is finding enough politicians, in power, who fit that description! For despite whatever they say publicly, most seem more concerned with repressing criminals rather than reducing crime, more possessive about preserving wealth rather than redistributing it, and more inclined to pay, albeit at reduced rates, unemployment benefit rather than to create employment. This is a great pity, for as will be argued in Chapter 7, evidence for the effectiveness of income redistribution and employment as means of reducing the 'unacceptably high levels of crime' exist. If only politicians in power would stop turning a blind eye to this in their feverish desire to scapegoat some imagined but convenient group of 'wicked, agitating, mindless, militant, drunk, hooligan-thugs'. If only . . . but then, what kind of world do these politicians really want to live in?

Recession and crimes of the powerful

For reasons associated with scarce funding, ideological bias and access to information, there has been much less research on corporate and police crime than on 'conventional' crimes committed mainly by the powerless. It is always easier to investigate, and even penetrate, the privacy of those who cannot hide behind bureaucratic barriers and privileged positions. This section is therefore going to be short and scanty compared with that on recession and 'conventional crimes'.

Recession and corporate crime

Although over the last decade there has been an enormous exposé of corporate crime, particularly in the USA, little of this has attempted to assess whether recession increases the incidence of these violations. Most studies have focused on one case, usually a dramatic example, such as the Pinto Car Scandal, when, according to Dowie (1977), the Ford Motor Company continued selling a car they knew to be dangerous and which may have been responsible for the untimely deaths of between 500 and 900 people; or the death of 26 miners in the Scotia Coal Company shaft under the Big Black Mountain in Kentucky when the company had already been

cited for the violation of 652 safety violations, at least sixty of
which were for failures to maintain adequate ventilation and
methane gas measurement procedures (Caudill, 1977); or the
Electrical Industries Price-Fixing Conspiracy when executives
from 29 leading corporations were either imprisoned or fined for
swindling customers out of a fortune (Geis, 1967); or one of the
endless list of despressing episodes in corporate history. Whilst
these convey the enormity and carnage of corporate violations,
they do not provide a window onto the possible relationship
between recession and crimes of the powerful. Indeed, despite a
blossoming literature on these crimes, only one study (Clinard and
Yeager, 1981) is directly related to the theory developed in the
previous chapter. These authors examined the records of all US
regulatory agencies and were able to obtain information on all
detected violations. They used this data as the dependent variable –
corporate crime – no matter whether it had attracted an official
response of persuasion or prosecution. Various economic measures, such as profitability, efficiency, liquidity, labour intensive-
ness, and growth rate, were used to measure the economic climate
facing both individual firms and all firms in particular industries.
These measures related to the years 1971–5 which although not a
long time-span, does none the less coincide with the oil-crisis
related recession of the early 1970s. For corporate crime, Clinard
and Yeager considered specific environmental, labour and manufacturing violations as well as an overall violation score. Although
it was not expected that these measures would account for all, or
even the major variation in corporate crimes, simply because the
theory of corporate crime is much more complex and cannot be
reduced to mere economism, they did reassuringly reveal a positive effect on the levels of violations. The authors discovered that:

> financial performance was found to be associated with illegal
> behaviour . . . firms in depressed industries as well as relatively
> poorly performing firms in all industries tend to violate the law
> to greater degrees. (p. 129)

They also found that firms with higher violation rates had lower
growth rates compared with low-violating firms, and that companies operating with labour intensive costs were more prone to
violate labour regulations (such as those related to health and

safety, work conditions and wages). Taken together, they concluded:

> the results suggest that, compared to non-violating corpora-
> tions, the violating firms are on average larger, less financially
> successful, experience relatively poorer growth rates and are
> more diversified.(p. 132)

It needs to be stressed that these results were of only moderate
statistical strength, but that would be expected, for 'threat to
capital accumulation' is only part of the theory of corporate crime,
and other factors certainly intervene to amplify or mute its effect.
None the less, it is clear from this major breakthrough in the study
of corporate crime that a firm's or industry's economic climate
does influence its propensity to violate regulations designed to
protect the rights of employees, consumers and the general public.
Clearly a more focused research project on this specific issue, and
covering a longer time-span, would be needed to enhance our
understanding of the relationships between recession and corporate crime.

There are no comparable studies for the UK. We shall therefore
have to rely on information provided by the Health and Safety
Executive and by the Wages Council. However, before these are
considered, it is important to point out that law evasion and law
revision are options available to potential corporate violators, and
since these opinions will undoubtedly be used, direct increases in
actual violations will be muted. None the less, some increase
during recession would be predicted from the theory advanced in
the previous chapter.

The Health and Safety Commission report that during the
period 1980–84 the number of enforcement notices rose from
8,637 to 8,824. This is a slight increase, but it has to be seen against
a background of fewer visits by inspectors. In fact, these visits fell
from 285,000 to 245,000 during this period. This meant that
enforcement notices, which in effect indicate that a regulation (or
regulations) are being violated, increased by 16 per cent from 30.9
to 35.9 per 1,000 visits. The Health and Safety Commission is only
one agency empowered to issue enforcement notices for violation
of regulations designed to protect employees. Local Authorities
also have a similar power. When their enforcement notices are

added to those of the Health and Safety Commission, a clear pattern of increasing violations emerges. Thus between 1975 and 1982 the total number of all enforcement notices rose from 7,599 to 16,005, an increase of over 110 per cent (Health and Safety Statistics, 1981–82, p. 14).

Another indicator of corporate violation of regulation is the number of fatal accidents and serious injuries sustained by employees. Although not all these are the result of employer neglect, recklessness or indifference, none the less the majority of them occur under the pressure of work routines laid down by employers. Although it is not possible to put an exact percentage on which proportion is due to employer negligence and which to employee accident, there is no reason to believe that this proportion would changed markedly from year to year. But what has changed markedly during the 1980s is the total number of such incidents. Thus from 1981 when there were 67.9 per 100,000 employees, to 1984 when the figure was 87.0 per 100,000, there was an increase of 28 per cent (Manufacturing and Service Industries Reports for 1981, 1982, 1983 and 1984.) This is a remarkable increase and it indicates clearly just how far health and safety conditions at work have deteriorated under the impact of recession.

Other data supporting the idea that employers tend to violate regulations more often under conditions of economic recession come from the Wages Council. Information from the Wages Inspectorate shows that from 1979 to 1985, the percentage of companies visited found to be paying one or more employees less than the *legal* minimum wage increased by nearly 10 per cent from 31.5 to 34.6. There was also a similar increase in enforcement notices issued to all checked establishments, i.e. whether by visit or correspondence. Since the total amount underpaid amounted to £2.5 million in 1984, this is clearly an important form of theft from employees, although, to be fair, it needs to be set against the estimated £18 million stolen by employees (see *Criminal Statistics*, 1984, p. 43). Thus despite a reduction in its resources, and in its inability to visit more than an eighth of establishments on its register, the Wages Inspectorate was still able to locate many offenders and show that they had become more numerous as the recession bit into the profitability of many businesses.

Environmental uncertainty and competition is one reason why corporations find themselves in financial difficulties. During a recession these difficulties increase and some companies are unable to pay their creditors. In these circumstances, a compulsory liquidation order might be made to wind up the business, and creditors, shareholders and customers frequently find that they are 'out of pocket'. Whenever this occurs, there is suspicion of mismanagement and occasionally fraud. These suspicions have increased recently, partly because of a few scandals that have been picked up by consumer programmes on TV, and also because the sheer number of compulsory liquidation orders has risen dramatically. In 1973, there were 1,080. Twelve years later in 1985, there were 5,761 – nearly a six-fold increase. An increasing number of frauds have emerged from these liquidation proceedings. Thus from 1977 to 1984, convictions for 'fraud by company directors' rose by 120 per cent from 31 to 69. These may be small numbers (although not a small increase) but nonetheless it has to be remembered that unlike many burglaries or robberies, liquidation normally involves considerable financial losses to many creditors often amounting to millions of pounds.

There have also been increases in the numbers found guilty for 'bankruptcy offences' – the 1984 total of 122 being *four* times higher than the 1977 figure. Numbers found guilty of 'false accounting' also rose by 21 per cent during this eight-year period.

Although all these data show increases in violations during the recent recession, it has to be remembered that they refer to cases proven in court or acted on by regulatory agencies. These are almost certainly far fewer than the total number of illegalities hidden in the depths of corporate bureaucracies.

Recession and police crime

A reflective viewing of the media coverage of demonstrations and workers–government confrontations, particularly in the UK, should provide persuasive evidence that police irregularities, especially brutality and violence, have increased over the last decade. The way in which the police brutalised, terrorised and violated mining communities during the miners–government confrontations in 1984 is too well documented to be casually dismissed. Similarly, police 'riots' at Lewisham, 1978, Grunwick, 1979, the National Graphical Association's dispute with publisher Eddie Shah in 1982, and the Oxford Street demonstration against the UK government's support for the American bombing of Libya, to mention a few, all combine to reinforce this suspicion that police illegality has increased.

However, despite this array of cases, they remain just that. Where, a sceptic might ask, is the substantial evidence that over recent years the incidence of police crime, particularly brutality and misbehaviour of civilians, has increased? Clearly, data on police convicted cannot be utilised because the number of police prosecuted for assault against the public has never been more than 2 per cent of those against whom formal complaints have been made. In addition half of those prosecuted were found 'not guilty'. Furthermore, those making a formal complaint are only an iceberg tip of those who consider the police have used unnecessary and illegal violence against them but who fail to take any action because the complaints procedure is generally considered to be so biased and ineffective. In the absence of valid data on police brutality, the only proxy is complaints actually made by the public and recorded by the police. These show a marked increase over the last seven years. For example, the number of complaints of assault rose from 2,483 in 1978 to 3,318 in 1984, and during that period the number of alleged 'oppressive/harassing conduct' increased from 1,495 to 3,380. However, during that period the number of police against whom a complaint could have been lodged, at least in terms of numbers available, increased from 109,000 to over 120,000. So even if the level of police brutality remained stable, the actual number of cases would have increased because there were more police. But when this possibility is considered, it can still be seen (see Table 3.4) that during the worse years of the recession, the rate of complaints against for police for assault, oppressive conduct or harassment, increased from 3.9 to 5.8 per 1,000 police. This represents a disturbing increase from 1978 to 1984 of over 40 per cent.

The alternative explanation, that these increases merely reflect the public's willingness to complain against the police, is not very persuasive. For such willingness to increase, the public would probably have to be convinced that the complaints procedures have become less impartial in their favoured treatment of the accused and hence more effective. But it is exactly this which has not changed recently, despite the government's attempts to tinker with the machinery to create the illusion of independence. The fact

Table 3.4   *Complaints of police brutality and harassment and recession*

	Complaints made by public of			Rate per 1000
Year	Assault	Harassment	Total	police
1978	2,483	1,495	3,978	3.9
1979	3,086	1,483	4,569	4.0
1980	3,067	1,695	4,762	4.0
1981	3,178	2,078	5,256	4.4
1982	3,363	2,236	5,599	4.7
1983	3,229	2,101	5,330	4.5
1984	3,318	3,380	6,698	5.8

is, despite the establishment of the Police Complaints Board in July 1977 and the Police Complaints Authority in April 1985, the rate of complaints being 'substantiated' by the investigation remains suspiciously small at less than 10 per cent. Of course the public may be unaware of this 'low' substantiation rate, but they will undoubtedly be aware that in the media debate about the complaint procedure, the tone has been consistently critical, particularly about the lack of independence – the police investigating themselves – and the 'poor' results. It was this constant criticism which pushed the government into tinkering with the formal appearance of the complaints procedures. In view of this, it is for those who favour an 'increased willingness' explanation of the steep rise in the number of citizens formally complaining about police brutality to reveal not only the argument for this, but the evidence which supports it. The conflict theory explanation offered in the last chapter does at least move beyond mere assertion and provides a rationale for expecting more police brutality, and the increase in complaints for this illegal behaviour have certainly moved in the predicted direction.

One American study also supports conflict theory's expectation that police brutality will increase with more material inequalities. Jacobs and Britt (1979) examined police-caused homicides from 1961 to 1970 in each State and computed the population at risk for each year so as to arrive at a standardised rate. They found considerable variations in this fatal type of police brutality: thus Georgia had a high score of nearly 40 per million persons killed by the police, but in New Hampshire it was just under 3 per million.

To account for and explain these wide variations, the authors correlated police-caused homicide rates against economic inequality, proportion of the population who were black, the number of police per capita, changes in the population flow, proportion of urban dwellers, and an index of violent crimes. A number of these factors did positively correlate with police-caused homicides, but when these were controlled for, there remained a strong association between inequality and police fatal brutality. They reported that the 'most important conclusion . . . [was] . . . that the unequal States were most likely to have the largest number of police-caused homicides' (p. 406).

Of course, one American study, and evidence of public complaints against British police, do not *prove* that the police are more illegally violent during economic crises, when unemployment increases and income inequalities widen, but these data are certainly consistent with such an argument. They support the view that the police are essentially part of the social control apparatus and when political consensus and super-sub-ordinate social relations are threatened, as they are during a recession, police violence, especially towards those groups perceived to be the most potentially threatening, will increase. The government, not being harmed by this anti-democratic turn of events, will not do anything effective to stop it, although it might, for public appearances, wring its hands occasionally, at least when it cannot avert its eyes, which is of course, its preferred and usual stance.

Conclusion on recession and crimes of the powerful

The evidence on recession and crimes of the powerful is much less substantial than that on 'conventional' crimes. None the less, scant as it is, there is some evidence, both in the USA and the UK, that as unemployment and income inequality worsened, there were more violations of regulations supposed to protect employees, consumers and the public. However, this is clearly an area where much more detailed research is needed before any firm conclusion can be drawn. In addition to examining changes in violations committed by 'legal companies' or their managers, there is also a need to consider crimes committed by respectable persons against their employers, or by various professionals, such as government officials, engineers, architects, doctors and others against clients. However, these 'crimes of the respectable' are well hidden (Doig, 1984) and much in-depth investigation would be needed before we know as much about them as we do about common, conventional crimes committed by the powerless.

4 The State and 'Problem Populations' During Recession

During the last ten years or so, both British and American governments have pursued similar 'law and order' policies which differed markedly from those of their predecessors. Before offering an explanation of these shifts, it is necessary to document them in much more detail than has been offered so far because their enormity is quite staggering. Clearly governments felt that there was a problem to which they had to respond positively; the nature of that response, and the problems, real or imagined, it was shaped to deal with, need to be considered carefully.

The network of social control grows

At the *hard* end of penal policy, the state's 'positive' response involves massive increases in public expenditure (i) to expand the prison estate, and encourage and facilitate a policy of *incarceration*, (ii) to expand the judiciary to process more people deemed fit for 'criminalisation', and (iii) to expand and 'militarise' the police force, ostensibly to contain a worsening 'crime problem', dampen down 'fear of crime' and maintain 'social order'.

This is not to view the state as an instrument of class domination which directs and finely orchestrates every move of social control agencies. This 'instrumentalist' view of the state is too crude. Instead, it is better to view the state as occupying a central position in a network of alliances formed on the basis of common interests and benefits. From this central vantage point, the criminal justice system, as part of the alliance, offers a reassuring view. It can be *relied* upon to play a significant part in preserving social order. With its ability to expand into areas not previously subject to its jurisdiction, its preparedness to deploy forces into expanded territory and increase the rates of apprehension, arrest and prosecution, its apparent willingness to partially ignore police disregard for law when their violations are against 'the enemy within' – like striking coalminers – and its capacity to increase the use of prison sentences, it is *one* of the first line defences available to the powerful. This is not to imply that the criminal justice system responds passively to political pressures. The view, enlarged on below, is that the judiciary, police and other social control people processing professional agencies are relatively autonomous institutions which have their own reasons for dealing more harshly with the unemployed and unemployables. It is the 'logic of their situation' and not state dictatorship that makes the courts, police and some professional agencies reliable and trustworthy allies.

But the expensive *hard* end cannot be expanded infinitely, and certainly not sufficiently to contain and control the swelling of persons criminalised or those deemed fit for criminalisation. Consequently the cheaper *soft* end of penal and control policies also has to be expanded. This involves dealing with two types of persons: those who have offended and those who *might* offend.

The *soft* end grows in part to accommodate those whose offences might have led them to prison, but who can be better 'treated' or 'helped' by serving an 'alternative', such as 'suspended sentence under supervision', 'community service order', and 'probation order'. Cohen, in *Visions of Social Control* (1985, p. 41), provides an illustrative list of the patchwork quilt of organisations, programmes, schemes and projects started up all over the North American continent and Britain in the name of 'diversion' and 'decarceration'. He also argues that these 'alternatives' become transmuted into 'adjuncts' so that the overall network of social control, including prisons, actually expands, in total contradiction to the professed aims of their advocates (Lemert, 1981). In other words, many 'offenders' who would never have been sent to prison, but would have been 'fined', cautioned or unconditionally released, end up being supervised in a community service project, on a probation order, or on a suspended sentence.

If various alternatives had been used genuinely, then the percentage of convicted persons sentenced to prison should have gone down. In fact, the opposite has occurred. In England and Wales, for example, the proportion of convicted persons being imprisoned without suspension (total or partial), has gone *up* from 11.8 in 1974 to 16.4 in 1984 (a staggering increase of 39 per cent in the incarceration rate), the respective percentages for community service order or probation order more than doubled from 6.6 to 15.5, and those fined went *down* from 51.5 to 41.5 (a drop of 19 per cent). The outcome is that proportionately more convicted persons are sentenced to some form of state supervision than a decade ago; in Cohen's imagery, the net of social control has widened.

There is a second group of individuals for whom the *soft* end of social control agencies also expand. These are people identified as *potential* offenders, whose circumstances, personalities, or the way they complete the Minnesota Multiphrase Personality Inventory or some similar questionnaire, enable 'experts' to identify them as being 'in need'. Since 'prevention is better than cure', as many as possible of this identified population ought to be, and have been, drafted into one of the bludgeoning schemes designed to 'treat', 'help', 'counsel', 'guide', or 'sensitise', such as TARGET (Treatment for Adolescents Requiring Guidance and Education Training), CPI (Critical Period Intervention), READY (Reaching Effectively Acting Out Delinquent Youths), and START (Short Term Adolescent Residential Training), (Cohen, 1985, p. 41). An important feature of these programmes etc. is that they are often run by or intimately linked to agencies administering the various 'alternatives to prison' schemes. Thus the line between offenders and non-offenders, once so clearly demarcated by the prison walls, now becomes totally blurred. Within the same community agency there might be petty offenders with longish criminal records, first offenders, 'pre-delinquents', persons 'at risk', and others simply in 'need'.

There is nothing in Britain (Hudson, 1985), or Canada (Hylton, 1981), or the USA (Austin and Krisberg, 1981, 1982), to support the idea that 'decarceration', 'diversion' and 'decriminalisation' has led to its social control network shrinking. Indeed, behind the rhetoric of these 'alternatives to prison' is the harsh reality of more state control. Not only does the total network of control agencies expand *physically*, but it also expands *territorially*. Persons not previously part of its domain now find themselves increasingly caught up in its machinations.

There's plenty of money for 'law and order'

This expansion of both the *hard* and *soft* ends of social control has to be funded and justified. It is at this point that the state and its media allies make an enormous contribution to the growth of a more authoritarian centralist state. It takes two forms: first the allocation of resources, which in addition to more money means more *power*; and second, the presentation of *ideological* justification for this allocation.

Over the last fifteen years British and American governments have allowed the police, courts, prisons and other control agencies to expand. This can be illustrated first by events in England and Wales. The police have:

1 grown from just under 93,000 in 1970 to over 120,000 by 1984, which represents a massive increase of nearly 30 per cent. In the spring of 1986, the British government allotted the Home Office sufficient additional funds to pay for the recruitment of a further 3,200 officers, bringing the expected total to around 124,000.

2 strengthened their technological and quasi-military capacities: for instance, the provision of water-cannons, CS gas, plastic bullets, riot shields, the establishment and deployment of Special Patrol Groups, whose appearance and tactics are more military than the familiar 'friendly' bobby, and more recently, during the government–coalminers confrontation, the emergence of a *de facto* 'national police force', have all transformed the British police.

3 enjoyed the extension of their discretionary powers of apprehension, interrogation, detention and arrest. For example, under the Police and Criminal Evidence Act, 1984, the police were granted greater powers to set up road-blocks; to stop and search; to enter premises and seize anything they consider evidence; to arrest, even on such minor grounds as refusal to give name or address or believing name and address given to be false; to prevent access of spouses, friends or legal representatives; to detain suspect for up to 36 hours without bringing a

charge and to enforce a body search. In addition, they have been granted increased discretion to arrest for carrying an offensive weapon – it could be anything the police *considered* to be offensive – and given wider powers in connection with serious arrestable offences, where the police are entitled to determine just what is 'serious'. Finally, the present government has announced its intention to submit to Parliament a Public Order Bill which will contain a new 'public disorder offence'. Conviction for this will almost certainly be dependent purely on the arresting officer's 'subjective' assessment that at the time of arrest, or just prior to it, the suspects had been behaving in a disorderly and threatening manner. Unless the 'codes of practice', also contained in the 1984 Act which are supposedly designed to record, monitor and contain the use and abuse of these powers, are given executive teeth, then the police over the last couple of years will have been granted powers which essentially reverse 1,000 years of developing British civil liberties.

As an integral part of the government's 'Law and Order' campaign, the criminal courts have:

1 increased their personnel. Thus during the period 1972–83, High Court Judges, Circuit Judges and Recorders increased by 41 per cent, from 628 to 887. Registrars increased by 27 per cent, from 134 to 170, and Magistrates by 26 per cent, from 20,539 to 25,934.
2 been given new powers of sentencing. For example, the Youth Custody Order made possible under the Criminal Justice Act, 1982, enables courts to sent 14–21-year-olds to prison rather than detention centres, attendance centres and borstals, thus driving a final nail into the coffin for the Children and Young Persons Act, 1969, under which courts' powers were partially transferred to local government social-work departments. The present government are also proposing to introduce a new sentence – *intermittent custody*. This would enable courts to imprison offenders for 8 hours during weekdays, or all weekend. Since ordinary prisons are already massively overcrowded, it has been proposed that the government consider restructuring schools and hospitals now lying idle and closed down because there is not enough public money to maintain them.

The Prison estate has also benefited from the government's campaign against crime. There has been:

1 an enormous rise in the number of prison officers. Thus in 1971 there were 18,500 and by 1984 this total had risen to nearly 28,000, an increase over 50 per cent. This represents an increase in the number of prison officers per prisoner. In 1971 there were 3.4 prisoners per officer, but by 1984 this had fallen to 2.4. Furthermore, the government is now proposing to increase prison staff by about 5,000.
2 a considerable expansion in prison cellular capacity to accommodate more and more prisoners. The present government's prison-building programme is staggering in size and *irrelevance*. By the end of 1985 there were active plans to construct 18 new prisons and refurbish a number of older prisons – there were no plans to close any down. The outcome will be an expanded capacity from about 38,700 to over 50,000 by the 1990s, an increase of nearly 30 per cent. Since most people in prison shouldn't be there, because their crimes were petty property offences, or they are mentally ill, or fine-defaulters too poor to pay their fine, or remanded unnecessarily (Wright, 1982), this programme simply in not needed if its primary purpose is to control serious crime and punish violent offenders.

Finally, other control agencies have expanded and had their resources increased:

1 The Probation and After Care Service has increased the total number of Probation Officers (in the field and in prisons) from 4,408 in 1979 to 5,010 in 1985, an increase of 14 per cent; and auxiliary, other professional and administrative staff have increased during this period by 61 per cent, from 3,556 to 5,722. In addition, real increases in funding went up during this period by an annual average of 5 per cent.
2 'Intermediate Treatment' programmes have multiplied. From an estimate budget of just £3 million in 1978/9 the cost of these programmes rose to an estimated £15.5 million by 1983/4 (Rogowski, 1985, p. 351). The majority of adolescents caught up in these programmes have not been judged guilty of any offence, but have been identified, by experts, as 'in need' or 'at risk' of

committing offences. This form of preventive intervention sails very close to being soft, subtle socialisation by employees of the state.

3 The Manpower Services Commission (MSC) has been the major agency propelled into dealing with the problem of 'youth unemployment'. Its budget rose from £120 million in 1974 to £1,628 million by 1984/5. The Youth Opportunity Programme, for which participants receive an *allowance* (not a wage) at little more than social-security level, has expanded from 216,000 entrants in 1979 to 550,000 by 1982. Pratt (1983) sees this as quite sinister. According to him:

> as youth unemployment continues to grow, so a further tier of intervention has been developed; the work experience programmes, etc. are themselves now likely to require prior participation in pre-entry schemes, such as 'work introduction' or 'work preparation' courses . . . detailed reports on participants' 'confidence', 'ability to mix', 'politeness', and so on are fed back to the careers service prior to consideration for suitability for a place on a Youth Opportunity Programme: *after* which, there have been suggestions for continued monitoring and provision of such facility as 'Youth Opportunities Centres' or 'Personal Guidance Bases': a return to unemployment simply redesignates the young as 'at risk': hence the need for detailed planning and structuring of the programmes to try and plug gaps, to try and ensure that schooling is followed by training, and training followed by, perhaps, supervision of leisure to watch out for disillusion and the development of criminal tendencies – to be remedied by further training. (p. 354)

A very similar pattern of changes in the criminal justice system occurred in the USA. For example, there was a massive prison-building programme in the 1970s. From 1955 to 1975 fifteen states more than *doubled* their prison capacity. In the case of South Carolina, it was by as much as 138 per cent (Nagel, 1977, p. 166). Some states, on the other hand, hardly increased their prison capacity and these tended to be the ones which had lower rates of unemployment. Thus of the fifteen high prison-construction states, eight were in the higher half of the states' unemployment league.

Of those with the low prison-construction programmes, only four were in this same division. This prison-building programme did not stop despite Nagel's plaintive plea for a moratorium. The response to overcrowding, which as in Britain became the central political issue of the prison debate, was to build more prisons. To help finance this, the 1981 *Task Force on Violent Crime* recommended a $2 billion subsidy towards state prison construction. According to Austin and Krisberg (1985):

> In the fiscal years 1982 and 1983, states allocated nearly $800 million to expand or improve prison capacity. An additional $2.2 billion was allocated for prison construction via bond issues or other revenue mechanisms . . . In 1982 state correction systems added 21,212 beds to the capacity and an additional 100,000 beds were either planned or under construction. (pp. 16–17)

The Attorney General's *Task Force on Violent Crime* also contained 64 recommendations for combating 'dangerous' crimes. These included increased use of 'dangerousness' as a criterion for selective incapacitation; use of preventive detention; revision of exclusionary rule to allow the introduction of illegally obtained evidence into court under some circumstances; restrictions of the rights of habeas corpus; greater concentration of federal law enforcement; more money for prisons; and the use of armed forces in controlling drug traffic (Davis, 1985, p. 121). Many of these ideas were incorporated directly or in a modified form in President Reagans's Criminal Justice Reform Act, 1982. This, and the later Extradition Act, 1983, were described by Calavita 1983 as 'forewarning of an erosion of due process and civil liberties in the years ahead' (p. 139).

Another major shift, not formally experienced in the UK, was the abandonment of 'rehabilitation' and its replacement by a co-opted version of 'just deserts', which simply became 'get tough'. This was exemplified by numerous states embracing the 'crime control model' advocated by many right-wing criminologists. This advocated: worrying less about the rights of accused and criminals; basing sentence on offence; stop coddling the guilty; impose determinate sentences; abolish parole; and expand incarceration and selective incapacitation (Cullen *et al.*, 1985). In addition to jettisoning 'rehabilitation', parole was also effectively abolished under the Sentencing Reform Act, 1984. This last measure, which is again not a move adopted in Britain, is bound to increase the average daily prisoner population because there will almost certainly be no compensatory reduction in the length of prison sentence. Indeed, the practical effect of many states adopting, or co-opting, the justice model (Greenberg and Humphries, 1980) is for the average prison sentence to rise.

There have also been substantial increases in the numbers of police and correctional officers. Thus the police increased by 74 per cent from 348,569 in 1965 to 606,223 in 1983. Of course, the population size has increased during this period, but even allowing for this, the number of police per 1,000 civilians rose from 18.0 to 25.9. Similarly, correctional officers rose from 110,700 in 1965 to 296,645 in 1984. These changes, plus massive investments in law enforcement (Quinney, 1980, pp. 126–39) and rapidly increasing militaristic capacity of the police (Crime and Social Justice Collective, 1977), brought about similar patterns of social control to those occurring in Britain. For example, at the *hard* end, the prison population increased by 48 per cent between 1973 and 1983, and at the same time the probation population increased by 63 per cent (Petersilia, 1985). There is no evidence that crime rates rose by these magnitudes during this decade. Indeed, evidence reviewed below suggests that crimes rates hardly rose at all! Thus, instead of being rational responses to increased crime, these changes signified the rise of what has been variously referred to as the 'punitive', 'exceptional', 'centralist', or 'authoritarian' state. Being irrational responses, or so it seems, this remoulding of the modern state does raise an intriguing question. How have British and American governments managed to 'justify' these massive shifts in power and resources without mentioning their attempts to monitor, demoralise, control and discipline the growing 'reserve army of labour' or those resisting attempts to 'South-Koreanise' the labour force? Both governments argued that the 'crime problem' is getting worse, and therefore demanded a warlike mobilisation of resources and human energy to reduce it. In addition, each portrayed itself as being pressurised by demands from those for whom 'fear of crime' has become a major anxiety, by demands from a worried general public, and by demands from the liberal establishment for more 'justice' and more 'community care'. The basis for these justifications needs to be examined carefully because if they turn out to be inflated rhetoric then the 'justification' for these changes still remains to be uncovered.

Justifications for shifts in power and resources

Justification one: 'serious crime' is getting worse

We are told almost daily by politicians, police, judges, journalists and TV commentators that our crime problem consists of such offences as murder, rape, robbery, assault, wounding, theft, handling stolen goods, arson and vandalism. Furthermore, and this is *the* cause of alarm and moral panic, these crimes have increased *dramatically* during our lifetime. Unless some drastic remedial action is pursued vigorously and ruthlessly, this crime problem will continue, so the story goes, to spiral out of control threatening the very fabric of our civilised way of life.

Most people listen to these orchestrated alarms. They don't want to be murdered, raped, robbed, assaulted, burgled or criminally victimised in any way. Consequently they are receptive to 'law and order' campaigners who claim that only with more punishment and more discipline will we be able to control this crime problem and thus avoid social disaster.

The evidence relevant to assessing the claim that crime is getting worse has already been considered in Chapter 1. Essentially it was concluded that whilst crime has increased, it has not done so at the alarmist rate suggested in 'crime recorded by the police' and taken up as gospel by 'law and order' enthusiasts.

Not only is there evidence that the 'crime problem' is not getting as bad as politicians, police and journalists like to imagine, but when these so-called serious crimes are examined, many of them do not look that serious.

The fact is, over half the recorded serious crimes refer to theft and handling stolen goods. Many of these crimes are trivial, involving trifling amounts of money or property. Thus in 1982, 46 per cent of theft (excluding theft from and of a motor vehicle) in England and Wales involved property worth less than £25. Burglary accounts for a further quarter of all other serious crimes. Yet nearly one-quarter of burglaries involved no property being stolen and a further 17 per cent involved property worth less than £25.

Robbery, a feared act, high on the agenda of serious crimes to be tackled, involved the loss of no money in 18 per cent of cases, and less than £25 in a further 26 per cent. Put another way, *two fifths of all serious recorded crime refers to offences involving property worth less than £25*. This may mean a lot to some individuals hard up against the wall of economic marginalisation, but in objective terms these are hardly crimes to be regarded as 'serious' and treated with the heavy hand of imprisonment.

Even if it is conceded that a substantial proportion of so-called 'serious' crime is in fact trivial – at least in an 'objective' sense – isn't it still true that Britain has a major problem of serious *violent* crimes? Well, it is true that even though violence against the person, including homicide (but excluding rape and sexual assault), is extremely rare, constituting just over 3 per cent of all serious recorded crimes, it has none the less increased in terms of absolute offences from 52,000 to 109,000 over the last decade or so. This looks like an alarming increase. However, within the broad category of violent crimes against the person, those crimes causing death or endangering life only increased from 5 to 6.5 thousand (that is, about 26 per cent), so that the biggest increase was confined to non-life-endangering woundings and assaults.

Finally, to take one other relevant example, mugging has occupied the centre stage in much of the 'crimes getting worse' debate. The media present *mugging* as though it were (i) an everyday occurrence, (ii) violent, (iii) victimising the elderly, (iv) victimising women, (v) committed by British West Indians who are imitating their American brothers, and (vi) a growing problem which requires repressive measures to control it. Yet when Home Office researcher Malcolm Ramsay (1982) looked at the 'reality' of mugging, he found it did not resemble its media image.

Mugging is rare. It is not a legal category but can be inferred from the number of robberies and thefts from the person. By sifting through police records of these two offences, Malcolm Ramsay was able to conclude that the rate of mugging in England and Wales for 1980 was no more than 30 per 100,000 of the population. Clearly this rate varied among different areas; thus in Greater Manchester it was 25, in the West Midlands it was 47, in Merseyside it was larger at 65 and in London it reached 104.

Although it is a rare event, this did not stop the *Daily Mirror* from asserting under the headline 'PLIGHT OF THE OLD AGE

PENSIONERS', that 'by tonight the lives of 266 people in Britain will have been transformed. They will have been the victims of the grim daily toll of violence. Most of them will be pensioners battered by muggers.' But this figure of 266 represents 97,246 cases of *violence against the person*, which are mainly assaults between teenagers, being divided by 365. Muggings do not even come under this official heading! There were, however, 43,781 cases of robbery and theft from the person, which means that even if all of these were muggings – which they most certainly were not – then it would be the equivalent of 120 per day, and not 266 as the *Mirror* declared.

Muggings are not necessary violent. In Ramsay's analysis of three police forces, only 3 per cent of victims required hospital treatment longer than twelve hours, and a further 19 per cent required an even shorter period of hospitalisation. In the majority of cases the victim was not physically hurt at all.

Pensioners may be mugged, but not more so than other age groups. Indeed, because the elderly take more precautions than other sections of the population, they put themselves 'at risk' less. Certainly Ramsay's evidence did not reflect the elderly being victimised more than younger people. If anything, young males had more to fear from other young males than did old ladies. Similarly, young black males had more to fear because they were mugged more often by adolescents like themselves.

Young black males may commit mugging. But again according to Ramsay's data, they do not do so at a rate exceeding their proportion of the local community. In other words, where the majority of local citizens are black, then the majority of muggers are black; where the majority are white, then whites form a majority of muggers.

Mugging is not a new phenomenon but, in one guise or another, has been with us for decades (Pearson, 1983). There is no reliable evidence that it is getting worse. The number of recorded robberies and thefts from the person are increasing, but serious doubts on the validity of these data have already been raised. Finally, there is no evidence that more repressive measures necessarily reduce the rate of muggings. Advocates of repression simply portray the lack of deterrence as *the* cause of mugging, whereas it is a minor cause beside economic, political and social marginalisation.

All this is not to deny that muggings exist and that they are a problem. Of course they are an acute problem, particularly for those living in inner-city areas where the likelihood of being victimised is greater. It would be callous to deny or ignore this. Yet the reality of mugging is far removed from the imagery of mugging as presented in the media.

To argue that politicians, police and journalists misrepresent the 'crime problem' and make it worse and larger than it really is, is not to dismiss it, or the very real suffering left in its wake. However, before a problem can be successfully resolved, it is necessary to see it 'realistically'. The move towards 'punishment', prison expansion, military-style policing, and more control both at the *hard* and *soft* ends, begins to resemble a paranoid panic, *if* these measures are directed at reducing the soaring 'crime problem'. For that particular problem does not seem to warrant such draconian measures.

The argument to be developed later in this chapter, is that the government is *not* responding to the 'crime problem', although it provides a reasonable excuse. Rather it is responding to its perception and anxiety that a particular and identifiable group – those most deprived by recession and government economic policies and still young and vigorous enough to resist – are potentially dangerous and have to be controlled and disciplined.

Justification two: 'fear of crime' is a major social problem

Maybe a second justification for the government's 'law and order' campaign is more persuasive. It suggests that this policy is merely a passive response to demands from those members of the public who 'fear crime'.

Certainly it is true that recent surveys, both in the UK (Clarke *et al.*, 1985; Smith, 1983) and the USA (Clemente and Kleiman, 1977; Garofalo, 1979), show that 'fear of crime' has become a major issue. However, as Maxfield's (1984) analysis of 1982 *British Crime Survey* shows, this 'fear of crime' is not evenly spread throughout the population. It is mainly experienced by women and the elderly living in inner-city areas. This pattern was replicated in the 1984 *British Crime Survey*. Thus nearly 12 per cent of the general population said they felt 'unsafe' walking in their neighbourhood after dark. This figure rose to 22 per cent when the question was put only to inner-city dwellers. Within these blighted areas it increased to 41 per cent for those living in bad housing conditions, and for women in these houses it rose to 49 per cent. Ironically it is young males living in these areas who are much more likely to be victimised by others like themselves. Considerable reliability can be placed on these results, because they reflect almost perfectly the same patterns discovered in North American surveys which have been conducted for a number of years and provide a very reliable data base (Balkin, 1979; Gordon *et al.*, 1980; Stafford and Galle, 1984; Yin, 1980, 1982).

Both American and British government claims to be concerned for the plight of inner-city victims have a hollow ring to them when it is realised that both governments have been willing to exacerbate the material problems experienced by these very same people. For example, in their analysis of the *New Class War*, Piven and Cloward (1982) clearly document that it is the unemployed, the unemployable and the working poor who are immediately and negatively affected by cutting back the cost of the welfare state. The 'brunt of these cuts falls on the public service employment, unemployment insurance, Medicaid, public welfare, low-income housing subsidies and the disability and food stamp programs' (p. 19). Since the recipients of these benefits overlap considerably with the groups of people who feel unsafe on the streets after dark, it raises doubts about the sincerity of government officials who claim that 'law and order' policies are responses to the demands of these citizens. Is it credible that a government is very responsive to the fears of these citizens when:

> Reagan himself has shown enormous animus toward those he perceives to be enemies of the kind of social order he thinks he deserves to rule. As governor of California, he classed black rioters as 'mad dogs' and insisted on cutting the already underfunded food budgets and mental institutions. He and his top appointees use a great deal of rhetoric about 'fraud' and 'malingering', and about benefits going to people for whom they were not intended, all of which leaves the clear implication that these 'abuses' have created a government fiscal crisis. Reagan appears to believe that the 'rabble' has captured the state and is plundering its resources, both to avoid working and to live better than those who do work. Productive people – like the

self-made millionaires who surround Reagan – must be restored to honour and power. (Piven and Cloward, p. 38)

Similarly, it is hardly credible that a British government which has imposed rate-capping, cuts in public expenditure, toughened up welfare benefit entitlements, and cracked down on 'scroungers' – all of which have contributed to making life in the inner-city hellish – should simultaneously pose as the saviour of these very same people by promising to protect them with a tough penal policy of more punishment and extending the arena of social control. If the government really cared about these inner-city dwellers' sufferings, why not do something now about housing conditions, public amenities and, above all, unemployment? It seems phoney for a government to present itself as being responsive to the 'fear of crime' while not being responsive to demands from those same people for 'more jobs, better housing, and improved environment'. How does a 'caring' government respond to only a part of the people's sufferings, yet remain indifferent to the rest? Maybe they do not care that much. Maybe their responsiveness to 'fear of crime' is purely a convenient gloss on what they feel they need to do anyway, not for the sake of inner-city dwellers, but for maintaining and creating the right conditions for capital accumulation. Part of these conditions consists of diffusing the threat posed by that section of the 'surplus population' perceived to be potentially or actually dangerous to productive relationships. 'Fear of crime' therefore provides a convenient excuse for intensifying and increasing the surveillance, apprehension, arrest and imprisonment of inner-city young males and for changing the criminal law so as to criminalise more of the ways in which this group might resist deteriorating economic circumstances.

Justification three: the general public demand it

Another excuse that governments provide for pursuing 'law and order' policies is that the general public demand it. This demand does not reflect a personal fear of being victimised, but a more global anxiety about our threatened 'way of life'. For most people, the alleged recent surge in crime, sensationalised by the media and puffed up by politicians, has been experienced as a potent threat to civilisation as we know it. Unless the state makes strenuous and firm efforts to stem the tide, we shall all be engulfed in a wave of lawlessness. At least, that is how it appears to those who demand a 'law and order' policy – so we are told. But just how numerous are these citizens who are worried sick about the 'crime problem'? Who belongs to this constituency and is it a group whose worries usually evoke governmental positive responses? Are 'law and order' policies adopted by the state really a shining example of 'democracy at work'?

Research in both the USA and the UK belies the view that behind the 'law and order' wagon is a massive public army pushing it forward towards the golden crime-reduced land of the future. This imagery may capture the truth for capital punishment, especially for the killing of police, but beyond that, there is mainly a wide variety of views, which themselves are not necessarily internally consistent or held with binding conviction. For example, Cullen and colleagues (1985) reported on statewide polls of Texas for the years 1977–82. 'Texas was chosen for analysis because it has a clear reputation as a "law and order" state with a harsh prison system' (p. 16). From the seven annual polls, it appears to Cullen *et al.* that:

> If Texans are punitive, they are not without their humanistic side . . . Responses . . . reveal that a substantial minority support the policy of releasing well-behaved inmates from prison prior to the end of their sentences. Similarly, there is no wholesale rejection of rehabilitation . . . treatment remains a legitimate correctional goal to most Texans . . . While Texans believe that more prisons should be built, they are equally in favour of simultaneously developing community corrections. Further, there is clear sentiment that nonviolent offenders are prime candidates for community supervision, and a substantial group believes that placement in programs should be individualised (as the rehabilitative ideal suggests) and not rigidly matched to the nature of the crime (as the punitive model would dictate). (p. 19)

It appears to these authors that politicians want, like Pontius Pilate, to wash their hands of responsibility and cast the blame on the force of public demand. But this is merely convenient political posturing, for:

Texans – a group hardly known for their liberalism – are neither gripped by fear nor unwilling to consider a range of correctional responses to the criminally wayward. The public 'will', in short, is much more complex and tolerant than politicians acknowledge. (p. 22)

Polls conducted in Britain by the Prison Reform Trust (Shaw, 1982) and the Home Office give support to this idea of the public being more malleable and flexible than described by 'law and order' apologists. The first poll reported a widespread acceptance for reparation and community service orders for reducing the prison population, as well as more liberality on sentencing than would be imagined. The author, Stephen Shaw, concluded:

On prisons and penal policy, the majority of our people are more liberal in their attitudes than has hitherto been believed. While one cannot argue that there is a great body of public opinion clamouring for reform of our prisons, there is no reason to suppose that there would not be public acceptance of a rational programme of change. (p. 26)

Data from the second British Crime Survey in 1984 revealed just how easy it is for politicians to use opinion polls selectively and thus give their claims for public support more credibility than they deserve. Thus although a majority of the public thought that courts ought to imprison more convicted burglars, they also *underestimated* what proportion of burglars are imprisoned. In other words, the so-called support for more-severe sentencing may be more a reflection of ignorance than a genuine desire for more 'law and order'. Furthermore, the survey found that a majority of the public supported the idea of more parole, shorter sentences, and alternatives to prison for non-violent offenders. As two Home Office researchers, Hough and Moxon (1985) put it:

These findings suggest that policy-makers and courts can treat with a degree of scepticism the claims often made by the media that public opinion demands a tougher line with offenders. The BCS offers no evidence to suggest widespread punitive attitudes amongst the public. If, as the results of the BCS suggest, opinion and practice are broadly in line, there is probably leeway to introduce more lenient or heavier sentences withouth losing public support. Support for more lenient sentences, however, would probably only be forthcoming if the public were better informed about current practice. (p. 171)

It appears that public opinion is the last refuge for the politically bankrupt. Justifications which use an imaginary public opinion to support them usually have something to hide. At this instance, it is not too hard to discover. In both the USA and the UK the recession has produced a growing number of economically marginalised people amongst whom ethnic minorities are over-represented. While it would be impossible for a government to justify 'law and order' policies as attempts to defuse the threat posed by these 'problem populations', it is easier to announce that public opinion demands something be done now about the growing crime problem. The media can be safely left to fill in the script and provide the characters. In this unfolding drama, equations are easily made between unemployment, black and crime, thus justifying increased policing againt the unemployed and the blacks as well as the imposition of stiffer sentences and the building of more prisons. But in making this response, government spokespersons hammer home the 'crime' part of the equation and leave other state officials quietly to get on dealing with the other parts – the unemployed and the blacks.

Before leaving this section, some consideration should be given to those people who do support 'law and order' policies. More support comes from 'people who tend to be older; less educated; and lower in income' (Corbett, 1981, p. 339); this seems an unlikely constituency for politicians, particularly Republican and Conservative politicians, to follow. Furthermore, if we are to believe that 'democracy is at work' and the 'common people's' wishes are heard by those in power, then what are we to make of the fact that poll after poll records that the problem about which people are *most* concerned is unemployment. Twice as many report being worried about this as they do about crime. If governments really respond to public pressure or anxiety, why has unemployment risen and risen in Britain and America over the last decade, and risen partly because both governments have pursued non-Keynesian economic policies which would predictably push up the numbers unemployed?

It all looks hollow and unpersuasive. Governments like to *appear* to be responsive to public pressure, but in doing so they interpret and even construct the dimensions of that opinion to shape what they are seeking to accomplish in the first place. Public opinion can be twisted and turned to anything politicians want. They are rarely driven by it, but instead cloak themselves in it to give themselves more credibility. Public demand is not the driving force behind the recent shift towards 'law and order' policies; the engine driving towards harsher penal policies is to be found in the relations of production and the casualties thrown aside by the logic of capital accumulation in an increasingly interdependent world economy.

Justification four: 'liberal enlightenment' is irresistible

If both British and American governments' claim to be responsive to pressures from the public is suspect, what about the other possibility that they are nudged along the path of penal reform by liberal-progressive conscience?

Changes at the *hard* end of social control are certainly presented by government officials as the triumphant 'return to justice', which originally was recommended by the American liberal establishment to redress the wrongs of (i) indeterminate sentencing, which condemned prisoners to the agony of never knowing when they would be released, (ii) the sham of rehabilitation, for it often turned out to be rhetoric masking the reality of 'coercive treatment' including participation in dangerous drug-testing experiments (Mitford, 1977), and (iii) the imprisonment of many whose crimes did not deserve such a harsh penalty but whose personal characteristics seemed just right for 'treatment' in prison (Fogel, 1975; Singer, 1979; Twentieth Century Fund Task Force on Criminal Justice, 1976; Von Hirsch, 1976).

The 'justice model' meant first 'punishing' the offender in strict accord with the seriousness of the offence. This necessitated a move towards determinate sentencing. Within this sentence there was always the possibility of 'mercy' – sentence reduction – and 'voluntary rehabilitation' – without any strings attached to parole or remission. But in principle the unity between offence and sentence was to be re-established, as it was before the advent of 'positivism' with its view that behaviour was determined and therefore individuals required 'treatment' or 'rehabilitation' for as long as it took. Although the liberal establishment believed the 'justice model' was more humane and fair, it soon became disillusioned with the interpretation of its ideas. For politicians and criminal justice personnel simply 'co-opted' the bit they liked, namely *punishment* (Greenberg and Humphries, 1980). It become more prison, for longer; luxuries such as 'educational facilities', 'rehabilitation units' or 'job-training' schemes were forgotten. 'Lock 'em up, and throw away the key' was the hellish termination for the reforms forged in the name of liberal benevolence and the 'justice model'. Both American and British governments seized the opportunity, created by the sudden windfall conversion of liberals to the justice of punishment, to shore up the criminal justice system and grant it more powers.

As for expanding the *soft* end, governments projected themselves as responsive to another set of liberal ideas. Institutions were inhumane, efficient, and counterproductive; it was better all round to 'treat' people in the community. The response was to enlarge 'community' programmes of all kinds, for offenders and *potential offenders*, and simultaneously expand the total network of social control but at a lower cost per unit because, as politicians saw it, the *only* attractive feature of 'community programmes' was that they were comparatively cheaper.

'We're a democratic government responsive to demands from the people' has the same hollow ring as 'we're tackling the growing crime problem.' Governments like to *appear* to be responsive to ideas and pressures from below, but behind this appearance is the reality of a cunning state at work.

If not these justifications, then what?

Government penal and social control policies, judicial sentencing practices, and policing patterns do not emerge from a vacuum; rather they reflect changing patterns of social relationships, particularly between those in positions of power and their subordinates. During the last decade or so, Anglo-American societies have experienced a deepening economic crisis producing very high levels of unemployment and widening income inequalities. In turn, these have affected the way governments, judiciaries and police have managed, controlled and 'criminalised' subordinate groups.

Marx saw capital accumulation as both the engine of capitalism and the cause of a major problem – what to do with the 'reserve army of labour' – for he argued that it 'constantly produces a population which is superfluous to capital's average requirements for its own valorization' (1977, p. 782). Some of the methods adopted by the state to deal with this human debris have been analysed by a number of contemporary 'radical' criminologists.

Thus Canadian academics Reasons and Kaplan (1975) view increasing admissions to prison as a response to rising unemployment, even though the response, being a 'latent function' of prisons, is not usually intended or entirely recognised as an important outcome of imprisonment. They believe that prisons serve functions generally overlooked or minimised by those who advocate their abolition; prisons, they believe, survive because they are 'functional for certain segments of society that may be either not served or ill-served by alternatives' (p. 371). One of the latent functions of imprisonment is that it brings about a reduction of the unemployment rate. They write:

> in a depressed economy prisons keep low income individuals out of the job market. Inmates are generally unskilled; if they were out in free society, they would be competing with other unskilled individuals for a steady shrinking supply of jobs. Imprisonment reduces the competition. Removing 200,000 unskilled persons from the labour market makes the economy look better; if they were not institutionalised, the unemployment rate would be higher. Thus the prison keeps the unemployment rate lower than it would be otherwise. (p. 372)

Whilst it is undoubtedly true that prisoners, many of whom prior to incarceration were unemployed, do not appear as unemployed persons and thereby keep total unemployment down, none the less, given the size of the prison population relative to the unemployed, this contribution must be minimal and is certainly not one to be emphasised.

The criminal justice system makes another contribution to solving the problem of human debris thrown on the rubbish dump by the logic of capital accumulation. Thus Mathiesen (1974) refers to this debris as 'unproductive elements', and views criminalisation and imprisonment as having both a physical and symbolic *expurgatory function*. He argued that:

> our social structure probably increasingly creates groups which are 'unproductive' [and] must rid itself [of these] elements, partly because their presence creates inefficiency in the system of production – it 'throws sand into the machinery' – and partly because the 'unproductive' brutally remind us of the fact that our productive system is not so successful after all. A society may get rid of its 'unproductive' elements in many ways. *One way* is to criminalize their activities and punish them by imprisoning them. (p. 77)

Quinney (1977) refers to this human debris as 'surplus population' and argues specifically that:

> criminal justice is the modern means of controlling [the] surplus population produced by later capitalist development [and that] control is especially acute in those periods when the economic crisis is most obvious during periods of depression and recession . . . A way of controlling this unemployed surplus population is simply and directly by confinement in prisons. (p. 134)

In a less blunt vein, Spitzer (1975) conceptualises this group as 'problem populations' who, he argues,

> tend to share a number of social characteristics but most important among these is the fact that their behaviour, personal qualities and/or position threaten the *social relationships of production* in capitalist societies. In other words, populations become generally eligible for management as deviant when they disturb, hinder or call into question . . . capitalist modes of appropriating the product of human labour . . . the social conditions under which capitalist production takes place . . . patterns of distribution and consumption in capitalist society . . . the process of socialization for productive and non-productive roles . . . and . . . the ideology which supports the functioning of capitalist society. (p. 642).

These 'problem populations', unrequired by the productive process but actually or symbolically threatening it, become perceived as nuisances eligible for state intervention. If they are 'social junk', as Spitzer graphically describes such groups as the mentally ill, old, sick or disabled, they have to be *managed*; if they are 'social dynamite', such as the unemployed or the unemployable, they have be be *controlled*.

The former groups represent a fiscal problem which has intensified with the growing inability of the modern capitalist state to generate sufficient surplus to pay for welfare programmes and simultaneously maintain costly defence budgets. In response to this fiscal crisis of the welfare state, which largely arises out of spending priorities and not because 'there is no money available', UK and US governments have attempted to reduce public-welfare spending, and as part of this objective they have pursued a policy of *decarceration*. This has meant removing people from mental hospitals and similar institutions, closing them down, and diverting potential patients by encouraging and legitimating 'community treatment', which is often a synonym for no treatment at all, and is of course, comparatively cheaper. It has also opened the gates for a 'new trade in lunacy', the *privatisation* of 'mental illness'. Those who can afford private-clinic and nursing-home fees have been able to secure 'treatment'. The remainder have been left to fend as best they can, and frequently this has been too much for them. In Scull's (1977) evaluation, the rhetoric of 'decarceration' stressing the humaneness of closing down 'hellish' institutions and returning people to community comforts, bears little resemblance to reality. Instead:

for thousands of the old, already suffering in varying degrees from mental confusion and deterioration, it has meant premature death. For others, it has meant that they have been left to rot and decay, physically and otherwise, in broken down welfare hostels or in what are termed, with Orwellian euphemism, 'personal care' nursing homes. For thousands of younger psychotics discharged into the streets, it has meant a nightmare existence in the blighted centers of our cities, amidst neighbourhoods crowded with prostitutes, ex-felons, addicts, alcoholics, and the other human rejects now repressively tolerated by our society. Here they eke out a precarious existence, supported by welfare checks they may not even know how to cash. They spend their days locked in or locked out of dilapidated 'community-based' boarding houses. And they find themselves alternately the prey to street criminals, and a source of nuisance and alarm to those 'normal' residents of the neighbourhood too poverty-stricken to leave. (pp. 1–2).

The latter groups – 'social dynamite' – present an acute problem of social control because they are actually or potentially more troublesome. Spitzer (1975) argues that this problem population – the able-bodied, mainly young unemployed and unemployable males, amongst whom ethnic minorities are over-represented – throws into question the ability of the capitalist mode of production to generate enough work and wealth, and this in turn creates a 'legitimacy' crisis. Furthermore, it is just this problem population who, because they can distance themselves from the consent to be governed, are likely to be perceived by those in positions of power and authority as potentially disruptive, thus constituting a threat to social discipline, law and order. Consequently, this problem population has to be eliminated, suppressed or controlled: the state has to respond 'positively'.

Although governments, both in Britain and North America, justify more punishment and expanded networks of social control in terms of reducing the 'crime problem' and responding to the 'fear of crime', 'public demand' or 'liberal-reformism', none of these accounts seem genuine. These accounts are glosses to conceal government anxiety about the 'social dynamite' part of the 'surplus population' thrown out of work by the recent recession. There are good reasons for this anxiety. Both governments are unashamedly aware that their economic policies are reducing the living standards of large sections of the community. In particular, they are acutely conscious that unemployment and unemployability are creating havoc, despair, disillusionment and alienation. They also realise that the burden of economic marginalisation is very unevenly distributed among regions, social classes, age-cohorts and ethnic groups, and that the concentration of unemployment, falling living standards, economic and political marginalisation, might be an explosive mixture. Government officials may argue in public that 'unemployment is no excuse' for rioting or committing any other crime, but in private, they may well wonder whether those bearing the burden of their economic policies can be relied upon to accept it magnanimously. Politics, like sociology, is not an exact science. Increasing people's opression, by reducing their living standards and imposing intolerable levels of unemployment without compensatory and hassle-free welfare benefits or hopes for a brighter employed future, may not necessarily lead to riotous assembly or criminal mayhem, but it *might*. As Lord Scarman (1982) warned:

> to ignore the existence of economic, social and political factors . . . without which the disturbances [in Brixton during early April, 1981] cannot be fully understood . . . is to put the nation in peril. (pp. 34–5)

Glimpsing this haunting possibility, and not being dissuaded by the contradictory and somewhat ambiguous research findings on the 'unemployment-causes-crime' hypothesis, successive British and American governments have actively striven to defuse this situation, not by pursuing policies of 'full-employment', but by screwing down the lid of social control. They have created a fertile soil in which a rapid growth towards more control of the most threatening part of the 'surplus population' can take place. This has been achieved by providing more police and the powers to gather up the economically marginalised, by increasing courts and their powers to sentence them, and by building and extending the prison estate to house them. Government officials have also provided the ideological rhetoric to urge criminal justice personnel forward. By arguing that the public is increasingly afraid of a crime problem which is itself getting worse by the minute, and by advocating more punishment in place of rehabilitation, more selective incapacitation instead of coddling offenders, governments created the right atmosphere for approaches to crime and criminals to shift towards a 'law and order' stance.

The outcome of these changes has been a steady drift towards a 'punitive' or 'exceptional' state, in which the power of state officials increases at the expense of citizens' legal rights and civil liberties. It is a state in which not only are more and more people (mainly the 'surplus population') locked up or caught up in the expanding control network, but it is one in which citizens attempting to protect their legal rights or defend their civil liberties are increasingly scapegoated as 'troublemakers' with 'anti-police' sentiments, and, like other 'moaning minnies' who have no respect for authority, are portrayed as the scourge of our society. The 'enemy within' is not a term to be dismissed lightly; it genuinely reflects the government's view that the country has indeed been invaded by groups of people who no longer have any respect for the law, who are no longer willing to be acquiescent, and whose beliefs are 'alien' to the traditional values that made Britain and America 'Great'. This enemy has to be dealt with. But British and American governments do not have to do this directly. The institutions, the practices and, above all, the mental frame of mind already created in minor state officials, do this 'dirty work' almost without anyone realising it. These governments have trusted, reliable allies, particularly in the judiciary, police and control agency professionals. These need not be part of an orchestrated plan. They merely respond to *their own particular problems* in ways which bring about results beneficial to the government. Being a major beneficiary, the government and, behind it, the interests it serves ultimately, need do nothing more than give an occasional wink and nod in the right direction. 'Law and Order' is simply the ideological shield behind which American and British governments have prepared for the worse contingencies as the recession deepens. In the 'war against crime', the police are not to be criticised and the prisons are to be used increasingly and extensively. These are resources any government can deploy with more effectiveness if it chooses. Governments in both the USA and the UK have seen the percentage in police demands for more powers and resources, and have accepted them. They have seen the advantage of a swing towards the 'justice model' with its emphasis on punishment and imprisonment. There was no need to plan a defence against potential disruption; it emerges, out of the woodwork as it were, from actors already primed to act in the logic of their own situation. Successive recent governments simply went along, floating on the tide of these actors' aggregated decisions.

This brings the argument to the micro level of analysis. How and why do judges, police, and welfare professionals, unwittingly or not, help to control and discipline 'problem populations' thrown up by the logic of capital accumulation?

5 The Criminal Justice System and 'Problem Populations'

Although there are numerous state officials in the criminal justice system, three groups will be analysed in this chapter. These will be: magistrates and judges; probation officers; and police. It will be shown that the unintended and unwitting contribution each makes to reducing anxieties created by the existence of a population surplus to the requirements of the productive system, flows from these officers making decisions guided by the 'logic' of their situation as they *perceive* it.

The courts and changing sentencing practices

Over the last decade or so, the criminal justice system has been faced with what it *believes* to be a growing problem of crime and a growing number of persons who need prison both to deter and incapacitate them. The belief in the 'crime problem' comes from an awareness that the number of crimes recorded by the police is increasing, and also from the increased numbers of persons being processed through the courts. However, the judicial response is not purely mechanical. It does not simply respond passively to an increased 'work-load' by maintaining the same sentencing practices. Instead, the judiciary responds actively, changing its practices to fit what it perceives to be a changed situation. Not only is it more receptive to the idea that Britain has been experiencing a massive crime wave over the last decade, but it is also more in touch with those social groups who clamour for more prisons, police and punishment. It therefore responds actively by *increasing* the use of prison sentences and *reducing* the use of non-supervisory sentences, such as fines or unconditional discharges. The outcome is the imposition of more sentences at the higher end of the punishment tariff *over and above* the changes in the volume and pattern of crime. This effect is not a mechanical response to the increased numbers being processed, but is essentially mediated by judicial attitudes and ideological positions which prepare a sufficiently large proportion of judges and magistrates to respond to deteriorating economic conditions by resorting more frequently to severe penal sanctions.

It is as though the judiciary were a barometer of anxiety levels felt by the superordinate class whenever class antagonisms deepen during times of economic crisis and recession. This effect would not be unexpected given *who* constitute the judiciary. After reviewing numerous surveys and reports on the social and educational backgrounds of members of the higher level judiciary, Griffiths (1977) concludes that:

> four out of five full-time professional judges are a products of public schools, and of Oxford and Cambridge. Very occasionally a brilliant lower-middle-class boy has won his place in this distinguished gathering. With very few exceptions judges are required to be selected from amongst practising barristers and until recently no one without a private income could survive the first years of practice. To become a successful barrister therefore it was necessary to have financial support and so the background had to be that of the reasonably well-to-do family which, as a matter of course, sent its sons to public schools and then either straight to the bar or first to Oxford or Cambridge. (pp. 28–9)

Is it any wonder, given their pedigree background, that those fine gentlemen who comprise the higher echelons of British justice, the Law Lords, Judges of the Queen's Bench, High Court Judges, Circuit Judges and Recorders, are inclined to make decisions consistent with the beliefs and prejudices of a narrow political spectrum. 'These judges have by their education and training and the pursuit of their profession as barristers, acquired a strikingly homogeneous collection of attitudes, beliefs and principles, which to them represent the public interest' (ibid, p. 193). But on reflection, *their* interpretation of public interests means preserving what they perceive to be the interests of the state and maintaining law and order as they perceive the state to have defined it; boiled down to its sticky essence, this amounts to protecting private property rights, which, given the enormous inequalities in property ownership, means protecting the privileged property sections of the community, and 'the promotion of certain political views normally associated with the Conservative Party' (ibid.)

At the other end of the British judiciary are stipendiary magistrates (of whom there are nearly 100) and lay magistrates (of whom there are over 25,000). These are the cart-horses of the criminal justice system. They lack the class and educational pedigree of the stable traditional upper/middle classes, but the bulk of them are culturally, socially and politically set apart from the vast majority of defendants who stand uneasily before them on the wrong side of the tipped scales of justice. Magistrates natural constituency is those concerned with the preservation of property. The knowledge that there are millions of idle hands on the streets, doubtless provokes anxiety in them. For many magistrates (and judges) believe that the unemployed are likely to help themselves to other people's property. They also believe that a major part of their judicial function is to be seen protecting private property. When to these beliefs is added the 'knowledge' that 'crime is getting worse' and the 'fear of crime' is becoming a major social problem – messages that politicians, via the media, communicate – then the judiciary are bound to become more sensitised to the dangers that lurk in high levels of unemployment. Consequently, it is very likely that their decisions, both in terms of verdicts (in magistrates courts where the vast bulk of cases are heard) and sentences, will be tinged with hostility and anxiety whenever they sense a deterioration in class relationships and a slackening of discipline-through-work (or school, or family) among the subordinate classes.

This is not to argue that the judiciary are given explicit instructions, or are part of a gigantic conspiracy, but merely that there is a class 'logic' not only *in* their situation, but *in the perception* of their situation. This 'logic' leads them to make decisions which *in the aggregate* may look like the result of a carefully orchestrated effort but is in fact nothing more than thousands of unrelated, but similar individual decisions. Furthermore, given the 'Constitutional

Independence' (but 'political reliability') of the judiciary, there will be no concerted effort to prevent or curtail the steady drift towards more frequent use of severe penal sanctions as judges and magistrates react to what they perceive as growing or potential disruption resulting from the upsurge in the volume of unemployment in particular and an intensification of class conflict in general. In other words, those who do not benefit from these decisions are in no position to change them, and those who do benefit have no interest in changing them.

American criminologist Jeffrey Reiman (1984, p. 114) argues that the superordinate class allows the judiciary to operate independently for two major reasons. First, by criminalising mainly working-class people, among whom the unemployed and ethnic minorities are over-represented, the judiciary both creates and sustains the idea that the 'crime problem' which threatens our middle-class civilised way of life, comes essentially from the 'lower orders'. This is a useful ideological fiction because it masks the enormous physical, economic and social costs caused by 'crimes of the powerful', such as corporate crime, commercial fraud and illegal industrial pollution. Second, by 'punishing' offenders, the courts render them morally defective and thereby help to preserve the social structure and particularly the differences in income and wealth from being implicated in the causation of 'conventional crimes'. Because of these two benefits – its crimes are ignored relatively, and its contribution to working-class crime is concealed – the superordinate class has no interest in changing the criminal justice system or preventing the judiciary from 'disciplining and deterring' the economically marginalised.

This does not necessarily mean that during times of rising unemployment the judiciary increases the severity of penal sanctions only against the unemployed; they may well extend imprisonment across the spectrum of persons found guilty, particularly as the majority of these are bound to be working class and/or ethnically oppressed. None the less, when passing sentences, the judiciary are likely to make fine distinctions even within these subordinate groups. If there is judicial anxiety during times of deteriorating economic conditions, then it would be those convicted persons from groups perceived to be actually or potentially disruptive who would feel the harsher side of judicial discretion. It is possible that even within the unemployed population the judiciary would see crucial distinctions.

For example, unemployed males are more likely to be perceived as problematic because in Western culture, work is not only believed to be the typical way in which males are disciplined but it is also their major source of identity and thus the process by which they build up a stake in conformity. Consequently when males are removed from or denied access to work, it is widely believed that they will have various anarchistic responses among which criminal behaviour is likely to figure quite strongly. These cultural meanings of work attributed to males are likely to have adverse effects on the way in which unemployed males are processed in the criminal justice system.

This is not to argue that when it comes to sentencing, magistrates and judges allow the offender's employment status to override the seriousness of his present offence and previous convictions (if they exist). But when they consider sentences for offenders whose offences and previous convictions are similar, they are still forced, because of prison accommodation and court welfare officers' reports, to take other factors into account. One of the most likely extra factors affecting the sentence imposed on a male offender will be whether or not he is employed. If he is not, the judiciary are more likely to view him as potentially more likely to commit other, particularly economic, offences, and consequently pass an immediate prison sentence. This severe sentence is imposed partly because the judiciary believe it will *incapacitate* him, and thus marginally reduce the crime rate, but also because this sentence may *deter* other unemployed males tempted by the possible economic gains of crime. That there is no such simple relationship between incarceration and crime rates (Biles, 1979, 1982; Bowker, 1981; Greenwood, 1983; McGuire and Sheehen, 1983; Nagel, 1977) is either unknown to the judiciary or fails to dissuade them from using their commonsense notions of crime-causation to guide them in sentencing unemployed males.

In contrast, and again because of institutionalised sexism, unemployed females can, and for the most part do, slip back into or take up the wife/mother social role and hence become subject to all the informal controls of *being* in the family, thus making criminalisation and imprisonment, as forms of social control, unlikely resources to be utilised by the judiciary. Furthermore, given the view held by a large proportion of the population that female employment leads to delinquent 'latch-key' children, it is unlikely that judges and magistrates will favour imprisoning unemployed mothers, for they will be seen as fulfilling their stereotypic gender-role and hence playing their informal part in delinquency control. Removing them to prison would interfere with this vital social service. Indeed, the gender-role of keeping the family together becomes all the more important during times of economic crisis and high unemployment; rapidly increasing the rate of imprisonment for unemployed mothers during such times would jeopardize the 'social reproductive' process, and thus further impair the chances of longer-term economic recovery (Braithwaite, 1980, p. 204). Whilst it is unlikely that the judiciary will necessarily be aware of this macro-functional relationship, the aggregation of their individual decisions not to imprison unemployed females unwittingly brings it about!

In addition to making a distinction between gender, the judiciary will also be affected by the offender's age. Thus young unemployed males will be perceived as potentially or actually more dangerous than older males simply because their resistance to adversity will have been less worn away by barren years of accommodative strategies to inequalities in the distribution of income and life chances (Parkin, 1971). They will have experienced less discipline at the work place, and their physical prowess and energy, attributes often considered prerequisites for 'conventional' crime, will still be in prime condition. There is a further reason why the judiciary might be affected by the suspect's age. It is 'common knowledge', no doubt shared by the judiciary, that youth and conventional crime are linked; the peak for these crimes tends to be in the mid-teens. This is also an age-group suffering from much higher than national average rates of unemployment. Consequently it can be expected that the association between unemployment and imprisonment will be greater for a population of younger compared with older males.

Finally, there are reasons why ethnic minorities, particularly young males, would be treated more harshly by the judiciary. Not only is the unemployment rate among this group two to three times higher than its white counterpart, but their demographic characteristics – they are disproportionately aged between 15 and 25 years old – also signal potentially high levels of criminal behaviour. So, as a group, the British black population are doubly vulnerable, first to higher levels of unemployment and second to higher levels of criminality because that is 'youth's speciality'. In addition, black youth is politically marginalised and therefore unwilling and incapable of attempting to struggle for change of the system from the inside.

When racial discrimination is added to these factors, and when there have already been urban riots in which unemployed British blacks figured prominently (Southgate and Field, 1982) – a fact blown up out of proportion in highly sensationalised media presentation – there are a whole bundle of reasons why the judiciary would view ethnic minorities as needing discipline. Indeed, in a recent Home Office publication, Stevens (1979, p. 16) appeared to predict and justify this when he wrote 'representation among those arrested and convicted is also likely to increase, and that the absolute numbers of blacks arrested and convicted will increase rapidly, in the 1980's and perhaps beyond'.

The judiciary would not necessarily have to be aware of these demographic characteristics and social changes, or their likely effects on delinquent behaviour. Individual judges and magistrates merely have to view many young offenders, particularly if they are also black and unemployed, as likely to commit further serious criminal acts, and that would justify imposing, in their 'learned opinion', a sentence of imprisonment.

In dispensing 'justice', magistrates and judges have to make fine distinctions between those convicted even for similar offences. They could not commit to prison all those found guilty of property offences. How are they to make these distinctions? I have argued above that the judiciary operates largely in terms of its theories of crime – what types of person are *really* criminal and therefore likely to re-offend. Since these theories, in one way or another, render the poor morally defective because they make 'wicked' decisions when others living in similar circumstances have the moral fibre to resist, then the courts feel justified in imposing harsher sentences. The process is not sinister. Indeed, when magistrates and judges experience not only a total increase in the 'work-load' but also a disproportionate *increase* in those perceived as being criminal and likely to re-offend – namely unemployed and unemployable males – then they are acting out of the best possible motives – to protect the public. Of course some magistrates may use this account cynically, being aware that behind it a certain amount of class warfare is being strategically waged. But there is no need to assume this is true of the majority; they are simply doing their job as they see it ought to be done and how the 'public' demand it. The economic elite, not being harmed by this, simply have no reason to stop it, and consequently the judiciary goes on making the poor criminals and ignoring the alternative possibility that poverty is a crime (Reiman, 1984, pp. 116–28). On the other hand, since the elite benefit from the criminal justice system, they are not without sufficient acumen to give it a boost in resources and power occasionally and a nudge in the Right direction.

Although this section has relied exclusively on data relating to England and Wales, the processes it describes also apply to the USA. Thus although judges in America are openly political appointees, that does not depart significantly from Britain where a not dissimilar process goes on behind closed doors. And just as British judges share a common set of cultural assumptions, so do the Florida judges studied by Frazier and Bock (1982). These researchers were impressed with the 'subculture of sentencing', based around 'law and order' views, to which these judges subscribed. Furthermore, there is little reason to consider that American judges do not have views on age, gender and race similar to those outlined above. Most of the research studies reviewed later reveal that these three social characteristics intrude into US court proceedings because judges consider them to be relevant. In addition, the predicted population growth for black males at risk of committing crime mirrors the British situation. Thus the 20–28 black male population is predicted to grow between 1980 and 1990 by 18 per cent, whereas the comparable white population is expected to grow by only 1 per cent (Austin and Krisberg, 1985, p. 25). Given the longstanding acceptance of the black=crime equation to the American white mind, these demographic predictions, like their British counterparts, are bound to percolate through to the criminal justice system.

The 'latent' contribution of probation officers to the expansion of social control

The importance of the Probation and After-Care Service, both in North America and Britain, has increased substantially over the last two decades. Murrah (1963) reports a prominent American judge commenting that 'of all the administrative aids available to the judge an adequate, comprehensive and complete presentence investigation is the best guide to intelligent sentencing' (p. 67). A similar enthusiastic evaluation can be found in Hogarth (1971) who reported a Canadian judge's view that 'the presentence report is one of the most important developments in Canadian criminal law during the twentieth century' (p. 246).

Although it is complicated to explain the Probation Service's lurch into prominence, two reasons, also relevant to evaluating the Service's contribution to controlling 'problem populations', stand out as deserving special consideration. These occurred in both North America and Britain, but for illustrative purposes the situation in England and Wales will be examined in detail.

Two changes in the criminal justice system over the last twenty years help to account for the rising importance of the Probation Service. First, the ascendancy of 'individualised justice', particularly for adolescents, which occurred during the late 1960s and early 1970s and was embodied in the 1969 Childrens and Young Persons Act, required courts to obtain much more detailed background information on suspects awaiting trial and offenders awaiting sentence. The Probation Service became the conduit along which this information flowed. Second, the proliferation of 'alternatives to prison', which accelerated with the introduction of parole in 1968 and the spread of community service orders from 1973 onwards, required the Probation Service to prepare many more social inquiry reports to assess whether probation or another 'alternative to prison' could be recommended. The Service thus became a centrally important agency shaping and influencing decisions affecting sentence and parole. It also became more involved with supervisory work beyond straightforward probation orders.

These changes resulted in a rapid numerical expansion of clients being supervised by probation officers. Thus the number of offenders received annually on a Probation Order increased from just under 24,000 in 1973 to 34,000 by 1983. The number of prisoners released on parole under licence to the Probation Service rose from 751 in 1968 to over 6,000 by the mid-1980s. Community Service Orders, many of which are supervised by the Service, increased to over 30,000 ten years after being made available to the courts. Finally, a proportion of the annual number of 30,000 offenders given a suspended prison sentence over recent years has been taken on as additional statutory work for the Service.

The path of increasing importance has not been smooth, or without 'unintended consequences', for the increased clientele and the deepening involvement in courts and prisons created a constant 'dilemma' for probation officers. It was the typical way in which this dilemma was solved that brought about the Probation Service's contribution to the expansion of social control and, unwittingly or not, contributed to the increasing number of persons, particularly the unemployed, being imprisoned. But first, the nature of the dilemma.

The Probation Service has a vested professional and occupational interest in advocating and demonstrating the relative effectiveness and cost-efficiency of 'alternatives to prison', particularly those with which it is intimately involved. In order to justify the allocation of state resources and secure their occupational existence, they need to prove that the services offered will, at worst (and hopefully results will be better than this), produce a rate of re-offending no higher than that among persons released from prison. Furthermore, they need to demonstrate that this superior comparative effectiveness can be achieved at a much lower cost per offender. Of course, this latter objective is easy to achieve – the daily cost of a British prisoner is at least twenty times higher than that of a probationer. The relative costs in America are not that dissimilar. Funke (1985) has estimated that the average cost of paying for a 500-bed prison is roughly $11.5 million per year. This would pay for nearly 20,000 probationers on a one-year order.

The former goal – effectiveness – is like 'hunting the snark'. Despite a wide variety of ingenious schemes for reforming, educating, helping, assisting, training, treating, supervising, befriending and counselling offenders, 'nothing seems to work'. At least that is the dismal conclusion arrived at by Martinson (1974) in his classic evaluation study of numerous attempts to measure the effectiveness of various methods to reduce recidivism. It would not be unreasonable to conclude from this that the Service, like other correctional/control agencies, lacks a proven technology or demonstrated professional expertise. None the less, the illusive goal of effectiveness has to be pursued. Consequently, probation officers have to aim, through their 'recommendations' to courts and prison Parole Boards, to secure not only sufficient clients, but also ones who are *suitable*. Numbers are clearly important because these can be welded as a bargaining lever to wrench more funds from central and local governments. The suitability of clients is essential if results flattering to the service and therefore enhancing their demands for more resources are to stand any chance of being achieved.

These professional and occupational interests do not fit easily with another feature of the Probation Service. As an integral part of the criminal justice system, it constantly has to secure its *credibility* with the courts and prisons. According to Walker and Beaumont (1981), there is a simple reason for this. They argued that 'Although official accounts concede probation officers' flexibility and discretion in the methods they use there is *an expectation that they will always act as agents of the court* (my emphasis) (p. 26). Being aware of this expectation, individual probation officers feel a strain towards appearing reasonable, fair and just to magistrates, judges and prison higher officials. Clearly a reputation for being soft, sentimental and 'out of touch with reality', will render a probation officer's recommendations impotent. To avoid this, officers need to develop a sensitivity to local courts and prison officials and, particularly with the former, a sixth sense in predicting what kind of sentence will be imposed, or at least the narrow range of possibilities under consideration. They also have to gauge whether the sentence will be imposed irrespective of any skilled written advocacy of an alternative. If they assess this to be likely, it would be prudent to write a report which flatters the court rather than waste time and effort pointlessly opposing it. Any probation officer who is seen to prioritise occupational interests by recommending probation orders, community orders or some other sentence with which they might become involved in a supervisory capacity, and is considered blinkered to the courts' sentencing practices, will not only incur its displeasure, but will lose personal

credibility and cast a shadow on the whole local Probation Service.
'Second-guessing' the sentence is difficult because within the
judiciary two 'systems of justice' reside as uneasy bedfellows. The
first, *individualised justice*, presumes that offenders are more
deprived than depraved, and that with skilful, professional insight,
each individual offender's personal problems can be identified
and, to some extent, ameliorated. Under this system, 'what' the
offender did becomes relegated to 'what' kind of problems the
offender confronted both at the time of the offence and prior to it.
In the determination of sentence, guilt becomes less important
than the offender's 'needs' and suitability for professional intervention. This requires fairly extensive interviewing to gather
sufficient information to form a recommendation.

The second system, sometimes called the *justice* or *tariff* model,
is based on the classical idea that the offence should determine
sanction. The more serious the offence, the more severe should be
the sanction. The offender is punished not because of personal
qualities, or the conditions surrounding the offence, but because
the offence itself deserves, indeed demands, a particular sanction.
There is no need to delve into the suspect's past or present
circumstances, or psychological characteristics. The primary and
overriding issue is the establishment of guilt. Once this is settled,
the sanction, in principle at least, should be determined automatically. Since under this system, judicial discretion is minimised, a
robot, properly programmed, could dispense justice!

Although these two systems of justice are distinct theoretically,
they are rarely realised in practice in a way that resembles their
pure form. Indeed, in the USA, and in the UK particularly, both
systems operate simultaneously. This creates a second strand in
the dilemma facing Probation Officers. Is the court likely to see a
particular case more in terms of the 'justice' or the 'individualised'
model?

With some cases this is no problem. At the most serious end of
the offence spectrum, the 'tariff'/'justice' system is likely to domi-
nate; at the trivial, first-offender, adolescent end, the 'individualised' model is likely to weigh more heavily in the minds of
magistrates. However, these are extremities. The majority of cases
are in between. In these, there is likely to be a fine balance
between elements incorporated from both models. The officer's
dilemma is how to guess this balance correctly so as not to lose

credibility with the courts (Roberts and Roberts, 1982; Rosecrance, 1985).

As in medicine, and other service-professions, dilemmas and
ambiguities are resolved by applying the same defensive principle,
'when in doubt, it is better to be safe than sorry'. When making
recommendations to the court, officers' discretion has to be tem-
pered by an awareness that they are its agents. As Walker and
Beaumont (1981) argue:

> the dominant influence in reports [by officers] is that they are
> written for an *audience* – the court. This determines the ap-
> proach taken, the content and the style. It also acts as a con-
> straint, determining the limit of material considered relevant.
> (p. 21)

In attempting to 'gauge' the court's mood, and in particular
predict whether it will lean towards the 'tariff' or 'individualised'
system of justice, and which type of sentence it might impose when
it has made this decision, probation officers will tend to be *cautious*. Their 'faces', and beyond that, their professional credibility,
depend upon it. Consequently, where there is ambiguity, and
there often is, they will tend towards making sentence recommendations which favour applying the 'tariff' model, and where, on a
prima-facie basis, this indicates imprisonment, recommend that
sentence.

This creeping conservatism, understandable in terms of preserving professional standing, has an 'unintended' effect, or as
sociologists call it, a 'latent function'. It might lead to more prison
sentences being recommended than the courts would have imposed otherwise, and in this way unwittingly contribute towards
increasing the control of 'surplus populations'.

This possibility is reinforced by a second consideration. In
attempting to select suitable clients, probation officers may move
slightly from the principled position of recommending an 'alternative to custody', particularly where the client is estimated by them
to be a poor risk and unlikely to respond well to their professional
services. In this circumstance, they might push the offender up the
'tariff' and recommend custody. In other words, some offenders,
who from another more 'individualised' perspective might look
like suitable cases for not being imprisoned, become, through the

process of officers protecting their professional and the Service's interests, transformed into just the opposite.

Thus the increased involvement of the Probation Service in the criminal justice system over the last two decades, an involvement premised on the basis of developing more genuine alternatives to imprisonment, has probably made a contribution, no doubt unintended and unwitting, to pushing up the number of persons sent to prison. It has done this by being too cautious, and *over-predicting* the number of cases for which courts would have handed down a prison sentence. The courts, having little reason not to accept these recommendations, go ahead and imprison the offender. If the interests of the courts, as perceived by magistrates, were threatened by these recommendations, they would lean heavily on the Service to change its practices, and maybe even lose a practitioner or two. But since the courts' interests are not harmed (just as the national interest, as perceived by the government, is not harmed by the courts' sentencing practices), they are, on the whole, willing 'to be influenced' by officers' correctly anticipated recommendations. It is the harmlessness of probation officers' sentence recommendations that explains the very high agreement between these and the actual sentence reported in research conducted in Britain (White, 1972), Canada (Hagan, 1975) and the USA (Carter and Wilkins, 1967; Neubauer, 1974; Myers, 1979), and not that the courts are unduly influenced against their judgement to accept them. Indeed, according to American criminologist John Rosecrance (1985):

> officers exert a minimal influence upon the sentencing process. . . [because]. . . when decision making is actually required, it is done by correlating a recommendation with informal but existing sentencing parameters. Knowledge of current sentencing concepts and policies allows the probation officer to select satisfactory or 'ball park' recommendations. Through a process of bureaucratic winnowing, only probation officers who are willing to provide such recommendations consistently are assigned to the presentence investigation unit. These officers are rewarded for their compliance and come to accept the prevailing sentencing parameters as 'natural'. (pp. 549–50)

By pushing more offenders into custody than they need have, the Service creates a problem for itself. It still has to secure sufficient numbers of clients to justify its own demands for financial resources. Officers find themselves filling this gap by recommending probation and/or community service orders to some offenders who would never previously have been given a supervisory sentence in the first place. These are offenders whom officers predict would be treated more in terms of the 'individualised' model of justice by the courts, and who, by virtue of their personal qualities, offer the service a strong possibility of not being 'failures'. Some at least of these would previously have been either fined, or given a conditional/unconditional discharge.

The results, doubtless unintended, of probation officers resolving the dilemma between securing occupational interests and gaining credibility in the courts, is that they contribute not only to widening the net of social control, but also to the increasing number of persons being sent to prison. They trawl into the net of social control persons who would not have been caught previously, and they shunt a proportion from the *soft* end, where they probably deserve to be, to the *hard* end, and thus contribute to the problem of prison overcrowding.

It would be wrong to exaggerate this contribution and thus distort reality too much. Nor would it be justifiable to argue that this contribution is greater than that made by magistrates and judges themselves, or by the next group of control agents to be examined, the police. But none the less it would be naive to assume that the Probation Service and its practitioners, although operating no doubt from benevolent motives, do not bring about consequences they never intended. Social life is too replete with ironies ('latent consequences') for any professional group to be exempt from this 'social fact'.

The police and the control of 'problem populations'

The contribution of the courts, with the Probation Service's assistance, to the problem of prison overcrowding, widening the net of social control, and damping down the potential threat, real or imagined, posed by 'problem populations', is only possible with 'a little help from their friends'. Through their deployment, arrest and prosecution practices, the police supply the judiciary with an increasing number of persons to process, and among these proportionately more are young, unemployed, and/or black. How and why do the police bring this result about?

The police have a particular image of themselves. First, they are the thin 'blue line' protecting upright respectable citizens from the tidal wave of criminality which, as they believe, occurred within the last twenty years and has become a major source of anxiety and worry in the community causing far too many people to stay at home behind bolted doors and locked windows. Second, they view themselves as the 'guardians of public morality'. Although the police realise that over many moral issues, particularly prostitution, homosexuality, abortion, pornography, alcohol and other drug consumption, there exist heated, volatile disagreements, none the less they tend to identify more with the conservative sides of these debates. Finally, they experience themselves as 'front-line troops' in a war against certain types of dissidents – marginalised, alienated and alien youth, terrorists, football hooligans, industrial agitators and militant trade-unionists – all of whom, so it appears to those suffering from cultural amnesia, have crawled out of the woodwork only recently. A close reading of either Stan Cohen's *Folk Devils and Moral Panics* (1972) or Geoff Pearson's *Hooligan* (1983) would soon cure this amnesia, but these studies, like other 'demystifying' sociological texts, are doomed to the fate of co-optation, parody or rude dismissal.

From the officers' perspective, these three images – 'protector', 'guardian' and 'defender' – coalesce to produce a view of police work as dangerous, socially isolating, and containing problems of authority, which not only undermine efficiency, but frequently poison police–public relationships. Despite these lurking dangers, the police perceive themselves as having a mandate to solve the 'problem of crime', reduce the 'fear of crime' and eliminate the 'enemy within'. To achieve these herculean tasks, the police cannot be too hindered by procedural niceties to protect the civil and legal rights of citizens. The warnings of politicians and journalists that social order, as we have known it, is under real threat, the demands of frightened citizens for more police and policing, and the legal system turning a permissive 'blind eye' to irregularities, all combine to give the police a secure sense of certainty that it is important, almost at any costs, to get the villains.

The three types of police work outlined above, and which in reality often overlap, require the police to develop routine methods for recognising certain types of persons as being 'typical criminals', 'symbolic assailants', 'purveyors of immorality' and 'political extremists'. For a number of reasons this rogues gallery will be lined with portraits drawn from a pastiche of class, sex and racial ingredients. In the first two 'typifications' particularly, the economically marginalised and ethnic minority males will figure prominently in the foreground.

There are two reasons for these 'stereotypic villains' being portrayed in this way. The first consists of external influences, and the second refers to occupational experiences and organisational needs.

By virtue of their training and general involvement in the acquisition of 'cultural common sense', the police come into contact with versions of criminological theories posing as explanations of criminal activity. The majority of these are 'types of person' accounts, which describe offenders as a pathological, almost subhuman species. They have brain, chromosome, glandular, psychological, or personality disorders; they are, in a word, *flawed*. Sociological theories, such as differential association, anomie, cultural transmission, and control, will definitely play 'second fiddle' to pathology theories, even though all propose some flawed environmental factors, such as bad friends, irresponsible parents, libertarian schools, disorganised neighbourhoods, or some combination of these. Both types of theories suppose that there exists a major 'set of facts to be explained'. These 'facts' are that crime is primarily a lower-class young male activity. Hence each theory is shaped to fit snugly around these 'facts', thus elevating the class/youth/male–crime relationships into *the* touchstones of criminology.

These theories have trickled down, in loosely translated form, from the academe to the minds of laypersons, including the police. Through the acquisition of this 'conventional wisdom', the police 'know' where to find criminals; they live in poor, inner-city areas where the lower-class, economically marginalised and ethnic minorities live semi-ghettoised existences. The police also 'know' how to recognise them: they are pathological or abnormal, or have corrupting friends, inadequate parents, weak teachers, or live in neighbourhoods lacking a sense of community; and above all they have been 'identified' previously either by expulsion from school, caught playing truant, involved with social work departments, or by past dealings with the police. This non-representative sample of

citizens becomes the front-line suspects methodically selected by
the police as being 'up to no good'.

Politicians and journalists scoop up deposits left by the popular-
isation of academic criminology and give them a reconstructed
interpretation to suit their own particular interests. Consider one
example – 'the scrounger'. The floodlights of engineered opinion
picked out the distinguishing features of this 'folk devil' as the
unemployed total broke through the barrier of post-war Keynesian
consensus welfarism in the late 1970s and early 1980s. An event on
2 September 1982 encapsulates the whole process. On that day,
'283 people who walked into an unemployment benefit office in
Oxford found themselves arrested by the police on suspicion of
fraud' (CHAR, 1983, p. 7). Newspapers used all the imagery of
the 'scrounger' to mediate this mass arrest to the public. Who were
these fiddlers? They were, according to the London's *Standard*,
'bands of highly organised claimants. . . roving round the country
conning "our" money out of the Department of Health and Social
Security'. Among them were such moral disreputables as 'seven
Irishmen', 'a gipsy couple', 'a top class stripper', 'an unmarried
mum' and, of course, 'blacks'. This last 'stereotype', a particularly
unpleasant racist slur, was depicted in a *Sun* cartoon. It showed
twelve accused claimants riding on a conveyor belt past a magistrates' bench. Four of the claimants were black. This proportion of
one-third totally misrepresented the actual ratio. According to
CHAR (1983), 'In reality, only 4 out of 283 people arrested. . .
were black; two were released without charge, one had his case
dismissed, and one was convicted' (p. 49).

Yet the damage was done. Readers of the *Sun* were led to
believe that blacks form a significantly large proportion of 'scroungers'. This further reinforced the black=crime equation, which
began with the mugging panic of the early 1970s (Hall *et al.*, 1978)
and climaxed with the *Daily Mail*'s screaming headline: BLACK
CRIME: THE ALARMING FIGURES. In this classic scare
story, policemen's leader Jim Jardine was reported to be calling
for at least another 5,000 officers to deal with the problem.
Readers were warned that things were deteriorating just like
'across the water in America'. Somehow guns were thrown in,
even though guns appear in a minute number of muggings. And
Mrs Jill Knight, Tory MP, claimed that the Home Secretary had
assured her that 'where serious criminals could be deported back

to their countries of origin they would be'. Of course, it was all misinformation. The data on which the story was based referred to only 3 per cent of serious crimes. The race of the vast majority of offenders was simply unknown. But this point was nicely concealed beneath the alarming headlines.

Furthermore, these 'scroungers' – 'lazy', 'idle' 'aliens' in our midst – were not the deserving poor. They were not poor at all! They were described as making a fortune. One was reported to have claimed £13,000 illegally even while driving round in an £8,000 sports car. Others had the nerve to insult respectable sensibilities by turning up to collect their dole money in taxis they could afford from the vast hoardings of their fraud or earnings from 'moonlighting' (the contradiction between 'idle' and 'moonlighting' not being apparent to either tabloid journalists or their readers!).

It was alleged to be an enormous fiddle. The *Daily Telegraph*, who claimed that 'one in 12 dole claims are fraudulent', could not put a precise monetary value on it. The *Express*, however, was able to ask whether it was '£100m.? £200m.? or £300m.?' and thus alert readers to its possible size. The *Sun* went further. One of its headlines revealed that 'Dole swindles cost £400m.' And the *Mail* put the cream on the claimants' fraudulent cake by asserting that £500 millions was involved!

The courts were quick to 'legitimate' police action against these deeply wicked scroungers. They heard the cases almost instantly, and handed down severe sentences. Of 139 guilty pleas, all were given a custodial sentence, only two of which were suspended, even though many were appearing in court for the first time and had not been advised by solicitors. Of nineteen pleading 'not guilty', four were finally convicted and given custodial sentences.

The Big Culprits, the Landlords who made a lot more money out of supplying bogus addresses for claimants in return for a 'fee', were ignored by the police, and no one in authority complained. But when claimants and/or their solicitors complained about police irregularities and violation of civil and legal rights, these were either dismissed or condemned to the rubbish tip of 'complaints through the proper channels'.

The lesson police learnt from this one incident – and it is merely a highly publicised example of daily confrontations between some members of the public and the police – is that certain social groups are stigmatised and scapegoated by politicians and the media. As such, they are condemned groups the police are permitted to arrest and criminalise. This segment, by coincidence, as Vonnegut would have it, happens to come from the inner-city lower-class areas, where the economically marginalised and disadvantaged ethnic minorities live. They are, in other words, the *same* people whose crimes form the 'facts to be explained' in mainstream criminological theories.

Selective deployment patterns adopted by the police result in officers, and especially new recruits 'on the beat', coming into direct and personal contact with a limited slice of 'deviant/criminal' life. These deployment policies, determined by higher management, interact with and reinforce media images of the typical criminal and politicians' warnings of our escalating crime problem. They focus on certain parts of urban areas, particularly those 'known' to contain criminal elements or where it is believed that violence is likely to break out. They also concentrate on 'public' places, where 'idle' hands spend most of the unoccupied days and nights. The outcome is that young unemployed males are frequently 'in the sights' of the police. Of course, the institution of 'privacy' which determines that police dwell mainly in public places is not constantly observed. The police frequently penetrate the 'privacy' of those persons living mainly in lower-class areas where the unemployed and ethnic minorities are concentrated?

As a consequence of these deployment patterns, directed as they are by theories of criminality, as well as organisational pragmatism and political cynicism, the police tend to concentrate on 'street' crimes, such as robbery, burglary, theft and assault. These crimes are undoubtedly committed more frequently by lower-class young males, and the unemployed and ethnic minorities are also over-represented in this group. The police will hardly ever meet upper-class criminals deeply involved in corporate violations of state regulations, government malfeasance, professional malpractice, embezzlement or security/insurance fraud. Only when respectable citizens untypically commit 'street' offences, are the police likely to become involved.

When it is realised the crime on which the police concentrate is only a slice of the total, the 'war against crime' takes on a slightly different colour. In this new light, it can be seen also as a 'war'

against those populations surplus to the requirements of the productive process and who are perceived by the state as being
willing, at least potentially, to resist. Indeed, if 'street' crime is a
form of resistance, albeit a totally 'irrational' form because it
victimises people in a similar predicament, then the state feels
some justification for this 'war' against the 'enemy within'.

The population on whom the police concentrate their attention
is likely to view itself as 'picked on', 'pushed around', 'unfairly
treated' and 'occupied by a police force increasingly resembling
the army'. These feelings constitute a massive 'sense of injustice'
and this undoubtedly colours police–public relations in parts of the
urban landscape. In these encounters, civilian behaviour is likely
to be perceived by the police as hostile, uncivil, unpleasant, and
above all, as threatening their authority and physical safety. No
wonder they are receptive to the media's portraits of 'thugs',
'bully-boys', 'granny bashers', 'louts' and 'hooligans'. These reflect, at least in a distorted form, their interpretation of experiences with young inner-city males, and thus reinforce and
'legitimate' police behaviour (and 'misbehaviour') towards them.

These deployment patterns have another effect which facilitates
the police adopting a 'tougher' stance towards certain social
groups. They are likely to come into contact with those sections of
the community amongst whom the 'fear of crime' is higher than
elsewhere. In the USA (Balkin, 1979; Braungart *et al.*, 1980;
Gordon *et al.*, 1980) and the UK (Clarke and Lewis, 1982; Maxfield, 1984) the old, women, and particularly old women living in
inner-city areas, report higher rates of being afraid to go out after
dark, and believe they can protect themselves less easily in a
neighbourhood they perceive as being unsafe and growing worse
all the time.

These respectable citizens – the old, women, and particularly
old women, who contribute little to serious crime and do not
threaten police authority – bring out the 'guardian' side of police
work. Fortified with this paternalistic, protective mission, the
police feel perfectly justified in taking a hard stance towards
people they perceive to be threatening the lives of these vulnerable
members of the population and destroying the fabric of the community they inhabit. Also, by drawing this cloak of 'protecting the
public' over their professional conscience, the police feel able to
practise a little 'vigilante' justice, or fall into the habit of charging

certain people with offences for which there is no real defence,
such as being disorderly, resisting arrest, using threatening behaviour towards an officer, and obstructing the highway (Cain and
Sadigh, 1982; MacBarnet, 1982). These tactics are very valuable
when the law is seen to be too soft and in need of a little help 'from
its friends' to get more right results.

Finally, the police, like any other organisation, needs to project
an image of itself as efficient, but hard-pressed. It needs the former
to mute criticism; it needs the latter to justify the allocation of
more financial resources and legal powers. To achieve these ob-
jects, it has to 'clear up' a sufficient number of crimes to satisfy the
public that the police are doing what they can. But at the same
time, the police have to appeal for more resources on the grounds
that they could do much better with modern equipment, improved
technology, and extended legal powers. In this careful balancing
act, it is essential to keep organisational costs down by arresting
and prosecuting suspects who are seen by the public to be acceptable targets for police intervention, and who, in addition, present
little trouble to bureaucratic routines and procedures. As Chambliss (1969) saw it, the principles governing the administration of
justice are simple. He suggested that:

> Those persons are arrested, tried and sentenced who can offer
> the fewest rewards for non-enforcement of the laws and who can
> be processed without creating undue strain of the organisations
> which comprise the legal system. (pp. 84–5)

Young, poor, unemployed, ethnic-minority males are the most
vulnerable to apprehension, arrest and prosecution, not because
they commit more crimes, although they certainly commit more
'street' crimes, but because *in addition* they are in no position to
protect themselves, present little trouble to the legal process, and
coincide with the media's image of 'villains', an image widely
accepted by the public. Thus, although the police have considerable discretion, they feel a strong need to employ it in a selective
manner. They do not want to upset their organisational superiors
and the work norms they formulate. They do not want to be seen
disregarding the fears of respectable old women in inner-city
neighbourhoods. They do not want to be seen in dereliction of

their mission to defend all that is good from the 'enemy within'. Finally, they do not want to jeopardise their careers by getting on badly with peers. For this host of reasons, police discretionary powers, wide in theory, take on a practical substance around a select group of routinely suspected citizens.

As the number of unemployed has grown over the last decade, it would be expected that unemployed suspects increase disproportionately in those arrested and prosecuted by the police. This is not because the police are the government's poodle and simply respond obediently to commands. The 'logic' of police work is such that it would lead to this result. Media representations, politicians' warnings, citizen complaints, occupational experiences, peer-group socialisation, and organisational norms for 'results', all dovetail to produce considerable pressure on constables to behave in highly predictable ways, despite their discretionary powers. At the receiving end of this predictable behaviour will be those conforming to 'folk devil' images, who pose problems for authority by their lack of respect and deference, and who are unable to offer much trouble to the smooth bureaucratic process of being criminalised. By sheer coincidence, as Vonnegut would have it, these just happen to be young, working-class males, amongst whom the unemployed and ethnic minorities will be over-represented. This is not to imply that most of these are 'angels' who have not committed any crime. But crimes, maybe different ones, are also committed by other types of persons from more 'respectable' backgrounds. However, the very nature of police discretion precludes full enforcement of the criminal law. The net police cast to trawl in suspects is so designed not to catch all offenders, but only some. Those caught may be presented as the worst, and most dangerous offenders, but that is more ideological than descriptive. Compared with corporate violations, government offences, and crimes committed by numerous respectable professional groups, these 'street' criminals are small fish. However, ideological messages have real consequences. 'Street' criminals are viewed as *the* criminals, and so the police feel justified in arresting and prosecuting them. This is reinforced by large sections of the public who believe this will do something about the 'crime problem'. It is also supported by politicians who see electoral advantage in waging a war against 'street' crime, as well as cynically seeing it as yet another weapon for controlling the 'social dynamite' part of the 'surplus population' and hence reducing the likelihood of resistance or rebellion.

Furthermore, ethnic minorities form a large part of this 'surplus population', and 'racial prejudice' both in the community and the police gives an unpleasant twist to economic marginalisation. As Reiner (1985) sees it:

> The young 'street'·population has always been the prime focus of police order maintenance and law enforcement work. The processes of racial disadvantage in housing, employment and education lead young blacks to be disproportionately involved in street culture. They may also become engaged in specific kinds of street crime. . . At the same time, the relative powerlessness of ethnic minorities and lower working-class youth means that the police may be less constrained and inhibited in dealing with them. In times of economic crisis and competition for jobs and other resources, the majority group (especially the white working class) might indeed benefit from the effects of over-policing the blacks, because black stigmatisation as criminal, the acquisition of criminal records, reduces their competitiveness. For all these reasons, the economically marginal ethnic minorities, and especially their youth, are prone to become 'police property'. (p. 136)

Once a group has been identified as 'police property', encounters between them and the police become tense and fraught; each approaches the other in terms of 'stereotypes' which although at first misleading, come, through a kind of self-fulfilling prophecy, to resemble the real thing. The police come to see the economically marginalised as 'criminal' and threatening; the economically marginalised come to see the police as prejudiced oppressors. The outcome is more economically marginalised persons being apprehended, arrested and prosecuted, a process which has intensified during the recent recession.

Conclusion: what this 'radical' view opposes and predicts

The ghost haunting this chapter is an alternative, more orthodox, and doubtlessly more appealing to commonsense explanation of the link between unemployment and imprisonment. According to this orthodox perspective, there is a very mechanistic relationship between unemployment and imprisonment. It proposes that rising unemployment pushes up the crime rate as more individuals are tempted to break the law, a temptation many of them are unable to resist because they lack sufficient moral fibre. (This personal failing is also a major convenient explanation for their being unemployed.) As the rate of crime increases, and assuming a constant rate of reporting crime by the public, and arrest and prosecution by the police, so there is an *automatic* increase in the work-load of the judiciary. As this work-load increases and as more people are convicted of crime, so naturally the judiciary send more people to prison.

While there is obviously some truth in this, particularly the expected increase in the number of prison sentences following more convictions, it has at least two serious flaws. First, the rates of reporting, arrest, conviction and imprisonment are unlikely to remain constant over time; indeed, they are likely to vary as economic circumstances change. During a time of increasing unemployment, it is reasonable to expect that:

1 reporting of crimes increases, partly because the 'fear of crime' intensifies – this occurs because people *believe* that 'unemployment causes crime', but also because more reporting pushes up the level of 'recorded crime' thereby fuelling the 'fear of crime'!

2 the number of police increases, partly because it attracts some of the unemployed, and partly because the government also *believe* that 'unemployment causes crime', or at least considers it should be prudent enough to increase the police force just in case;

3 the police are likely to adopt a tougher policy towards people in high areas of unemployment because they too *believe* that 'unemployment causes crime' and that these areas might become unmanageable;

4 the judiciary will increase the use of imprisonment and other supervisory sentences, although not simply as a mechanical response to any increase in the numbers convicted, but because they believe this to be a rational means of helping to reduce a crime problem which they perceive is increasing

because they too *believe* that the level of unemployment
affects the level of criminal activity;
5   the government, despite whatever public pronouncements it
makes, quietly colludes in all these responses, thus significantly influencing the relationship between unemployment
and imprisonment.

The 'radical' view developed in this chapter considers that
unemployment and imprisonment are linked, but instead of looking at crime and conviction rates as the mediating factors, it has
focused on the *belief* that 'unemployment causes crime' and how
this belief directly or subtly affects judicial sentencing practice,
probation officers' sentence recommendations, and police deployment, apprehension, arrest and prosecution policies.

The second related flaw in the orthodox perspective is that the
relationship between unemployment and crime is nowhere near as
simple as is commonly claimed. The response to unemployment
depends very much of what it *means* to those experiencing it. This
varies across age, gender, class and ethnic divisions. It is also
affected by the actual and perceived *duration* of unemployment,
and what is believed to have *caused* it. Crime is only likely to be a
response among those unemployed who blame the economic system rather than themselves, who perceive that they will be unemployed for a long time, or become unemployable, who fail to see
an institutional way of changing the situation, and who are willing
to resist rather than acquiesce, even if that means breaking the
law. Even then, whether crime occurs or not would depend upon
many other factors, which is why numerous attempts to demonstrate an empirical relationship between unemployment and crime
have produced, as Chapter 3 argued, ambiguous and inconsistent
results.

Nevertheless, it is clear that many people *believe* that 'unemployment causes crime'. This belief is important for understanding
the increasing prison population, because magistrates and judges
deliberating over a sentence, probation officers considering which
sentence to recommend, and police considering whether to arrest
and prosecute, may well be influenced by their *belief*, or by their
belief that others *believe*, that 'unemployment causes crime'. This
of course is not to argue that unemployment becomes the major
determinant of police, probation or judicial decisions. That would

be an absurd position to propose. None the less, each of these state agents has to use discretionary power. They cannot simply proceed on the basis of whether or not a crime was committed. They need to make decisions on its seriousness, mitigating circumstances, plausible defence, and take into account a host of other organisational and occupational considerations. In this matrix of extra-legal factors, the suspects' personal characteristics, including age, sex, race and employment status are taken into account. As unemployment increases, more unemployed persons get caught up in the network of legal control. Their employment status will play a part, maybe only marginal, in affecting the decisions control agents have to make about eventual disposition. None the less, the marginal contribution to many individual cases adds up. When aggregated these individual cases show that the proportion of the imprisoned population who were previously unemployed increases, a proportion in excess of that predictable from simple increases in the number of persons convicted.

It is important to stress once again that this is not a conspiracy theory. The important minor figures in this drama – the judges, magistrates, probation officers and the police – all act in 'logic of their situation'. Each have beliefs – although these are not dissimilar – experiences, occupational and organisation needs, and these combine to make behaviour patterned and predictable. It is the 'unintended consequences' of these individual decisions which, when aggregated, mount up to an increasing prison population, a widening of the net of social control, and a damping-down of the potential threat of 'social dynamite'. The government rests content with these 'unintended consequences' because their 'latent function' does not harm them or the interests they protect. Indeed, they tend to benefit from this 'latent function' and that is why they occasionally give the criminal justice system, broadly conceived, more personnel and resources to get the job done.

Figure 5.1 represents both the orthodox and 'radical' perspectives on the relationships between unemployment, crime and punishment. From it, certain hypotheses can be deduced, and these will be tested against the best available research findings in the next chapter.

As the recession deepened over the last decade, so the government felt the need to become more 'coercive'. As part of this 'coerciveness' it allowed, and occasionally nudged, the judiciary to

Figure 5.1 *Two models of unemployment–crime–punishment*

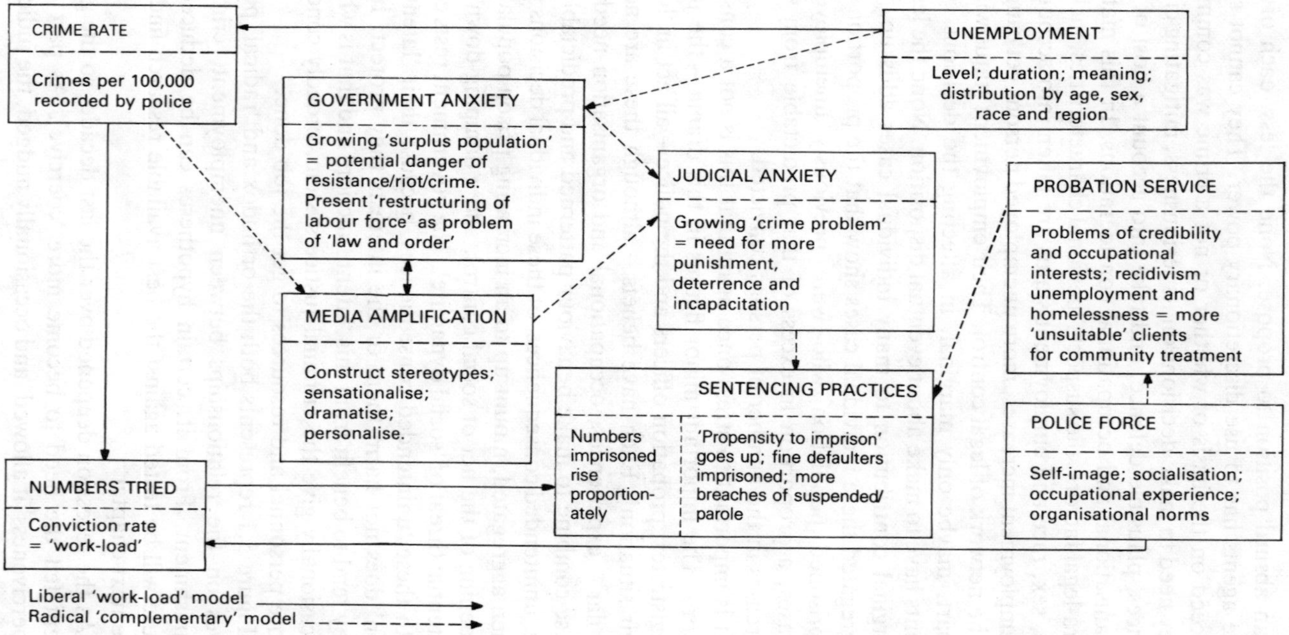

UNEMPLOYMENT

Level; duration; meaning; distribution by age, sex, race and region

PROBATION SERVICE

Problems of credibility and occupational interests; recidivism unemployment and homelessness = more 'unsuitable' clients for community treatment

POLICE FORCE

Self-image; socialisation; occupational experience; organisational norms

JUDICIAL ANXIETY

Growing 'crime problem' = need for more punishment, deterrence and incapacitation

SENTENCING PRACTICES

'Propensity to imprison' goes up; fine defaulters imprisoned; more breaches of suspended/parole

Numbers imprisoned rise proportionately

GOVERNMENT ANXIETY

Growing 'surplus population' = potential danger of resistance/riot/crime.

Present 'restructuring of labour force' as problem of 'law and order'

MEDIA AMPLIFICATION

Construct stereotypes; sensationalise; dramatise; personalise.

CRIME RATE

Crimes per 100,000 recorded by police

NUMBERS TRIED

Conviction rate = 'work-load'

Liberal 'work-load' model ————
Radical 'complementary' model – – – – –

make more custodial or supervisory sentences. For its part, the judiciary were sufficiently anxious about the growing crime problem to respond by stiffening its sentencing policies. Thus the following hypothesis could be deduced:

1 *The rate of imprisonment has increased in recent years over and above that predictable from increases in the numbers convicted.*

The Probation Service, being primarily an agent of the court and wanting to maintain its credibility, found itself anticipating the court's drift towards more custodial sentences and hence sought to align sentence recommendations to this. A second hypothesis can therefore be deduced:

2 *If the person for whom the probation officer is writing a social inquiry report is unemployed, and other things, such as offence and prior record, being equal, this fact will result in a recommended sentence higher up the 'tariff'.*

Finally, the police, being sensitive to politicians, respectable citizens, the media portraits of 'villains', and organisational norms, will be influenced by the suspect's employment status. Thus, the third hypothesis is:

3 *When deciding what to do with a suspect, the police will be influenced by employment status and impose a harsher disposition. Other things being equal, the unemployed are more like to be apprehended, arrested and prosecuted.*

The next chapter will examine evidence relevant to testing these hypotheses, although it will do so in reverse order. It will start with evidence on police decision-making, it will turn to sentence recommendations made by probation officers, and finally it will consider court sentences. The outcome of these decisions, when aggregated, will then be tested on national macro data.

6 Does Recession Lead to More Imprisonment?

Attempts by social scientists to document the criminal justice system's discriminatory practices against powerless social groups has a long and honourable history. The primary motivation urging this effort forward was a *vision of justice*. In the centre of this vision was equality before the law and even-handed treatment to all, irrespective of race, creed, or colour. Beyond this vision of *justice for all* was the principle that power is a constant nightmare in democratic societies. Evil, immoral and wicked people will always create havoc; democratic institutions, with their planned insistence on balance of powers, responsibility, accountability and removability, provide some guarantee that the harm people do will be limited and short-lived. But this guarantee can only be enjoyed if democratic citizens are constantly vigilant. Knowledge is the key to this vigilance. If citizens are kept in the dark about what people in positions of power are doing, then they are unable to criticise them effectively. This is why governments and people in power attempt to guard their actions zealously with notions of state security, national defence, official secrets, confidential memorandum and classified material. It simply would not do, in a free society, for citizens to know all that they ought! They might then exercise their democratic duty, namely to shine the searchlight of informed criticism on power-holders.

It is in the context of this constant struggle between the duty of democratic citizens and power-holders' attempts to conceal their activities, that the search for discrimination in the criminal justice system has to be located. Other portrayals are mainly ideological smokescreens. Thus the idea that the police always have to be defended and any criticism is 'anti-police' is essentially anti-democratic hypocrisy. The police have only limited and specific

162

powers; these are to be employed in appropriate and proper ways. Because police, like any other power-holders, have to be account- able, citizens need to be informed of *any* systematic departure from the laws, norms and moral expectations that govern and guide police behaviour. Social scientists, attempting to document police discriminatory practices, are merely performing a service to citizens in a democratic society. They are providing them with 'knowledge', the necessary antidote to creeping authoritarianism. Similarly the view that judges and other court officials deserve our support does not cover 'whatever they do'. They too, like the police, have to be subject to constant scrutiny and criticism to prevent them straying from the path of righteousness. If they are discovered to treat similar suspects/offenders differently, and do so systematically, they then deserve to be exposed to public account.

The following examines three vital moments in the criminal justice system: police decision-making, probation officers' sen- tence recommendations, and judges' sentences. As far as possible, it seeks to review the most recent empirical research to see if these moments in the criminal justice system are coloured by the 'sus- pects'/offender's employment status and whether this form of dis- crimination has become more marked during the recent recession. In this way, hypotheses presented at the end of Chapter 5 can be tested.

Police and the unemployed 'suspect'

There are three decision-making sites on which police discrimina- tion could occur: 'on the street' encounters; the decision to arrest; and in Britain (although not the USA) the decision to prosecute. The current concern is whether there exists police discrimination against the 'surplus population', particularly young unemployed males amongst whom ethnic minorities are over-represented.

Evidence certainly exists that police discriminate against ethnic minorities who experience rates of unemployment far above the national average. This is particularly true for young black males. Furthermore, many of those employed are in low-paid, insecure, part-time jobs and so are on the razor edge of economic margin- alisation. For this reason, it is essential, when considering whether police discriminate against that part of the 'surplus population' that Spitzer (1975) refers to as 'social dynamite', that evidence of discrimination against ethnic minorities is included. At the worst, ethnic-minority status is a proxy for 'surplus population'.

Liska and Tausig (1979) reviewed thirteen American studies on race and police decisions, and concluded that these 'show racial differences at all decision-making levels, although the differentials are not always substantially or statistically significant . . . [Although] the differentials for race are always stronger than for social class' (p. 197). It is necessary to bring this evaluation up to date not because completion is good *per se*, but because more recent studies were carried out during a period of higher unemployment and some of these were British. They are therefore a better test of the 'police discriminate against "problem population" ' hypothesis which forms the background justification for this analysis.

Before analysing recent studies on police–public encounters the relationship between 'race and the war on crime' can be used to set the scene. In a very interesting study by Jackson and Carroll (1981) it was shown that while crime has important effects on the size of police budgets, so do other factors, such as social and economic inequality. Thus they discovered that across 90 major cities in the USA police resources and personnel numbers were influenced by the size of the ethnic-minority group, their extent of political mobilisation, and the income differences between blacks and whites. This relationship held even when a statistical control was made for the number of riots over the preceding decade, the city total population, and population density. They concluded that 'police expenditures are a resource that is mobilised or expanded when a minority group appears threatening to the dominant group' (p. 303). It is against this background of increased expenditure for policing areas with higher proportions of ethnic minorities, and presumably higher levels of unemployment, that police–public encounters have to be seen.

Since the Liska and Tausig evaluation (marginally updated by Box, 1981, p. 185), a further six studies on police and 'black' suspects have been located. Landau and Nathan (1983), in a study of police cautioning of adolescents in five areas of the London Metropolitan Police District during later 1978, found that although 'present offence' and 'prior police contact' were important determinants of cautioning, none the less, 'white juveniles were less likely to be cautioned (as opposed to prosecuted) than their black counterparts' (p. 136). This complemented an earlier study of the same data which examined whether or not the 'suspect' was immediately charged or referred to a police juvenile bureau for further consideration (Landau, 1981). Whilst previous criminal activity and type of offence play a major role in determining this police decision, area, age, and ethnic group also have a significant effect. 'With regard to ethnic group, it was found that blacks involved in crimes of violence, burglary and "public disorder" offences are treated more harshly than their white counterparts' (p. 129).

Another British study examined the offences for which different ethnic groups were charged (Cain and Sadigh, 1982). In a courtroom observation study carried out mainly during 1978–9 in a south London magistrates court, they discovered that:

> of the West Indian defendants, 46.6 per cent were charged as a result of *pro-active policing*, compared with 30.1 per cent of the white defendants. Examples of such charges, which depend on police officers rather than victims taking the initiative, are motoring offences, drunkenness, being a suspicious person, or obstructing the police. (p. 88)

Cain and Sadigh also found another relevant difference. While nearly half of the West Indians were under 21, this was true for only 12 per cent of the whites. This finding is consistent with the idea that it is *young* marginalised males who are more vulnerable to discriminatory policing.

It is important to realise that these charges resulting from pro-active policing reflect in part the way in which police in London (and presumably elsewhere) use their 'stop and search' powers. In a Home Office study (Willis, 1983) it was found that police use their wide discretionary power of 'stop and search' much more frequently against the young black population. For example, in the London borough of Kensington, the annual rate of stops for the whole population was 31 per 100, while for young males aged 16–24 it was 123, and for young black males it was 298. Similar wide differences were found in Peckham, another London Borough, and two other towns, Watford and Luton. It might be objected that the blacks are stopped more frequently because they commit more crimes. However, in the Willis study it was concluded that 'blacks, and particularly young black males, are much more likely to be stopped and searched by the police than whites. Nevertheless, the proportion of persons stopped who are subsequently prosecuted is the same for blacks as for whites' (p. 4).

Of course there could be other reasons for these differential rates of 'stopping and searching', such as 'suspicious behaviour', 'lack of civility', 'poor demeanour' and 'rudeness'. But if the levels of police prejudice documented by Smith and Gray of the Policy Studies Institute (1983) are accurate, then discriminatory practices against young blacks are not necessarily provoked by the adolescents' behaviour. Furthermore, in the absence of a well-utilised and effective complaints system against the police machinery, police soon realise that 'harassing' young blacks is unlikely to result in any disciplinary action.

An American study deserves a mention. Smith and Visher (1981) reported on the results of an observational study involving 900 police patrol shifts producing information on 5,688 police–citizen encounters during 1971 in Missouri, New York and Florida. They used an advanced statistical technique called 'probit' to see if the suspect's race affected police decision to arrest even if other factors, including demeanour and offence seriousness, were simultaneously controlled. They concluded that 'black suspects are more likely to be arrested' (p. 172).

Finally, another American study (Dannefer and Schutt, 1982) analysed nearly 2,000 cases disposed by the police in 1973 and 1975 in two New Jersey counties: River County, one of the most populous and heavily urban counties in the state, and Woodlawn County, a nearby largely suburban county. A long-linear analysis of the effects of race and the other variables on dispositions by the police revealed that 'race is the most important predictor' (p. 1123). Although these numerous studies on police decisions are relevant to the argument that during a recession the criminal justice system becomes more punitive, particularly towards the 'social dynamite' part of the economically marginalised population, they really only complement those studies which have directly concentrated on the unemployed and their treatment by the police. Unfortunately, only two of these have been located.

An American study (Thornberry and Farnworth, 1982) shows very clearly that the unemployed are disproportionately arrested.

In this longitudinal research, which consisted of 567 subjects drawn from the original sample of nearly 10,000 males born in 1945, the authors employed measures of self-reported crime, arrest, and job instability. The self-reported crime data was divided into three types: the total amount of all offences; crimes reported in the UCR annual statistics (i.e. 'index' crimes); and violent crimes. The only measure of criminal activity relating to job instability (defined as 'the total number of periods of unemployment over the ten year of the follow-up interview') was the total which included minor and status offences as well as 'index' and violent. Even then, this relationship only held for whites and not blacks. Yet when the arrest data is examined a totally different picture emerges. For those with histories of job instability, there is a statistically significant higher proportion of arrests for *both* whites and blacks, and for 'index' offences separately as well as total offences. There is also a relationship between job instability and arrest for violent offences for blacks only, which is statistically significant at the 10 per cent level. These data are entirely consistent with the argument that arrests are not determined entirely by criminal activity but are influenced also by people's employment status, especially among the ethnic minorities. In other words, in a society like ours where certain imaginary equations, such as black =crime, and unemployment=lazy=black are accepted by a proportion of the population, it is easy to see how these beliefs have real and unpleasant consequences.

This conclusion is echoed in a British research study carried out for the Home Office by Stevens and Willis (1979). They analysed arrests in the Metropolitan Police District (London) in 1975, and discovered that Britains of West Indian origin are wildly over-represented. Thus although blacks constituted only 4 per cent of the population, they constituted 40 per cent of the populations arrested for 'sus' (being a suspected person), and 37.1 per cent for other violent theft, 28.7 for robbery, 20.7 per cent for assault, and 11 per cent for other indictable arrests. Three possible explanations of this were considered: (i) blacks are over-represented among groups which are prone to arrest – for example the young; (ii) blacks are particularly likely to be picked up (rightly or wrongly) by the police; and (iii) even allowing for these special factors, blacks are disproportionately involved in crime. In order to examine the first of these possibilities, the authors examined unemployment rates in each police district and correlated this with arrests. They discovered that the white unemployment rates are a good indicator for both white and black arrest rates. Their suggestion was that:

> the white unemployment rate may be acting as a measure for the general economic deprivation of an area, and therefore that the more economically run-down area, the more likely that area is to have both high black, Asian and white arrest rates. (pp. 21–2)

However, they warn that:

> great care must obviously be exercised in making any causal inferences . . . One possible interpretation might be that although for all three groups there is good evidence of an association between social deprivation and arrests, the kind of deprivation that is significant varies for the three groups. (p. 27)

Put another way, the police are likely to arrest proportionately more young males in areas of high unemployment and this cannot be entirely accounted for by any differences in criminal activity.

Recent evidence from America and Britain supports the hypothesis that the police discriminate against those social groups who have become economically marginalised during the recent recession. In particular, the unemployed, among whom ethnic minorities are over-represented, are treated more harshly and are arrested and referred to court more often. There, court officials may compound their difficulties.

Probation officers' sentence recommendations and unemployment

There have been a number of studies attempting to discover if, when writing a Social Inquiry Report, probation officers are influenced by the client's social characteristics (Carter and Wilkins, 1967; Hagan, 1975; Horan, Myers and Farnworth, 1983; Katz, 1982; Myers, 1979; Walsh, 1985; Unnever *et al.*, 1980). However, very few studies have focused on the client's employment status. Those that have, provide some support for the hypothesis that officers are influenced, at the margin, by whether or not the client is unemployed.

In an early, statistically unsophisticated study, Curry (1975) analysed 129 individuals who had appeared in the District Courts of Texas County during 1973. His analysis supports the view that probation officers are influenced by the offender's employment status, although not too much reliance should be put on this because no regression analysis was carried out. Curry concluded:

> whether the defendant was employed at the time of the pre-sentence report was significantly related to the probation department's decision. Eighty-nine percent of those employed were recommended for probation; only sixty-five percent of those unemployed were so recommended . . . It appears . . . that a defendant may significantly increase his chances for probation if he can hold onto his job after arrest and conviction, or if unemployed, find a job prior to sentencing. (p. 71)

A study by Frazier *et al.*, (1983) of 309 pre-sentence reports prepared by probation officers for one of the six county judicial districts in Florida between 1972 and 1975 reported a slight but significant relationship between sentence recommendation and client's employment status. In Florida, the Probation and Parole Commission requires the investigating officer to list the offender's criminal history, education, employment status and history, family status and history, physical health and mental health, and residence. These reports contain a wealth of detailed information on personal characteristics. In the analysis, the sentence recommendations were dichotomised into incarceration and non-incarceration (and the method of estimation used was a logistic regression technique). Of all the legal and extra-legal variables, only five were significantly related to sentence recommendation. The extra-legal variables were gender, age and employment status, and of these the last was the most important. In Frazier's words, 'those who are employed are more likely to receive non-incarceration recommendations' (p. 313).

This conclusion was made *after* the effects of legally relevant variables, offence and previous convictions, had been controlled. However, an earlier Canadian study (Hagan *et al.*, 1979) did not report results entirely consistent with this. This research was based on 504 adult felony conviction cases in the King County Superior Court in 1973. Their results, they suggest, support both the

Marxian perspective which stresses the intrusion of personal characteristics into the sentencing process, and the Durkheimian tradition which centres more on the legal variables because these capture the 'moral outrage' of the community. They write:

> our findings indicate that being female, white, *having a stable work history* and family ties increase the likelihood of a deferred sentence and reduce the likelihood of an incarceration sentence. All of these effects are judged to be statistically significant . . . [However] . . . these effects are uniformly reduced when the variables suggested by the consensus perspective – offence severity, prior record and use of a weapon and violence – are introduced into the equation (my emphasis). (p. 517)

A recent American study appears to lean towards supporting Frazier and his colleagues. Although attempting to examine whether probation officer's gender made any difference to sentencing recommendations, Kruttschnitt (1985) also measured the effect of various offender characteristics, including employment status. The data derived from the records of nearly 3,000 felony offenders who were convicted in Hennepin County, Minnesota between January 1965 and December 1980. A half of her sample had been unemployed prior to conviction. Her results (derived from a regression analysis controlling for interaction effects between independent variables) are consistent with the hypothesised relationship between employment status and sentence recommendation. She wrote:

> recommendations for severe sentences are more likely to go to those offenders who have been convicted of the more severe offences, who were jailed prior to adjudication, and who had other cases awaiting them on the court dockets. Additionally, those offenders who are *male*, non-white, *unemployed*, have few if any children, and have lengthy arrest and probation records, are accorded the more severe recommendations . . . Taken together, these findings support [the] notion that probation officers may act as a conduit for the influence of extra-legal factors in the determination of sentence severity (my emphasis). (p. 295)

However, it was also predicted that as the recession deepened, probation officers, anticipating the courts' growing anxiety, would recommend more severe sentences for unemployed clients. This was not supported by Kruttschnitt's results. She trichotomised her data into three time-periods, 1965–69, 1970–73, and 1974–80. These correspond to periods of low, medium and high unemployment in the American context. Her results show that probation officers were uniformly influenced by the client's employment status and there was no discernible change over time. This is the only study with a time factor built into it. Clearly other studies are needed to clinch the issue one way or another.

Although experimental studies do not enable the hypothesis to be tested strictly, they do none the less indicate which type of considerations probation officers take into account when making sentence recommendations. One such experiment was carried out by Papandreou *et al.* (1982) on 205 probation officers employed in New South Wales, South Australia and the Northern Territory during October and December 1979. They presented each officer with a series of case histories containing a description of a serious offence, such as stealing, wilful damage and manslaughter, and included various combinations of other legal and extra-legal factors. From their analyses of officers' replies to these fictional cases, the authors concluded:

> the present study found that the employment of offenders was of some importance to the recommendations made by probation officers. Although the effect of employment was found to be somewhat erratic, unemployed offenders were generally treated more severely than employed ones. There was a tendency for employed offenders to be recommended for fine rather than bonds, probation or imprisonment. (p. 216)

Despite this apparent support, it has to be stressed that these researchers merely show that employment status of clients influences officers' sentence recommendation. They do not indicate *why* this occurs. Whether it is because of officers' beliefs about 'unemployment and crime', or the likely court sentence, or some other factors, is left to speculation. However, this relationship does have 'latent consequences' which could be avoided.

For example, the effect of 'second guessing' court sentences, which has been argued to be a feature of probation officers' practical role, can be deleterious for some offenders, particularly those whose extra-legal characteristics, such as sex, age, and employment status, are utilised as clues to sentence outcome. Cautious probation officers, not wanting to risk their credibility with the court, will tend to over-predict the court sentence and in that way influence the court to increase the sentence it would have imposed. This possibility was empirically supported in a recent study by Walsh (1985). He examined 31 probation officers serving a metropolitan Ohio county court in the years 1978–81, and the sentence recommendations they made in 416 cases. He was able to show that some officers, particularly those he classified as 'conservative' in their ideas and attitudes towards crime and criminals, tended to 'force' up court sentences by recommendations which were slightly harsher than the judge was initially contemplating. It appears, he wrote:

> that both conservative and liberal officers did a particularly good job in conveying their attitudes to the courts . . . on average, cases processed by conservative officers received somewhat harsher sentences than recommended, and that cases processed by liberal officers received somewhat more lenient sentence than recommended. (p. 298)

Walsh concluded that 'probation officers play an important role, perhaps the major role, in the determination of sentencing outcome' (p. 301). Thus 'second guessing' may not be without serious 'latent consequences'. In gauging the judge's likely sentence, some officers recommend a sentence harsher that the court would impose if left to its own devices. However, faced with a recommendation, the court tends to go along with it. The outcome is that the average sentence is higher up the 'tariff' than it would have been.

This conclusion is supported by a British experimental study (Hine *et al.*, 1978). These researchers 'doctored' actual social inquiry reports to vary the degree of social information they contained and then presented them for 'sentence' to magistrates. They discovered that magistrates were influenced by officer's recommendations:

because sentencers hold the views of probation officers in 'high regard' . . . [Therefore] . . . if officers who wrote the recommendations were anticipating the wishes of the courts the consequences for the offenders where custody was recommended could be unfortunate. (p. 99)

Indeed they could. In a later review of this experiment, Roberts and Roberts (1982) argue that 'at worst as many as half those subject to custodial recommendations would not have received a custodial sentence if a report had not been prepared' (p. 87).

Officers should therefore be made more aware and sensitised to their 'informal', as opposed to 'formal', power. Rather than officers passively anticipating judges' decisions, they appear to *influence* them. This influence could be channelled into reducing the number of custodial sentences and reducing the number of unemployed persons incarcerated.

Sentencing and unemployment

There are two ways of providing an answer to the intriguing question 'do courts take the defendant's employment status into account when deciding which sentence to impose?'. The first consists of examining as many courts as possible to discover the influence in individual cases of social characteristics, including employment status, on the sentence. In contrast to this micro approach, the second method consists of examining variations in the rate of unemployment and imprisonment *over time* or *cross-sectionally* whilst controlling for as many confounding factors, such as changes in the crime/conviction rates, as possible. Both approaches to the question have their methodological problems and these will be considered as the evidence from each is shifted. A cautionary note, however, is required: it is an easy question to put, but difficult to answer!

Courts and sentencing the unemployed

There is a long tradition in sentencing research to discover which factors influence judges. This was partly inspired by the wide disparities in sentences handed down by different judges and by the imposition of different sentences on offenders guilty of very similar offences. It was also inspired by the 'heretical' idea that judges might be influenced by offenders' race, or social class, or gender, or some other personal/social attributes. Indeed, those making early sorties into courtrooms came back with stories of sentencing chaos and contradictions. An American philosopher, William James, advocated making a distinction whenever a contradiction was encountered. The dominant attempt to impose some order on this chaos of sentencing has been to take this advice, and make a distinction between *legal* and *extra-legal* variables. The first refers to factors the courts *should* take into consideration, either because they are formally written into legal procedures and practices, or because there is a common adherence to the classical notion that offence and punishment should be closely aligned and therefore 'what' the person did should be the criterion determining sentence. The second refers to factors the courts ought not strictly to take into account in a *systematic fashion*. This reference to 'systematic' incorporation is important because notions of *individualised justice* permit the taking into account of unique circumstances surrounding the offence and offender. But when 'systematic' patterns emerge, then questions of justice give way to accusations of 'bias'. Thus if such factors as social class, race, gender and employment status become systematically incorporated in a predictable pattern, such that the lower class, minority ethnic groups, males, and unemployed risk being more severely sentenced compared with others who have committed similar crimes and have similar previous conviction records, but dissimilar social characteristics, then allegations of 'judicial bias' would seem justifiable.

Traditionally, research on sentencing that attempts to discover if 'bias' exists, has concentrated on class, race and gender (Box, 1981, pp. 180–98). Very little research has examined the possible influence of the offender's employment status. Furthermore, most of this research was conducted at a time of relatively full employment, and only recently at the height of the current recession has the issue of unemployment and its multiple effects been considered by social scientists. For these two reasons, only eleven studies on the influence of employment status on sentencing have been discovered. These lend some support to the view that the unemployed offender is more severely sanctioned, but this evidence has to be examined carefully.

An interesting study on sentencing disparity was carried out by Frazier and Bock (1982). They were testing the argument that individual characteristics of judges may have a greater influence on sentencing than offender's social characteristics. Previous research (Austin and Williams, 1977; Hagan, 1975) certainly gave credence to the view that 'judges who hold views strongly favouring "law and order" are more inclined than others to base sentence on strictly legal factors, and they are less likely to be lenient toward minority offenders' (p. 258). Furthermore, the idea that individual judges contribute to sentence variability appeals to common sense. It appears obvious that a judge's social, economic and cultural background will influence sentencing behaviour. However, in Frazier and Bock's analysis of 229 cases heard by 7 judges employed in one six-county judicial district of Florida in 1972–3 they were unable to discover any relationship between sentencing disparity and judges' characteristics. Rather, they found that:

net of the influence of other variables, sex, *employment status*, offence severity, and days in pretrial detention are related to sentence severity . . . Females, *the employed*, those who have low offence-severity score, and offenders who have not been held long in jail awaiting trial are likely to receive the most lenient sentences (my emphasis). (p. 263)

In Frazier and Bock's view, there develops among judges a 'subculture of sentencing' which partly reflects the common cultural background. This leads them to have fairly conservative and punitive views on ethnic minorities, the unemployed and the poor.

A previous study (Unnever *et al.*, 1980) used a different method of analysis, but on the same data, came, not surprisingly, to a similar conclusion:

in addition to race, age, *employment status* and number of adult arrests are also important . . . being *employed* is associated with a much greater likelihood of receiving probation . . . The finding that younger persons and the *unemployed* were more likely to receive prison sentences than older employed persons is at least consistent with conflict theory (my emphasis). (p. 202)

It might be thought that this Florida-based study consisted of too few cases, and that generalisations based on the sentencing practices of only seven judges are not feasible. At best this research should be regarded as indicative. However, sample size is not a problem with the next study.

An analysis by Cohen and Klugel (1978) of nearly two and half thousand cases in Denver (Colorado) and four and a half thousand in Memphis (Tennessee), during a two-month period of 1967, showed that juvenile courts handled 'idle' adolescents – who constituted 14 per cent of their sample – differently from 'active' (i.e. in school or work) adolescents. The former were given more severe sentences, even when prior record was controlled. According to the authors, 'present activity seems best interpretable as an indicator of a stereotypical perception by a court official that the juvenile is delinquency prone' (p. 172). Presumably this means that judges view 'idle' kids as needing more punishment to deter or incapacitate them.

In a later study, the same authors (Cohen and Klugel, 1979) examined the decision whether or not to detain an adolescent in custody prior to adjudication. For this analysis they used data from the same two locations but had a slightly larger sample size. They found that the factors most likely to determine this were prior record, *present activity* (i.e. 'idle' versus 'active'), and sex of offender. This decision was important because adolescents who had been in detention prior to adjudication were found to receive harsher sentences later. Thus employment status had an indirect effect on sentence. It first affected detention prior to ajudication, and this factor in turn influenced sentence.

A similar conclusion on the *indirect* influence of social factors was revealed in Lotz and Hewitt's (1977) analysis of 504 persons convicted of a felony in 1973 in King County, Washington, 'the most populous county in the Pacific Northwest'. One of the variables they explored was 'work stability', which whilst not being identical to unemployment catches a similar factor; although this should not be stressed too strongly as 70 per cent of their sample was classified as 'unstable'. The authors included this variable because the courts view persons with stable work histories as less likely to reoffend and more socially bonded. Such offenders would not need a severe sentence.

Lotz and Hewitt's preliminary analysis revealed that 19 per cent with unsteady work histories received imprisonment compared with only 4 per cent of those with a steady work history. This considerable difference was narrowed after a more sophisticated regression analysis was carried out on the data. This led the authors to conclude that:

> each of the legally irrelevant variables has a neglible *direct* effect. Instead their effects are, at best indirect, being transmitted via offence-related variables or through presentence recommendations . . . Aside from sex, the only [variables] strongly related to sentence are *work history* and dependency (my emphasis). (pp. 47–8)

This is an important conclusion because, in many cases, the final charge that an offender has to face is the result of 'plea bargaining'. Offenders with more social power, and that includes the employed in comparison with the unemployed, would be able to secure a better bargain and hence plea to a less serious charge. Subsequent research, not sensitive to this, would conclude that unemployment was not important because the seriousness of the offence was the main determinant of sentence. But since employment status affects the seriousness of the offence it means that the *indirect* effect of unemployment can be missed easily. Furthermore, as Lotz and Hewitt (and many other researchers mentioned above) point out, unemployment can affect probation officers' sentence recommendations. Since these recommendations have a significant effect on sentence, unemployment can in this way have an *indirect* effect on sentencing.

A study by Landes (1974) was very sensitive to the first of these issues. He analysed 858 defendants in New York County who appeared in court in 1971. From this he discovered that 'employment in legal activities and the amount of earnings from legal employment have significant negative effects on the size of the defendant's bond'. Bond size was very important because it almost determined whether the suspect was granted pre-trial liberty. This in turn was important because defendants not released on bail were, as a consequence of their detention, more likely to be convicted and more likely to receive longer prison sentences than comparable defendants released on bail. Thus although the final sentence was not related directly to employment status, it was *indirectly* affected by the absence of bail, which was itself determined by the size of bond, which in turn was influenced in part by the suspect's employment status.

Two other American criminologists, Carter and Clelland (1979), were critical of much previous research on sentence disparity because social class was poorly measured. They wanted a measure that was theoretically relevant to the conflict/neo-marxist perspective. In their study of 350 cases appearing in juvenile courts in a metropolitan area of southeastern USA they were able to obtain a 'subjective' assessment of the offender's class from the court social worker. It appears that in making this assessment, the court social worker classified as 'lower class':

> the chronically unemployed as well as persons dependent upon state or federal aid [and in addition] those who did not accept middle class values of hardwork, deferred gratification, and achievement. [This measurement of social class] combines emphasis on membership in the surplus labour force and lumpen-proletarian values. (p. 101)

A regression analysis revealed that 'lower class' persons (as used above) received more severe sentences, especially for status/victimless offences. Carter and Clelland considered this fact to be consistent with the neo-marxist argument that the criminal law incorporates violations against the moral order, and these are related, in a protective way, to the productive system. These laws tend to make illegal many pleasures, often related to sex and drugs, which can be pursued hedonistically without prior labour to earn the 'coins' necessary for buying fun. That is, youths prioritising leisure pursuits without first *earning* the right to them, are viewed as particularly threatening to the productive system because they symbolically and actually reverse the work–leisure, labour–fun relationships on which our society is based. It is for this reason that the 'surplus lumpenproletariat' juveniles appearing in court and found guilty of these offences receive harsher sentences.

They also discovered that the relationship between 'social class' and sentence severity for 'conventional' offences, such as burglary and robbery, was muted because of the statistical importance of probation officers' recommendations. A secondary analysis revealed that these recommendations were considerably harsher for 'unstable' working-class adolescents. In other words, for 'conventional' offences, the effect of unemployment on sentencing was indirect through the probation officer's recommendation.

One final supportive study is Kruttschnitt (1984). Although interested in exploring the effect of gender on sentencing, she also incorporated other social factors, including employment, because 'holding down a job represents not only economic power, but also social integration' and both these may affect sentence outcome. Here data consisted of 523 females and 504 males convicted of either theft, forgery, or drug law violations between the years 1972 and 1976, in Hennepin County, Minnesota. The level of unemployment in this sample was 56.8 per cent and 50 per cent respectively. Kruttschnitt showed that offenders' chances of receiving light sentences were increased if (i) they had no outstanding court cases, (ii) they were convicted of an offence that carried a light maximum penalty, (iii) they had few prior arrests, (v) *they were employed*, and (v) they were female. The influence of unemployment on sentence severity held equally for men and women.

Against these seven studies have to be weighed four others, one British and three American, which came to different conclusions. The first (Farrington and Morris, 1983) was conducted on 408 persons sentenced for Theft Act offences between 1 January and 31 July 1979, including 110 women. Like Kruttschnitt, these authors were primarily interested in the sentencing disparity between males and females. But in order to examine this properly, they incorporated other variables including employment status. In their sample just over 25 per cent were unemployed. An initial analysis of percentage of offenders receiving more severe sentences showed that employment status was statistically significant for men (52 per cent of the unemployed received a severe sentence compared with 36 per cent of the employed). The respective percentages for women were 27 and 17. However, in a regression analysis, it was discovered that employment was nowhere near as significant a predictor of sentencing severity as other variables, such as type of offence, current problems (like drug/alcohol consumption patterns), number of previous convictions, and legal presentations.

The second (Clarke and Koch, 1976) examined 798 defendants in Mechlenburg County, North Carolina, arrested in 1971 for burglary, breaking and entering, and larceny. In this sample, 19 per cent were classified as unemployed prior to being arrested, although the employment status of a further 21 per cent was 'unknown'. In a preliminary analysis, 27 per cent of the unemployed were imprisoned compared with 15 per cent of those with jobs. However, further complicated class-tabulations produced different results. These led the authors to write that 'race, age and employment are of slight or no importance', and in particular, 'employment is of little or no importance once income and [offence, criminal history and arrest promptness] are in the model' (p. 77).

The other American study (Chiricos *et al.*, 1972) failed to discover a relationship between unemployment and verdict (it did not examine length of prison sentence as a measure of severity). In a sample of 2,419 consecutive felony cases received by the Florida Probation and Parole Commission during the period 1 July 1969 to 28 February 1970, they found 20 per cent were unemployed. However, whereas 36.6 per cent of these were found guilty, this was not different from the 33.8 per cent of full-time workers found guilty.

Finally, there is one maverick American study, and that is by Bernstein and colleagues (1977). They examined 1,213 male defendants on a felony charge appearing in a court in New York State from December 1974 to March 1975. Of these, 29 per cent had been unemployed for more than six months and a further 29 per cent had been unemployed for less than six months. The researchers became interested in unemployment because 'employment stability rather than income was observed to be a question often raised in court'. They discovered that:

> the likelihood that a convicted defendant will receive a more severe sentence is increased if (i) the defendant is charged with robbery; (ii) has a heavier record of previous convictions; (iii) has been *employed* for a longer rather than a shorter period of time (my emphasis). (p. 753)

Their *ad hominem* explanation for this quirky finding was that judges considered those with a history of job stability had less reason to commit offences and so deserved more punishment than those whose work instability gave them some, albeit little, excuse.

Before ending this review of court sentencing and unemployed offenders, a number of points ought to be made. First, it is essential to be sensitive to *indirect* as well as direct influences, as current offence and probation officer's recommendations often mask the influence of offender's employment status. Second, despite the fact that the majority of these researchers – 7 to 4 – support the hypothesis that employment status influences sentencing, the evidence does not mean that the unemployed invariably get a more severe sentence. Clearly employment status is only *one* factor taken into account by judges and magistrates. It may make only a marginal difference. It is certainly not being claimed that it makes all the difference. None the less, this marginal difference, when aggregated, makes a considerable impact on the relationship between unemployment and imprisonment rates, as the next section should reveal. Third, the reader will have noticed that, for most of these studies, mention was made of the proportion of offenders who were unemployed. In each study there was an enormous difference between this and the proportion of the general population unemployed. This fact requires some comment. Although the unemployed commit more 'conventional' crime than the employed, as the evidence reviewed in Chapter 3 revealed, they do not commit that much more crime. This suggests that the criminal justice system, like a damaged vacuum cleaner, sucks in proportionately more unemployed offenders and creates the impression that their contribution to crime is greater than in reality. Having sucked them in, it then turns the screw another rachet by imposing more severe sanctions, and especially committing proportionately more of them to prison. Finally, there is the question of race. The analysis so far has concentrated entirely on the unemployed. But ethnic minorities form a disproportionately large part of the economically marginalised population. Furthermore, the 'war against crime' often becomes identified as a 'war against minority' because of the convenient black = crime equation.

Box (1981) reviewed much of the literature on race and sentencing prior to 1980 and found they were statistically related. Since then, several studies mostly confirm that black offenders both in the USA and the UK are more likely to be sent to prison or given longer prison sentences, even when legally relevant variables are controlled.

Thus Thompson and Zingraff (1981) examined sentences on armed robbers in a southeastern state for the years 1969, 1973 and

1977. These years represent different moments in the recession, and so if criminal justice becomes more discriminatory, then the relationship between race and sentencing severity ought to get stronger as these time periods are examined in sequence. That is exactly what the authors found; the relationship was indeed stronger in 1977 when ethnic-minority-status offenders were more severely punished.

A similar result was reported by Curran (1983). He analysed 543 offenders sentenced in Dade County, Florida for the years 1965–6, 1971 and 1975–6. He found that the relationship between race and sentencing severity was higher in the final two years when the recession had bitten deeper.

Spohn *et al.* (1981) are very critical of most previous studies because they are marred *by having too few cases*, a relatively small number of offences, inadequate controls for 'legal' and 'extra-legal' variables, inadequate measures of severity and inappropriate statistical techniques. Seeking to avoid these weaknesses, they analysed 2,366 male defendants who appeared in Metro City (a city in the Northeast and one of the largest in the USA) during the period 1969–79. They found that race had no direct influence on sentence severity, but it did have *indirect* influences because black defendants were less likely to have been granted bail and because they were less likely to be represented by a private attorney. In addition they found that race had *direct* and *indirect* influences on the decision to imprison. 'Black defendants are 20 per cent more likely than white defendants to be incarcerated' (p. 83) after all statistical controls have been introduced. This should concern all those interested in justice for all, because:

> even though race accounts for 'only' 4 per cent of the variation in our study in the decision to incarcerate, the tremendous difference between being imprisoned and being free makes a difference which is substantial and disturbing. (p. 86)

A study by Nagel (1983) appears to contradict the above results, because she found, after analysing 5,594 felony and misdemeanor cases in one borough of the city of New York between December 1974 and March 1975, that race was not statistically significant as a predictor of sentence severity. It was, though, in the predicted direction. However, in her sample only 12.3 per cent of the defendants were white, which not only indicates that most of the system discriminatory practices had been exhausted by this stage, but also it made genuine comparisons between races difficult.

Taking the evidence as a whole, it supports the hypothesis that sentencing severity is related to the defendant's employment status. It is also related to the defendant's race. Since blacks suffer from much higher rates of unemployment, sentencing severity is probably related to the fact that they are both black and unemployed.

Another, complementary, method of testing the hypothesis that employment status affects the decision to incarcerate and for how long, is to see whether the rate of *incarceration* increases as the *rate* of unemployment increases. The next section will address itself to this.

Unemployment and imprisonment

During the 1970s six studies were published documenting a relationship between unemployment and imprisonment. Three related to the USA (Jankovic, 1977; Robinson *et al.*, 1974; Yeager, 1979), and the others covered Australia (Grabosky, 1979), Britain (Brenner, 1976) and Canada (Greenberg, 1977). Since these were in agreement, there is little point in replicating each of their conclusions. However, three are worth a brief mention because they attempted to compare the predictive accuracy of the 'radical' model with that of the 'work-load' model which views increases in prison sentences as a mechanical response to increases in numbers convicted.

Greenberg (1977) examined the relationship between unemployment rates and prisoner admissions per 100,000 population in Canada during the period 1950–72 and reported:

the correlation between the per capita rate of admissions to prison and the per capita rate of conviction is approximately 0.01, in total disagreement with the 'work-load' model according to which the judiciary responds mechanically to changes in the rate of crime. [And consequently, the] high rates of commitment to prison during periods of unemployment . . . cannot be explained as a passive judicial response to a larger caseload. (p. 647)

Yeager (1979) analysed US data for the period 1952–74, and even after controlling for the conviction rate (i.e. the 'work-load' measure) he concluded that:

the results showed that the unemployed rate alone explains 54 per cent of the variation in the prison population sentenced during the years 1952–1974 . . . so that a 1 per cent increase in male unemployment results in 1,395 additional prisoners in Federal penal institutions. (p. 588)

Jankovic (1977) took the number of arrests as his measure for testing the 'work-load' model, and examined unemployment and imprisonment for both state and federal levels, and also supplemented this with an analysis of monthly statistics for Sunshine County California, from January 1969 to December 1976. His findings were consistent with the hypothesis that unemployment leads to more imprisonment over and above that predicted from the increased levels of arrests, but this only held during the period 1949–74 and only for state and not Federal prisons. The contradictory results of Yeager and Jankovic are a mystery (at the moment).

These, and earlier studies (Dobbins and Bass, 1958; Stern, 1940), lend considerable credence to the view that imprisonment increased during periods of recession as part of the state's drift towards the reimposition of control and discipline. This rarity, a virtual consensus from a variety of research reports, was disturbed by six further research studies in the 1980s, two of which are generally supportive, two of which are ambiguous, and the remaining two are very critical.

Box and Hale's studies (1982, 1984) come, not surprisingly, very close to testing the hypothesised relationship proposed in Chapter 4. Specifically, they tested to see if the relationship between unemployment and prison admissions under sentence held for the total population, and whether they were more pronounced for men compared with women, and young men compared with older men. After analysis time-series data for England and Wales for the period 1952–81, and controlling for two 'work-load' factors – recorded crime levels and conviction rates – they concluded that:

the total population under immediate sentence of imprisonment was sensitive to the level of unemployment even after controlling for crime levels and conviction rates. This effect was stronger for the male population alone and still stronger for young males. One crude and very simplistic way of rendering our results would be say that as the unemployment rate increased by 1,000 so the number of persons sent to prison over the number expected due to increases in crime levels and conviction rates was eight, for the male population it was eleven and for young males it was seventeen. This does not of course mean that unemployment is the major determinant of imprisonment; clearly the crime and conviction rates have that honour. None the less, it is clear that the number of persons immediately imprisoned, and hence the average daily prison population, would not be as high if the judiciary did not increasingly imprison persons in excess of that warranted by the conviction rate. (1984, p. 218)

The remaining proportion of the prison population under sentence omitted from the above analysis were fine-defaulters. These too would be expected to rise with levels of unemployment, either because the offender is simply unable to pay the fine, or because unemployment has so loosened his or her social bonds that imprisonment may be a preferred cost to paying a relatively exorbitant fine. For the purpose of exploring that possibility, Box and Hale felt there was no need to control for 'work-load' variables because the types of crime committed by fine-defaulters did not warrant imprisonment in the first place.

It is quite clear from official prison statistics that the number of imprisoned fine-defaulters has risen dramatically recently, particularly for young offenders, and despite the fact that the proportion of all convicted persons being fined dropped from 51.3 per cent in 1973 to 41.5 per cent in 1984. Thus in 1952 fine-defaulters were 14 per cent of the received-under-sentence prison population – this rose to nearly 25 per cent by 1984. For young offenders, it increased over the same period from just under 4 per cent to 13 per cent, which is over a 300 per cent increase. Not only is the total number of fine-defaulters being sent to prison going up as the recession bites, but the proportion of all convicted persons fined who then become defaulters also increased over the period 1974–84, from 7 per cent to 20 per cent for those under 21 years of age, and from 8 per cent to 14 per cent for those over 21 years of age (Home Office, 1985, p. 89). The correlations between unemployment and imprisoned fine-defaulters for the total, male, and young populations were respectively 0.85, 0.87 and 0.95, which are all highly significant.

Box and Hale argued that their data were strengthened by a recent Home Office survey covering 138 British towns. After allowing for the size of court, a factor inversely related to fine-enforcement performance, Moxon (1983) stated that 'there remained a strong and statistically significant correlation between committal rates [for fine-defaulting] and local unemployment levels' (p. 38). An observation study conducted in Nottinghamshire magistrates courts on behalf of the National Association of Probation Officers (NAPO, 1984) further reinforced this position by showing that the unemployed were something like 75 per cent of imprisoned fine-defaulters, although they constituted a small proportion of all those fined.

Summing up this research on unemployment, fine-defaulting and imprisonment, Box and Hale concluded, rather colourfully:

> Apparently, the judiciary are not taking the offenders' economic means sufficiently into account. Consequently, whether the court intends it or not, the unemployed receive a taste of prison which lasts, on average, for three weeks, and swells the average daily prison population by about 4 per cent. Imprisonment may, through the eyes of many magistrates, appear to be just what idle, lazy, and parasitic scroungers deserve, since by refusing to modify fines in strict proportion to the offender's ability to pay, magistrates demonstrate their willingness to allow increasing numbers of fine defaulters to end up in prison. (p. 219)

Kellough, Brickley and Greenaway (1980) analysed data from Manitoba, Canada for the inter-war years. They made crucial distinctions between years of high and low unemployment and years of high and low political dissent. Their most interesting finding was that rates of incarceration for different offences did not remain the same irrespective of the economic/political circumstances. During both depressed periods and years of high dissent the major increase in the rate of incarceration was for social control offences. Social control offences are typically those where the standard of proof required for conviction is much less than for property or violent offences; typically it requires the arresting officer to swear that an offence took place. This evidence, particularly for these types of offences, is notoriously hard to refute. Thus rates of incarceration went up in Canada during these years partly because the criminal justice system imprisoned more offenders charged with crimes for which the authorities could easily convict. Kellough and his colleagues also discovered that the rates of incarceration for different social classes did not remain similar during these years. In particular, the rates of incarceration increased more for lower-class offenders than their middle/upper class counterparts. This increase was especially marked for lower-class offenders against public order. From their results these authors felt able to conclude that:

> because incarcerations for less serious offences are mainly responsible for high prison populations, because any increase in incarceration for property offences is borne by the lowest-socio-economic groups, and because incarcerations for offences against the person remain stable, support is given to the contention that the repression represented by imprisonment is more related to peculiar economic and political circumstances of the time than to inexplicable 'crime waves'. (p. 269)

Contrasting with the strong support of these papers is the ambiguous results reported in the following four. Wallace (1980) analysed US state prison population per 100,000 general population for the years 1970–76 and controlled for other variables, such as amount of money spent on corrections, welfare payments, crime rate, and regional differences, particularly north–south. Instead of using the unemployment rate, however, Wallace chose the labour force participation rate. This was probably a fatal weakness, since many people not at work will be voluntary retirers, housewives, students, 'self-employed', and other mainly older non-registered non-workers most of whom will not be perceived as potentially threatening. In other words, there is not a strong theoretical case for using labour force participation rate for examining the recession–imprisonment relationship. For this reason, it is not surprising that Wallace discovered only a slight relationship between the two, and that *changes* in the labour force participation rate 'fail to predict inmate increases or decreases' (p. 63).

Another study with ambiguous results was conducted by Marenin, Pisciotta and Juliani (1983). They examined fifty US states for the years 1958–78, used both numbers unemployed and unemployment rate as independent variables, and controlled for crime rate as measured by UCR data. Although initially reporting a correlation between inmates and total unemployment consistent with the results of Jankovic and Yeager, they made the following damaging criticism:

> In contrast with earlier studies which used a single measure of unemployment . . . this analysis clearly demonstrates that the higher correlation . . . is largely an artifact of the measures of unemployment selected. Specifically, the correlation of inmates with *percentage unemployed* as opposed to inmates with total unemployed reduces the relationship for the entire U.S. from .76 to [an insignificant] .07 (my emphasis). (p. 44)

However, they also examined the fifty states separately. Their results show that it is dangerous to generalise across the whole of the country, for 'the correlation of convicts received with number of unemployed ranges from a +.76 for North Carolina to a −.45 for Iowa; the correlations between percentage unemployed and number received range for a high of +.72 for North Carolina to a −.51 for Alaska' (p. 45). Furthermore, once they introduced the crime rate as a control they found that while in some states unemployment accounted for changes in numbers received and total prison population, in others these changes were best explained as responses to changes in 'work-load'. Their conclusions were essentially a plea for more research to clarify better the social, economic and political reasons underlying these different patterns.

Carroll and Doubet (1983) can be reported briefly. On aggregated data from forty-five US states they reported no relationship (beta − .02) between unemployment rate and state prison admission rates. But since they were primarily concerned with other issues they made no comment about this result.

Much more substantial is the research of Galster and Scaturo (1985). Their study on fifty US states for 1976–81 not only used unemployment rate and controlled for total and violent crime rates, but it also had a refined measure of incarceration rate allowing for parolees, unconditional releases and court commit-ments. They summarise the major finding tersely:

> contrary to predictions derived from neo-Marxian paradigm, states with high unemployment rates generally had lower rates of prison commitments, controlling for crime rates. (p. 170)

However, they also disaggregated the data and, as they see it, one of their most important findings derived from this, for:

> in the South the relationships predicted by neo-Marxists are borne out (a) for incarceration rates in four of six years, (b) for court commitments to prison four of six years, and (c) for conditional releases from prison in three of six years. It is also noteworthy that virtually all of these supportive observations occurred in more recent years during which there was the claimed switch to the 'generic justice' model of penology. (p. 171)

Speculating about this, they suggested that lower welfare benefits and more stringent requirements for entitlement in the south resulted in the criminal justice system having a greater 'control' function than in other states with better welfare systems.

Inequality and imprisonment

It is easy to summarise research on income inequality and impris-onment, for only one study, Jacobs (1979), has been located. He was particularly interested in testing the idea that economic elites become anxious particularly about property offences when income inequalities are comparatively wide or widening. To accomplish this, he correlated imprisonment admission rate (measured as the total number of admissions divided by the total number of crimes known to the police) against the Gini coefficient in fifty US states for the year 1960. After controlling for percent urbanisation, percent law enforcement officers, absolute level of resources and immigration, he concluded that:

> inequality was the only significant predictor of imprisonment for larceny and . . . differences in economic advantage and power

have substantial independent effects on the imprisonment ratios
for burglary and larceny. (p. 520)

Conclusion

Three hypotheses, derived from the radical theorising presented in
Chapters 4 and 5, have been tested against available research
evidence drawn from numerous American and British studies.
Although there is some ambiguity and inconsistency in this body of
research literature, on balance it supports the view that unemployment status influences police decisions to apprehend, arrest and
prosecute, it shapes probation officer's sentence recommendations, and has a detrimental effect on the type and severity of court
sentence. This of course does *not* mean that irrespective of other
factors, particularly offence and prior record, unemployment status *determines* decisions in the criminal justice system. However,
although these decisions are only marginally influenced by the
suspect's/offender's employment status, they do, when aggregated, produce a macro-relationship between one effect of recession – unemployment – and one type of social control –
imprisonment. This relationship partially accounts for the 'overcrowding' in both American and British prisons. But it is the
political and ideological climate that explains the production of
this relationship and the currently favoured solution to prison
'overcrowding' which is to construct more and more prisons.

This raises the issue of whether or not this theory is historically
specific, i.e. whether it only applies to contemporary North
America and Britain. If it does, then the relationship between
recession and imprisonment is not inevitable nor mechanistic, but
is mediated or even muted by political ideology.

For example, Greenberg (1980), whose research on Canadian
data was seminal in highlighting a relationship between unemployment and imprisonment rates, failed to discover a similar relationship in Poland for the periods 1924–39, and 1955–76. He argued
that an important factor accounting for this result was the Polish
government's policy of periodic amnesty. These were politically
motivated and occurred in 1932, 1936, 1956, 1964, 1969 and 1974.

However, it might be premature and imprudent to dismiss the
relationship between unemployment and imprisonment as being
nothing more than the product of political ideology. The Nether-

lands, for example, have been held up by many writers as an example of *reductionism* in practice (Rutherford, 1984; Tulkens, 1979). The basis for this claim is that the prison population fell from 4,075 (or 38 per 100,000 population) to 2,356 (or 17 per 100,000 population). Furthermore, during this period the rate of recorded crimes was increasing almost as fast as the British rate. However, since then, and particularly in the 1980s, the prison population again climbed. By 1980 it was 3,203, and in September 1984 had risen to 4,880 (34 per 100,000 population). This was still among the lowest national rate of imprisonment per capita for European countries, but it does represent a total reverse picture of that celebrated as an ideal by 'reductionists'. It may be a simple coincidence but the Netherlands has experienced one of the largest increases in unemployment of all the European countries. From 1979 when it was around 5.0 it rose sharply to over 15.0 by 1985. On the other hand, the government which had been dominated by the Social Democratic Party for years suddenly changed in the early 1980s and was replaced by a Centre Right Coalition whose preferences for a more 'law and order' penal policy are obviously reflected in the increased prison population, an increase which primarily consists of young offenders among whom drug-related offenders figure prominently. The relationship between unemployment and drug-related offending makes it more than likely that the recent upsurge in the Dutch prison population has something to do with the sudden and dramatic increase in youthful unemployment.

There is one anomaly which needs to be considered. Apparently, during the inter-war years, when the 'Great Depression' occurred, a penal policy of 'reductionism' was pursued in England and Wales. This appears to contradict a major thesis of this book, namely that as unemployment rises, the prison population should increase. Therefore, it is necessary to have a closer look both at the data and the context.

It is certainly true that the England and Wales prison population (rate per 100,000 inhabitants) fell from 63 in 1908 to 30 by 1938. But this drop occurred during the first ten years, and from 1923 onwards it remained *stable* at around 30. Similarly, total receptions into prison, taking 1908 to equal 100, fell to 14 by 1918, then rose to 28 by 1923 and remained fairly constant until the *late* 1930s when the worst of the depression was over. A major reason for the 'reduction' after 1908 was primarily because Winston Churchill proved to be a remarkably liberal Home Secretary during his brief period of tenure from February 1910 to October 1911 (Rutherford, 1984, p. 124). This political climate, plus the effects of the First World War, resulted in the prison population falling. But during the height of the 'Great Depression' the prison population appeared stable. Even so, this does not appear to fit easily with a major thesis in this book. However, it needs to be recalled that at no time was it argued that a mechanistic relationship existed between unemployment levels and imprisonment. Any relationship was mediated by at least two important factors: first, the *meaning* of unemployment, both to those experiencing it directly and to those observing it from positions of political and economic power; second, the position of the British economy in the context of the world economy. On both counts, the inter-war period was markedly different from the recession of the late 1970s and 1980s.

Although unemployment levels were high, the duration of unemployment was low. The depressed areas of traditional manufacturing may have experienced high levels of unemployment, but there were expanding areas of new industries in the South. Furthermore, because of the rapid development of new towns, it was possible for the unemployed to move south, unlike now, when marked differences in housing prices make it virtually impossible to 'get on yer bike' and find jobs and homes. In the 1930s there was great optimism among the working classes that the Labour Party, which had only had two brief periods in office, would be returned to power and create a new industrial climate. For these reasons, the deep mood of desperation which hangs like a cloud over the present generation of long-term unemployed, did not exist to the same extent fifty years ago. The motivation for resistance, including criminal activity, was not therefore so present.

On the other side of the fence, the political and economically powerful did not view the unemployed as so much of a potential threat to social order, because Britain's position in the world economy was nowhere near as desperate as it is now, and the domestic economic expansion brought jobs and hope in many parts of Britain – thus blunting the sharper teeth of high unemployment. Consequently, the need to restructure the labour force, so obvious now, was not in evidence then, and therefore the need to criminalise and imprison potential resistors did not rise so high on the political agenda. In any case, the 'enemy within' was not as menacing as the 'enemy without' – the rise of the Third Reich during the 1930s posed a much more serious threat to the British ruling elite than did the unemployed. Indeed, the unemployed, despite their material predicament, could be relied upon to rally to the flag of patriotism, which was increasingly waved as the Germany military machine became more threatening.

So those additional factors which bring about a relationship between unemployment and imprisonment in contemporary Britain were much less in evidence during the inter-war period. The anomaly of the inter-war period is therefore more apparent than real. Consequently, the prison population remained stable and did not increase.

Clearly more comparative research between other industrialised countries needs to be carried out before the importance of government mediating the relationship between unemployment and imprisonment can be better assessed.

7 Conclusions and Policy Implications

The two major issues taken up in this book – crime and punishment during the recent recession – have already been summarised in chapter conclusions, and do not need further repetition. However, they do require *contextualising*. It is important to see these issues against the wider context of academic debates over the 'causes of crime' and the 'politics of prison overcrowding and abolition'. After that, some *implications*, particularly for crime and penal policies in a democratic society, need to be considered.

Reaffirming aetiology – the bride's story

A book like this, which attempts to look backward and forward simultaneously, is an obvious target for criticism. It displays an old-fashioned, and therefore contemptible, concern with aetiology – the 'causes of crime'. The Sixties, which inherited the rich legacy of Merton (and through him Durkheim), Sutherland (who created fertile soil for symbolic interactionist accounts of crime to flourish), and the Chicago School (with its emphasis on social disorganisation), became a euphoric and prolific period for theorising on the *social* causes of crime. The works of Cloward and Ohlin (1960), Cohen (1955), Becker (1963), Lemert (1967) and Matza (1964, 1969) became the clarion calls for vast armies of researchers, who poured out of the expanded tertiary educational system and beavered away to sharpen, test and apply these theoretical developments. The causes of crime, be they anomie and opportunity, subcultural learning, drift and desperation, labelling and reaction, formed the main courses on this rapidly expanding and exciting criminological menu. Yet by the end of the decade the death-bell had been tolled not only for Hippies, with their utopian hopes of love and peace, but also for this more modest down-to-earth criminologists' concern with aetiology. Although the bell-ringers, Morris and Hawkins (1969), rudely dismissed the endless rolls of money spent on causal research as having been flushed down the bog-hole of erroneous ideas, their denunciation only gained currency because they captured the mood of a defeated generation. These authors' forlorn sound was aeons removed from the optimistic babble of the mid-Sixties when nearly every criminologist, able-bodied or not, was drafted into the President's Commission on Crime and Violence, with its endless battalions of Task Forces dispatched to turn over every stone of American social structure and history to discover the causes of crime so that its incidence might be reduced substantially. They were defeated, or at least believed they were, by human perversity. Despite the widespread translation of opportunity, subcultural and labelling theories into public policies, levels of recorded crime continued to rise like Agincourt arrows until they burst the multi-coloured theoretical balloons of the Sixties. It does not matter now that this pessimistic belief was misguided and misplaced. The lack of fit between policies and theories, so apparent now but not at all obvious then, did nothing to stop the spirit withering.

Of course academic concerns are not killed off so easily. The quest for the 'causes of crime' continued, but in a dull, pedestrian form, far removed from any access to the machinery of state. Criminologists buried their heads in 'control theory' with its emphasis on situational, subjective factors so they should not be forced to see the social and structural causes of crime; whilst others, like renegade Arthurian Knights, abandoned the quest completely. 'Crime and Its Causes' were no longer One; instead the prevention of crime through environmental manipulation was the new calling, for which James Q. Wilson (1975, 1982) was a leading American spokesperson and Home Office researcher Ron Clarke (1980; Clarke and Mayhew, 1980) was a major British advocate.

A small group of British academics (Kinsey *et al.*, 1986; Lea and Young, 1984; Matthews and Young, 1986; Young, 1986), sailing under 'Realist Criminology' as a flag of convenience, have recently denounced these 'no-hopers' and reasserted the need to explore the 'causes of crime'. However, these 'realists' have displayed a disturbing ambiguity between emphasising the contribution made by 'material circumstances' and 'cultural meanings'. Thus in Lea and Young's (1984) *Law and Order*, 'relative deprivation' is proffered as *the* motivational engine of 'conventional' crime. While this subjective factor undoubtedly plays a part in causing crime, it is indeed curious, particularly in view of the materialism in the *New Criminology* (Taylor *et al.*, 1973), to divorce it from objective material circumstances. This is not to argue that these circumstances directly and invariably determine subjective feelings, but it certainly dismisses any argument that they are causally unrelated. Instead it reasserts that material circumstances are primary, and these shape subjective feelings, such as 'relative deprivation' and 'thwarted ambition'. It may not be a one-to-one relationship. But to argue that people *in our culture* who are absolutely worse off than they were or expected to be, and who are still young enough to both resent and resist this, will not have a stronger tendency towards deviance, seems curious to say the least. Of course not all people who become worse off, either because of unemployment or widening income inequalities, turn to crime. But without these objective circumstances it is difficult to see how such motivational elements as 'relative deprivation' or 'thwarted ambition' might be generated. For that reason, the 'causes of crime', in this book, are firmly rooted in material circumstances, although that is not to argue for one minute that these necessarily by themselves cause crime.

In not merely paying respect to this virtual wasteland of criminological theorising, but in actually resurrecting ideas thought buried under the tombstone of 'Nothing Works', this book invites the label of being 'old fashioned'. It even wets the glue on the back of this label by being a stickler for research and its empirical results. Nothing gets more up the nose of some contemporary criminologists than the assertion that ideas, no matter how orthodox in their pedigree or dizzying in their complexity, have to be abandoned if the results of 'hypothesis testing' research fails to support them. Whilst not making anything other than a humble claim, at least this book has attempted to remain faithful to Merton's (1957) prescribed interplay between theory formulation, research, and reformulation.

On the other hand, this book is 'terribly' fashionable, or at least promiscuous, which might, in certain social groups, amount to the same thing. It does not attempt to construct either a theory of crime or penal policy from any 'purist' position. Instead it adopts a position of 'integration'; as prescribed for the bride, something old, something new, something borrowed, something blue. Thus the theory of crime causation does not reduce itself to mere economism; it postulates that economic conditions are important, maybe even necessary in any theory, but it also brings in elements of labelling, control, and what passed for radical theory a few years ago. Theory integration is currently in vogue, at least in American criminological journals, and to that extent the theory in this book is voguish – as well as being old-fashioned.

Similarly, the 'theory of penal policies' developed in Chapters 4 and 5, whilst paying its respects to the Marxist traditions laid down by Rusche and Kirchheimer (1939), Bonger (1916), and maybe even 'The Doctor' (Marx) himself, quickly moved onto a micro-analysis whose theoretical roots owe more to the Weberian, and hence phenomenological, tradition. The key term in analysing the behaviour of judges, probation officers and police is not 'material-ism' but 'meaning'. What 'meanings' do decisions taken by these state officials have *for* them? Again this willingness to sacrifice purity and fuse Marxist and Weberian traditions exposes this book to unflattering critical comments. Yet from one point of view this fusion was necessary. Any attempt to stick doggedly to a structural account of the relationship between recession and changing penal policies would inevitably have been sucked into the quicksand of functionalism and conspiracy theory. Wanting to avoid both of these, the theory was strengthened at its core by grafting onto to it an answer to the question, 'how do actors bring about results of which they may be dimly aware, and in their more enlightened moments would not even support?' In pursuing this, it was hoped to avoid a naive trap into which, according to Young (1986), many 'left idealists' easily fall. He believes that:

It is a strange world, bourgeois economists may argue about the logic of capital – as do Marxist economists – but seemingly a local police chief has no problem in understanding what capital requires of him nor does the lone school teacher facing a disruptive class. (p. 19)

In this book's theory, there is no question of judges, magis-trates, probation officers or police necessarily having to under-stand the nature and contemporary crisis of capital accumulation or the need to restructure labour. Their decisions were explained purely in terms of the 'logic' of their situations; they understood their problems, not capital's, and took decisions on the basis of this understanding. It was the 'latent and unintended' consequences of these actions – a further old-fashioned concept – that widened the net of social control, forced up the prison population, and disciplined part of the 'surplus population'. By the device of focusing on 'latent consequences', and by arguing that government officials do not interfere when subordinates act in relatively harmless ways – to the government that is – it was hoped that this book would also avoid another naivety of 'left idealism'. For, again according to Young (1986):

> What is striking about left idealist theorising about the state is its almost unwitting functionalist mode of explanation coupled with a strong instrumentalist notion that the operation of every agency or action of powerful individuals is linked in some one-to-one fashion to the needs of the ruling class and capital and that all of the state agencies gear frictionlessly together to promote capitalism. (p. 17)

Mertonian functionalism, a variant of which is adopted in this book, was never this naive. The perfect harmony between capital's interests, the state and its agencies was never assumed. Indeed, it is wryly amusing to observe the current British government, which wants to limit public expenditure and yet expand the prison system. Their solution to this problem in the spring of 1986 was to reduce prison expenditure by effectively slashing prison officers' take-home pay. This, predictably, led to militant action on the part of the Prison Officers Association. When its members took industrial action, it enabled prisoners to express their resentments, and the subsequent 'riots' caused millions of pounds worth of damage. The government, realising that the POA had a point, not only withdrew the plan to cut their take-home pay but also found itself with a bill for damages caused by prisoners. Such is the irony of unintended consequences!

From this one example alone (and it could be repeated a thousandfold), it would be naive in the extreme to assume that all parts of the system worked in a harmonious fashion. Instead, the argument in this book is that governments muddle along, taking advantage of opportunities, welcoming and encouraging collective behaviour of which it approves or from which it derives benefits, and attempting to force along 'reforms' to allay anxieties shared by itself and sections of its supporters. It therefore does not have an instrumental view of the state nor is it guilty of naive functionalism. For what has been argued here is that government policy is as much a reaction to events as a creator of them; as much a recipient of the consequences of others' decisions as a dictator of them.

Policy implications

There are two areas addressed in this book which lend themselves to state intervention and amelioration – the causes of crime and the causes of imprisonment. Since in principle a government could tackle both these issues, it has the means to substantially reduce the level of crime victimisation and the number of persons condemned to prisons.

Reducing crime

Before making some simple and obvious recommendations for reducing 'conventional crime', it needs to be stressed, or repeated, that for many crimes, particularly crimes of the powerful, employment is a necessary prerequisite – for some, work is criminogenic! Corporate, business and professions' crimes continue irrespective of whether 3 or 33 per cent of the manual labour force are unemployed. There is also a need to emphasis the results of research on unemployment and crime. Briefly, although they lend weight to there being a relationship, it was not so enormous as to account for all 'conventional' crime, and the evidence was not always consistent or unambiguous. For income inequality and crime, however, the evidence was much stronger and indicated that any social policy which does not aim to narrow these inequalities would not reduce crime. Finally, unemployment and income inequality only appear to lead to crime when they occur within a cultural context which infuses them with an acute sense of 'failure' and 'rejection' and these in turn produce to a sense of 'relative deprivation' or 'thwarted ambition'. Without these subjective states, the motivation towards crime would be absent.

The theory developed in Chapter 2 also stressed other factors, such as inadequate social controls, social reaction and individual response, which amplify or mute the relationship between unemployment/income-inequality and crime. Thus any policy which simply focused on unemployment and inequality and did nothing, say, to prevent the 'marginalisation' of criminals via imprisonment and stigmatisation, would not be very effective. Thus a shopping list of reforms almost suggest themselves:

(1) *Reduce the level of unemployment, particularly long-term unemployment.* Although the call for more employment is intrinsically compelling, it may have an additional effect – the reduction of the amount of 'conventional' crime. But it needs to be remembered that Britain's and the United States' chances of returning to 'full employment' are weak given their deteriorating and arguably irreversible (Jordan, 1982) positions in the international economy. Furthermore, as the economic system becomes more computerised and capital-intensive, a large, and maybe expanding, pool of unemployable people will be created. The problems of this group can be substantially reduced if they are not stigmatised as 'scroungers', 'lazy' or 'parasites' and if they are afforded full civilian rights. Although they may be without a 'job' they can still enjoy the fulfilment of 'work' if they have the material resources and educational skills to occupy their time with some of the myriad 'projects' which give human beings in our culture a sense of engrossment, achievement, and self-realisation. Expanding the tertiary educational system seems an essential prerequisite for transforming the 'jobless' into 'work-centred'. It is more realistic therefore to look beyond job-sharing, shorter hours, and longer holidays, indeed to look *beyond employment* and anticipate a society where jobs are exceptional and yet everyone works (Bohm, 1983). There is little point in blindly arguing for a 'right to work' (meaning a paid job). For as Harrison (1983) reminds us, employment for many workers:

is a drudgery, routine, exploitation, subjection to arbitrary authority, and for many add noise, danger, chemicals, unsocial hours, all this sandwiched between two harrowing odysseys on public transport. Unemployment could be a liberation from all this, a chance for people to cultivate new interests, to join in community action and politics, to improve their home or their neighbourhood, to be with their children, to relate to their spouse in a more liberated way. *In reality it rarely delivers*. (pp. 117–8)

This sting in the tail has to be removed. Planning for a 'work-centred' society (where all receive a decent social wage) to gradually replace a 'job-centred' one (where only a majority earn enough to live decently) is not only essential for increasing human happiness, but it will also have the added benefit of reducing the incidence of criminal victimisation.

(2) As Sundance Kid said to Butch Cassidy as they were being hotly pursued by a posse of Pinkerton detectives, 'If they paid me to stop robbing banks what they're paying them to stop me robbing banks, I'd stop robbing banks!' In the context of the evidence presented earlier, this is surely an apt injunction. *The current grotesque levels of income inequalities, where some receive £40 or less per week and others £4,000 or more, have to be reduced; no human being is morally worth that much more than another.* Capitalism, as a system for producing wealth, may be unparalleled. But the motivation to produce wealth can be satisfied adequately and generously even if the system of distributing wealth is altered to enable those with comparatively little to obtain more. There might, of course, come a time, if redistribution proceeds too quickly or sharply, when those threatened by it will themselves turn to forms of crime as a mode of resistance. The middle classes, who have never been disinclined to lie, cheat, swindle and defraud, might be propelled to adopt more violent forms of criminal activity if they experience a rapid 'proletarianisation'. It is also possible that if the relatively worse off come to expect quick and substantial economic improvements, they will be even more bitterly resentful if the delivery is late or too slow. Furthermore, any policy of lifting people out of poverty must be aimed at the *whole* group and not simply a meritorious few. For if that happens:

> those who remain poor become more atypical, and therefore suffer greater relative deprivation . . . programmes which set out to lift target groups out of poverty do not normally succeed in doing so. More often, they raise expectations which they cannot fulfil, adding yet another disappointment to the long line

of disappointments inflicted upon the people they set out to help. (Braithwaite, 1979, p. 231)

Thus any policy designed to reduce income inequalities would have to be gradualist and educational. Cultural norms of 'acquisitiveness' and 'competitiveness' would need to be relegated against the rising stars of 'equality' and 'co-operativeness. Maybe at that stage, *wealth* inequalities can be looked at, for these vast and morally indefensible differences are also criminogenic.

It could be argued that if a realist view of unemployment is adopted and people are educated to appreciate the distinction between jobs and work and that the latter is more fulfilling, and that if income inequalities are narrowed considerably directly through social wages being raised to a decent, civilised level, and indirectly through a variety of tax subsidies, then the incidence of crime should drop substantially. This does not raise the ghost of a 'crime-free' society that haunted the *New Criminology* (Taylor *et al.*, 1973). It simply makes the modest claim that crime levels will be reduced. Of course this is not the only argument against high unemployment and large material inequalities. There are other, more morally compelling, reasons why these differences should be narrowed and employment increased, but they are not part of this book.

Even with less unemployment and fairer income distributions, crime would not be reduced that much if additional policies were not adopted to reinforce them.

(3) Control theorists have demonstrated that lack of 'commitment' is an important precursor of criminal activity. *Commitment, particularly in school, can be substantially increased by making educational curricula 'relevant' and by dropping the invidious 'successful'/'unsuccessful' labels currently attached to those destined for jobs and those about to join the dole queue.* So long as schools are geared towards calibrating children for the world of jobs, then children labelled as 'failures' are bound to be resentful, bitter, alienated and delinquent. In a society like ours, where jobs will become scarcer, schools should be reconstituted to be fundamentally about training 'for life'. If a major socialising institution, like schools, communicates to a section of youth that society 'dismisses' them, it can be no wonder this 'disowned' youth commits crimes. The rhetoric question 'Why shouldn't they?' almost

becomes irresistible. Without anything to lose, it is difficult to provide a positive reason why they should not at least commit some property offences. But what a sad answer that is! Yet unless there is a fundamental and urgent reconsideration of how schools should be reconstructed in the light of fewer and fewer jobs being available, it may be the only realistic one available. It would, however, be much more sensible and constructive if schools were transformed from institutions for training a minority for an ever-shrinking job market to ones training all pupils to be self-actualising citizens.

(4) Labelling theorists have demonstrated that imprisonment and discrimination against ex-prisoners 'marginalises' and hence condemns a section of the community who have become embroiled with the juvenile and adult criminal justice systems to a twilight life of further deviance (Box, 1981, ch. 7). These hard cases are not beyond rehabilitation or redemption, as the case of Jimmy Boyle (1977) demonstrates. But this is not achieved by paying ex-prisoners a social wage for six months after release, or by locating them in a low-paid, dull, boring and alienating job. Results from American programmes which have attempted to reduce recidivism by paying or employing ex-prisoners, have not been encouraging (Beck *et al.*, 1980). The way to prevent the vicious cycle of crime – prison – marginalisation is, first, to *imprison far fewer offenders* (about which more below), and second, to *pursue a genuine policy of rehabilitation within the prison for those fewer offenders whose crimes justify imprisonment.* The reaffirmation of rehabilitation over punishment should be high on any honest politician's guide to crime control (Cullen and Gilbert, 1982). It does not mean imposing work-discipline through sewing mail-bags or other meaningless routine activities, but should involve the best available courses in 'life-skills', 'assertiveness training' and self-development.

Reducing unemployment in the short run and moving beyond employment in the long run, when associated by actual narrowing of income inequalities, restructured schools for 'life training', and reductions in the 'marginalisation' of convicted persons, are all simple, obvious, *but* in the light of current research knowledge, *effective* ways of reducing the incidence of 'conventional' crime. Curiously, the reduction of crimes of the powerful may require that some of these policies be applied in reverse!

(5) Crimes of the powerful flourish in an atmosphere of indul-
gence'; the law really is, like a box of Christmas chocolates, 'soft at
the centre'. These crimes are also the child of a Frankenstein
marriage between 'competitive individualism' and 'moral indifference'. This suggests that *ways have to be found and implemented
for detecting, prosecuting, convicting and imprisoning more corporate and professional offenders than are currently caught up in the
criminal justice system.* This is not too difficult. Braithwaite (1984,
pp. 290–383) and Box (1983, pp. 63–79) have already put forward
a long shopping-list of legal and judicial reforms which would, if
carried out with sufficient political will, reduce the incidence of
corporate crimes and other crimes of domination. Briefly, law-
enforcement agencies need to be strengthened with more personnel and resources. They need greater powers of surveillance,
search and investigation. In order to penetrate the walls of se-
crecy, industrial spies should be employed and corporate whistle-
blowers encouraged and protected. Judicial processes need to be
altered to enable the successful prosecutions of corporate offenders to increase. This may mean having different procedural
rules for corporations, particularly those multi-nationals whose
financial resources are often greater than national states'. Thus
regulatory agencies, such as the Health and Safety Executive (UK)
or the Food and Drug Administration (USA), could be given more
powers to impose fixed penalties, thus avoiding complex, time-
consuming, uncertain and expensive prosecutions. The 'right to
jury' could be abolished for those cases where corporations are
prosecuted, but this should not be extended to cover individual
managers or directors prosecuted in their own right. Strict liability
could be extended. A recent report in *Justice* revealed that by 1975
there were over 7,000 separate criminal offences in Britain, *more
than half of which did not require any proof of intent.* This could be
increased to cover more corporate and organisational offences. In
these complex cases, 'beyond a reasonable doubt' could be replaced by 'on the balance of probabilities'; this would help to
secure more convictions in areas where the current level is abys-
mally low. Defendants in these cases would not be allowed to
spend more than a certain amount and certainly less than could be
used to impair seriously the prosecution's effectiveness. This
simply reverses the concept of 'legal aid' for the poor to make
them more equal with the state; reduce the economic power of the

rich to make them more equal with the state. A full range of sanctions, including probation orders, community service orders, compensation, reparation and targeted repentance to victims and potential victims (Fisse and Braithwaite, 1983), should be made available to criminal courts. Finally, 'nationalisation' for guilty corporations and imprisonment for people convicted of these types of crimes, where the victims are numerous and the objective levels of injury incalculably large, should become more frequent.

Clearly this last suggestion has important implications for penal policies to which we can now turn.

The politics of 'overcrowding' and the abolition of prisons

From a democratic socialist perspective, brutality, including un-lawful killing, by prison staff against prisoners, coercive drugging of 'unmitigated nuisances', capricious and malicious discipline amounting to additional imprisonment without the protection of 'due process', the destruction of marriages, families and prisoners' lives beyond a point justified by the offence, and the 'invisibility' of the system in which these 'violations of human rights' are commit-ted, are all more serious problems than mere overcrowding. Yet it is overcrowding which has formed the central public debate, both in the UK and the USA, over the last fifteen years.

Of course, overcrowding is a problem. It stretches kitchen, laundry, bath, exercise and work facilities. In turn, these problems not only create immense strains on the relationship between administrators and prison officers, but also between the latter and prisoners, and between prisoners themselves. They also create additional psychological problems for survival in what would be, even under 'normal' circumstances, a hellish place to live.

But what has been the outcome of this debate in Britain? Ostensibly every Home Secretary from Roy Jenkins to Douglas Hurd has created the appearance of being concerned to bring down the 'dangerously' high level of prison overcrowding. They have not succeeded in transforming this appearance into reality. This is partly because good intentions were allowed to be sub-verted by a judiciary determined to preserve its independence (but still remain reliable in the Right quarters), and anxious to tackle the apparent growing crime problem by imposing stiffer penalties on more and more offenders.

For example, the Criminal Justice Act, 1967 introduced a suspended sentence of imprisonment. This was supposed to be an alternative to imprisonment. However, the courts were allowed to thwart this ambition. They frequently imposed this sentence as an alternative to a fine or a probation order. Thus the imposition of a fine has dropped by nearly one-fifth in the last ten years whilst the proportion of convicted persons imprisoned has increased. Furthermore, the judiciary increased the length of suspended sentence, so that when someone re-offended, they went to prison for longer. This last effect not only pushed up the prison population but was exacerbated by the Court of Appeal's ruling that the new and activated sentences should run consecutively and not concurrently (Bottoms, 1981).

This same Act introduced parole. However, the hopes that this would seriously reduce the prison population have not been realised. The numbers released on parole rose quite sharply to 5,218 in 1977 and then remained more or less static for the next six years, despite more people being in prison. It was not until the Home Secretary implemented a section of the 1982 Criminal Justice Act, in July 1984, that a one-off contribution to prison overcrowding was experienced. In that year the qualifying period for parole was reduced from twelve to six months, although a prisoner still had to complete one-third of their sentence. Because of this the total number of prisoners released on parole doubled from 5,363 in 1983 to 11,909 in 1984. But even this was not enough to bring about a reduction in the prison population. Furthermore, within the figure of nearly 12,000 parolees there was a large backlog of cases. In future years the number paroled will predictably drop back.

The Bail Act, 1976 was intended to secure the diversion of thousands of untried suspects from prison, but it has only marginally affected the number of persons remanded in custody. It is true that shortly after this Act the number of suspects remanded in custody fell, but from 1980 onwards they rose again until 1984 when they returned to their 1975 level of around 53,000. But this bland picture of stability masks a fundamental change. During this ten-year period the average number of days in custody rapidly increased; from 25 to 51 days for men and 15 to 34 days for women. The outcome was that the average daily remanded prison population *doubled* from 3,500 to over 7,000! Not only have the judiciary been allowed to thwart the intention behind the Bail Act, but they still remand many citizens unnecessarily. Thus in 1984, nearly 4 per cent of remanded prisoners were subsequently found to be 'not guilty'. In addition, just over one-quarter were subsequently given a non-custodial sentence. Sometimes this was because they had already spent sufficient time in prisons, but in many cases this was because the severity of their crime did not deserve imprisonment.

The Criminal Law Act, 1977 removed simple drunkenness from the list of offences punishable by imprisonment. The magistrates responded by imposing fines unpayable by persons inclined to be drunk and disorderly and therefore 'without the wherewithal'. The outcome was that the same number found guilty of being 'simply drunk' in a public place, ended up in prisons as fine-defaulters. Thus in 1977 the total imprisoned for 'drunkenness', either immediately or in default of fine, was 2,478. But six years later it was still over 2,500 despite the intention behind the Act. Only in 1984 did a significant drop to 1,500 materialise.

The Criminal Justice Act, 1982 abolished imprisonment for the offence of loitering for the purpose of prostitution. Yet that has not prevented prostitutes being fined the maximum £200. Since those convicted are likely to be the least successful 'street walkers', these fines, whose total soon mounts up with subsequent court appearances, frequently and *predictably* exceed their ability to pay. Thus in 1984, 271 females convicted of offences related to prostitution ended up in prison as fine-defaulters.

Curiously, in February 1984 the Home Secretary announced that maximum fines in magistrates courts were to be doubled! Without arguing that magistrates would take full advantage of this increased power, there will doubtless be an increase in the average fine level and therefore a substantial increase in imprisoned fine-defaulters. Whether this outcome is averted by the Home Secretary granting courts the power to impose a community service order on fine-defaulters, as he suggested he might in a recent speech to Liverpool magistrates (Dean, 1984), remains to be seen.

The introduction of the partially suspended sentence, which was created under the Criminal Law Act, 1977 and implemented in 1982, has failed to achieve a reduction in the prison population. Home Office researchers examined 600 partially suspended sentences imposed in the fourth quarter of 1982 and concluded that 'possibly up to half these sentences replaced fully suspended sentence of imprisonment or non-custodial sentences' (Dean, 1983). The outcome of this sentencing practice is that more persons are imprisoned than was ever intended by those implementing this alternative to immediate imprisonment.

After the *Butler Report on Mentally Abnormal Offenders*, 1975, the government urged every Regional Health Authority to build a secure hospital establishment to relieve the prison system of over 1,000 mentally ill prisoners. But even now, over ten years later, the number of such prisoners has hardly dropped because the Health Authorities have not been willing, or able financially, to respond positively. In the *Government's Reply to the Fourth Report from the Home Affairs Committee* (Cmnd 8446), it was stated that they were still waiting for one of the fourteen Regional Health Authorities in England to provide plans for establishing secure accommodation. As of mid-1982, one 30 bed unit was open, building in progress would, when complete, provide a further 160 places, and building to begin in 1983 would add another 136 places. By 1985 they had still not reached 500 places. Furthermore, there is every indication that the government will have to prevent resolutely any attempt by mental-hospital authorities to disgorge their more troublesome patients into these more secure units and thus thwart any attempt to reduce significantly the number of mentally ill prisoners.

The recent history of government attempts to reduce the prison population is a history of 'tinkering'. Each Home Secretary has in turn drawn back from taking the most obvious and practical steps with the disingenuous excuse that he cannot legislate for the judiciary – its 'independence' is inviolable. It can be encouraged, exhorted, informed, reasoned with, but never instructed. The result is that major reforms are completely avoided, and every minor reform is weakened or sabotaged. For example, in 1981, Whitelaw proposed to reduce the prison population by an estimated 7,000 through granting parole after one-third of a prison sentence. But the Magistrates' Association Sentencing of Offenders Committee strongly opposed this move and threatened to retaliate by committing more offenders to Crown Court for sentence – a move calculated to secure longer sentences to offset early parole. By mid-1982 Whitelaw backed off, the plan was dropped and instead 'partially suspended sentences' created under Section

47 of the Criminal Law Act, 1977 were introduced as a poor and ineffective compromise (Ryan, 1983).

Of course, the central issue is that too many persons are sentenced to prison, and for too long (Fitzmaurice and Pease, 1982). The government could drastically reduce the prison population. It could (i) remove minor offences from the list of those subject to criminal law (e.g., drunkenness in public, sexual offences between consenting young persons, cannabis consumption); (ii) remove some offences from the list of those punishable by imprisonment (e.g., fine and maintenance defaulters, vagrants, beggars, and indeed all summary offences); (iii) prevent the imprisonment of certain types, such as the mentally ill or disordered, the persistent petty but socially inadequate offender, the undefended offender on the *Gideon* principle that the state shall not deprive any person of liberty unless that person's best defence has been presented by a legally qualified or competent person, those awaiting deportation, all first offenders and no one under the age of 18, except for violent offences; (iv) require the police to caution more suspects and only prosecute after convincing an independent judicial office that this course of action would be in the public interest; (v) increase bail hostels, institute a national programme of registered medical practitioners willing to provide examination of suspects in the community, and provide sufficient funds to speed up the period of time on remand in custody; (vi) increase the extent of suspended sentences to cover all periods of imprisonment, with the exception of a 'life' sentence; (vii) introduce day-fines, which would in turn reduce the number of fine-defaulters and, by heavily fining those more capable of paying, reduce the pressure to imprison where the present fine level is incommensurate with the offence's seriousness; (viii) pressurise the Regional Health Authorities to push ahead more quickly with the provision of more secure units; (ix) educate judges and magistrates to realise the limited objective – punishment – prisons can achieve, and to regard alternatives to prison, especially community service orders, probation orders, day centres and weekend attendance centres, as genuine *alternatives* to be used more often for those who would otherwise be imprisoned, and not, as is currently suspected, as an *additional* way of bringing more persons under state control (Cohen, 1985).

In addition, and even more important, the government could introduce new maxima levels of sentencing below the present levels and persuade the judiciary to aim for an average comparable with the present average on a pro rata basis. The Council of Europe (1985) recently published up-to-date information of the imprisonment rate per 100,000 population for twenty-one countries. The UK came third in the league with 96.5 whilst Turkey (139) and Austria (109) occupied the places above. There is no question that *the* reason why Britain has this high prison population is because the average sentence is much longer than in the vast majority of European countries. Furthermore, in terms of the comparable crime problems or the levels of recidivism, this marked difference in the average length of imprisonment seems unjustifiable. The government could, by directly engineering a shorter average prison sentence, reduce the prison population. If it *wanted* to act even quicker, because the crisis is now and not in the future, it could activate its powers under the Criminal Justice Act, 1982, and grant a six months' amnesty to all but those guilty of serious violent offences. The effect, 'at a stroke', would be to reduce the prison population drastically. But the present government appears to have no intention of doing so. Instead, its simplistic solution to the problem of prison overcrowding is to build more and more expensive, unnecessary and counter-productive prisons. The reasons for this response have already been elaborated. What is now quite clear is that the 'politics of overcrowding' have not been the lever for a reductionist programme, but have been paraded as the justification for an *expansionist* programme. This is true both for Britain and America.

Yet it need not be. A reductionist programme is feasible, liberal, humane and, most important of all, does not constitute a threat either to the public or to the economic system (Rutherford, 1984). It is necessary that this goal, however desirable, be achieved 'fairly'. Justice must not be compromised, the judiciary must not become merely an extension of the governing political party, and the public must not be endangered or ignored.

Justice demands that offenders receive a punishment commensurate with the seriousness of their offence. However, the present tariff level is not inviolable, and is certainly not the only possible interpretation of what constitutes a suitable gradation of punishments for different offences. If through administrative, legislative or judicial reforms, the average severity level of the tariff were reduced, justice would still be preserved – the commensurate relationship between offence and punishment would be left intact. The 'independence' of the judiciary is meant to stand between the citizen and the state to make certain that arbitrary or politically inspired punishments are not meted out. This 'independence' is not compromised merely by the state reducing the average length of prison sentence, or providing educational courses for the judiciary on the 'uses of imprisonment'. The judiciary would still be left to conduct its own business of establishing guilt and handing down a just punishment 'within the law'.

The public need not be endangered. It has been documented that the crime rate would not increase as a result of offenders being imprisoned for shorter periods, released earlier than at present, or diverted entirely into some alternative punitive scheme. The public need to be reassured; the evidence needed to achieve this is available, it merely has to be publicised effectively. Furthermore, if the government widened its criminal compensation scheme and made direct victim-restitution more central to our criminal justice system, then the sense of public outrage and indignation which might follow the implementation of the above ideas, especially if whipped up by the 'law and order' brigade and its media supporters, might be forestalled.

The means of reducing the prison population exist – indeed they have been presented to various governments ever since Roy Jenkins raised the alarm over fifteen years ago. Unfortunately, the history of the last decade's penal policy has been a history of government reluctance to do very much constructive, except construct more prisons! Is this because the above reforms are the utopian dreams of barmy radicals or the ivory-tower musings of starry-eyed academics? Hardly, for without exception these reforms come from a liberal consensus consisting of such official bodies as the Advisory Council on the Penal System, the Committee of Inquiry into the United Kingdom Prison Service, the House of Commons Expenditure Committee, and the Parliamentary All-Party Penal Affairs Group. These have been joined by, or echo the ideas of, the National Association for the Care and Resettlement of Offenders, the Conference of Chief Probation Officers, the National Association of Probation Officers, and the British Association of Social Workers. In addition, such libertarian/reformist groups as the Howard League for Prison Reform, the Prison Reform Trust, the National Council for Civil

Liberties and Radical Alternatives to Prison, have joined the chorus calling for the above ideas to be implemented with passion and urgency.

The problem is that Britain (and America also) has had governments lacking either the courage to implement these liberal reforms or the willpower to take on the pressure groups which would resist them. For example, in Britain, the Magistrates, the Association of Prison Officers and the Police Federation would all resist any attempt to curtail their powers or reduce their human resources. Various governments, and particularly the recent Thatcher government, have not only been reluctant to force a head-on collision, but these pressure groups are allies a government could not afford to antagonise, particularly if the main adversary is organised labour and the unemployed. In these circumstances, the government has chosen not to alienate these allies. Indeed, the recent government – POA dispute was quickly defused because it directly brought home to the government just how much it needs allies in its 'fight against crime' which is an essential ingredient in its hidden policy of restructuring the British labour force.

There is therefore little prospect of the present British (or the American for that matter) government changing the major platform of its penal policy, which is to build more prisons and allow the judiciary to fill, indeed over-fill, them. This is not because the nature of late capitalism would not allow a prison reduction. The reductionist programme runs up against not stubborn capitalism but governments who lack courage, willpower and are anxious about resistance and riots. It is the government's interpretation of the needs of late capitalism and not late capitalism itself which mediates, and therefore makes larger what might be a small mechanistic relationship between unemployment and imprisonment.

The 'reductionist' policy advocated here should not be confused with an 'abolitionist' position. The prison plays both an important *symbolic* and *concrete* function. Symbolically, prison demarcates between those behaviours society collectively condemns as being the worst imaginable and those it permits with varying degrees of tolerance. In doing this, the prison clarifies, maintains and reinforces the moral boundaries of a society. It is difficult to imagine any other institution performing this function so well and effectively. The criticism of prison inherent in this book is that it performs this function badly because it includes behaviours which are trivial when compared with some it excludes. But a prison system consistently devoted to the symbolic condemnation of those behaviours which *objectively* are most injurious to us, is highly commendable. It practice, this would mean removing many petty, minor property offences from the list of imprisonable crimes and including many crimes of economic and political domination. In a reduced, but reformed prison, there would be many more offenders drawn from privileged ranks, such as corporate directors, government officials, and members of respectable professions, while many contemporary prisoners who are poor would be dealt with in the community.

Prisons also play a concrete part in containing the crime problem. While locked up, offenders cannot prey on members of the public, and to that limited extent the level of crime is kept down. Since a reduced but reformed prison system would contain many 'dangerous' and 'violent' offenders, their incapacitation would be an unmitigated blessing.

The criticism of this book is not that governments have not abolished prisons, but that they have neither reduced nor reformed them even though their 'moral duty' to do so was plainly evident. They have instead expanded them as a pragmatic precaution and abandoned their 'moral duties'.

Bibliography

Allison, J. P. (1972) 'Economic factors and the rate of crime', *Land Economics*, 48: 193–6.

Austin, J. and Krisberg, B. (1981) 'Wider, stronger and different nets; the dialectics of criminal justice reform', *J. Research Crime and Delinq.*, 18: 165–96.

Austin, J. and Krisberg, B. (1982) 'The unmet promise of alternatives to incarceration', *Crime and Delinq.*, 28: 374–409.

Austin, J. and Krisberg, B. (1985) 'Incarceration in the U.S.: the extent and future of the prison', *Annals Amer. Acad. Political and Social Sci.*, 478: 15–30.

Austin, W. and Williams, T. A. (1977) 'A survey of judges' responses to simulated legal cases', *J. Criminal Law and Criminology*, 68: 306–16.

Avio, K. L. and Clark, C. S. (1976) *Property Crime in Canada: An Econometric Study* (Toronto University Press).

Bailey, W. (1984) 'Poverty, inequality and city homicide rates: some not so unexpected findings', *Criminology*, 22: 531–50.

Baldock, J. (1980) 'Why prison's population has grown larger and younger', *Howard Journal*, 19: 142–55.

Balkin, S. (1979) 'Victimization rates, safety and fear of crime', *Social Problems*, 26: 343–58.

Bartel, A. P. (1979) 'Women and Crime', *Economic Inquiry*, 17: 29–51.

Bechdolt, B. V. (1975) 'Cross-sectional analysis of socioeconomic determinants of urban crime', *Review of Social Economy*, 33: 132–40.

Beck, R. A., Lenihan, K. J. and Rossi, P. H. (1980) 'Crime and poverty', *Amer. Sociol. Rev.*, 45: 766–86.

Becker, G. S. (1968) 'Crime and punishment: an economic approach', *J. Political Economy*, 76: 169–217.

Becker, H. S. (1963) *The Outsiders* (New York: Free Press).

Benson, M. L. (1984) 'The fall from grace', *Criminology*, 22: 573–94.

Bequai, A. (1978) *White-Collar Crime: A Twentieth Century Crisis* (Lexington: Heath).

Berman, D. M. (1978) *Death on the Job* (New York: Monthly Press).

Bernstein, I. N., Kelly, W. R. and Poyle, P. A. (1977) 'Societal reactions to deviants: the case of criminal defendants', *Amer. Sociol. Rev.*, 42: 743–55.

Biles, D. (1979) 'Crime and use of prisons', *Federal Probation*, 43: 39–43.

Biles, D. (1982) 'Crime and imprisonment', *Aust. & New Zealand J. Criminology*, 23: 166–72.

Bishop, D. M. (1984) 'Legal and extralegal barriers to delinquency', *Criminology*, 22: 403–19.

Blau, J. R. and Blau, P. M. (1982) 'The cost of inequality: metropolitan structure and violent crime', *Amer. Sociol. Rev.*, 47: 114–29.

Block, R. (1979) 'Community, environment and violent crime', *Criminology*, 17: 46–57.

Bodenheimer, T. S. (1984) 'Prescriptions for death', *Crime and Social Justice*, 19: 108–12.

Bogen, D. (1944) 'Juvenile delinquency and economic trends', *Amer. Sociol. Rev.*, 9: 178–84.

Bohm, R. M. (1983) 'Beyond employment: toward a radical solution to the crime problem', *Crime and Social Justice*, 21–22: 213–22.

Bonger, W. (1916) *Criminality and Economic Conditions* (Chicago: Little, Brown).

Booth, A., Johnson, D. R. and Choldin, H. M. (1977) 'Correlates of city crime rates: victimization surveys versus official statistics', *Social Problems*, 25: 187–97.

Boshier, R. (1974) 'Does conviction affect employment opportunities?', *Brit. J. Criminology*, 14: 264–8.

Bottoms, A. E. (1981) 'The suspended sentence in England, 1967–1978', *Brit. J. Criminology*, 21: 1–26.

Bowker, L. H. (1981) 'Crime and the use of prisons in the U.S.: a time series analysis', *Crime and Delinq.*, 27: 206–12.

Box, S. (1981) *Deviance, Reality and Society*, 2nd edn (London: Holt, Rinehart & Winston).

Box, S. (1983) *Power, Crime and Mystification* (London: Tavistock).

Box, S. and Hale, C. (1982) 'Economic crisis and the rising prisoner population in England and Wales', *Crime and Social Justice*, 17: 20–35.

Box, S. and Hale, C. (1984) 'Liberation/emancipation, economic marginalisation, or less chivalry', *Criminology*, 22: 473–97.

Box, S. and Hale, C. (1985) 'Unemployment, imprisonment and prison overcrowding', *Contemporary Crises*, 9: 209–28.

Boyle, J. (1977) *A Sense of Freedom* (London: Pan).

Braithwaite, J. (1979) *Inequality, Crime and Public Policy* (London: Routledge & Kegan Paul).

Braithwaite, J. (1980) 'The political economy of punishment', in E. L. Wheelwright and K. Buckley (eds), *Essays in the Political Economy of Australian Capitalism* (Sydney: ANZ Books).

Braithwaite, J. (1984) *Corporate Crime in the Pharmaceutical Industry* (London: Routledge & Kegan Paul).

Braithwaite, J. and Braithwaite, V. (1980) 'Effects of income inequality and social democracy on homicide', *Brit. J. Criminology*, 20: 45–53.

Braungart, M. M., Braungart R. G. and Hoyer, W. J. (1980) 'Age, sex and social factors in the fear of crime', *Sociological Focus*, 13: 55–66.

Brenner, H. (1976) 'Time-series analysis: effects of the economy on criminal behaviour and the administration of criminal justice', in U.N. Social Defence Research Institute, *Economic Crises and Crime* (Rome: U.N. Publication No 15).

Brenner, H. (1978) 'Review of Fox's "Forecasting Crime"', *J. Criminal Law and Criminology*, 70: 273–4.

Brown, M. J., McCulloch, J. W. and Hiscox, J. (1972) 'Criminal offences in an urban area and their associated social variables', *Brit. J. Criminology*, 12: 250–68.

Buikhuisen, W. and Dijsterhuis, F. P. H. (1971) 'Delinquency and stigmatisation', *Brit. J. Criminology*, 11: 185–96.

Cain, M. and Sadigh, S. (1982) 'Racism, the police and community policing', *J. Law and Society*, 9: 87–102.

Calavita, K. (1983) 'The demise of the Occupational Safety and Health Administration', *Social Problems*, 30: 437–48.

Calvin, A. D. (1981) 'Unemployment among black youths, demographics and crime', *Crime and Delinquency*, 27: 234–44.

Carper, J. (1975) *Eating May Be Dangerous To Your Health* (New Jersey: Prentice-Hall).

Carr-Hill, R. A. and Stern, N. H. (1979) *Crime, The Police and Criminal Statistics* (New York: Academic Press).

Carroll, L. and Doubet, M. B. (1983) 'U.S. social structure and imprisonment', *Criminology*, 21: 449–56.

Carroll, L. and Jackson, P. I. (1983) 'Inequality, opportunity and crime rates in central cities', *Criminology*, 21: 178–94.

Carter, R. (1967) 'The presentence report and the decision-making process', *J. Research Crime and Deling.*, 4: 203–11.

Carter, R. and Wilkins, L. (1967) 'Some factors in sentencing policy', *J. Criminal Law, Criminology and Police Sci.*, 58: 503–14.

Carter, T. and Clelland, D. (1979) 'A neo-marxian critique, formulation and test of juvenile dispositions as a function of social class', *Social Problems*, 27: 96–198.

Caudill, H. M. (1977) 'Dead laws and dead men', *Nation*, 226: 492–7.

Chambliss, W. J. (1969) *Crime and the Legal Process* (New York: McGraw-Hill).

Chambliss, W. J. and Seidman, R. B. (1971) *Law, Order and Power* (Reading: Addison-Wesley).

Chapman, J. I. (1976) 'An economic model of crime and police', *J. Research Crime and Delinq.*, 13: 48–63.

CHAR (1983) *Poor Law* (London: Campaign For Single Homeless People).

Chester, C. R. (1976) 'Perceived relative deprivation as a cause of property crime', *Crime and Delinquency*, 22: 17–30.

Chiricos, G., Jackson, P. D. and Waldo, G. P. (1972) 'Inequality in the imposition of a criminal label', *Social Problems*, 19: 553–72.

Christenson, S. (1981) 'Our black prisons', *Crime and Delinq.*, 27: 364–75.

Cicourel, A. V. (1968) *Social Organisation of Juvenile Justice* (New York: Wiley).

Clark, R. (1970) *Crime in America* (New York: Simon & Schuster).
Clarke, A. H. and Lewis, M. (1982) 'Fear of crime among the elderly', *Brit. J. Criminology*, 22: 49–62.
Clarke, R. (1980) 'Situational crime prevention', *Brit. J. Criminology*, 20: 136–47.
Clarke, R., Ekblom, P., Hough, M. and Mayhew, P. (1985) 'Elderly victims of crime and exposure to risk', *Howard Journal*, 24: 1–9.
Clarke, R. and Mayhew, P. (eds) (1980) *Designing Out Crime* (London: HMSO).
Clarke, S. H. and Koch, G. C. (1976) 'The influence of income and other factors on whether criminal defendants go to prison', *Law and Society Rev.*, 11: 57–92.
Clemente, F. and Kleiman, M. (1977) 'Fear of crime in U.S.', *Social Forces*, 56: 519–31.
Clinard, M. B. and Yeager, P. C. (1981) *Corporate Crime* (New York: Free Press).
Cloward, R. A. and Ohlin, L. (1960) *Delinquency and Opportunity* (New York: Free Press).
Cloward, R. A. and Piven, F. F. (1979) 'Female protest: the channeling of female innovation resistance', *Signs,* 4: 661–9.
Coggan, G. and Walker, M. (1982) *Frightened For My Life: An Account of Deaths in British Prisons* (London: Fontana).
Cohen, A. K. (1955) *Delinquent Boys* (New York: Macmillan).
Cohen, L. E. and Klugel, R. J. (1978) 'Determinants of juvenile court dispositions', *Amer. Sociol. Rev.*, 43: 162–76.
Cohen, L. E. and Klugel, R. J. (1979) 'The detention decision', *Social Forces*, 58: 146–61.
Cohen, L. E. and Felson, M. (1979) 'Social change and crime rate trends', *Amer. Sociol. Rev.*, 44: 588–607.
Cohen, L. E., Felson, M. and Land, K. C. (1980) 'Property crime rates in the U.S.: a macrodynamic analysis, 1947–1977', *Amer. J. Sociol.*, 86: 90–118.
Cohen, L. E. and Land, K. C. (1984) 'Discrepancies between crime reports and crime surveys', *Criminology*, 22: 499–530.
Cohen, S. (1972) *Folk Devils and Moral Panics* (London: MacGibbon & Kee).
Cohen, S. (1985) *Visions of Social Control* (London: Polity Press).
Cohen, S. and Taylor, L. (1976) *Prison Secrets* (London: NCCL/RAP).
Colledge, M. and Bartholomew, R. (1980) 'The long-term unemployed', *Employment Gazette*, 88: 9–12.
Conklin, J. E. (1977) *Illegal But Not Criminal* (New Jersey: Spectrum).
Cook, P. J. and Zarkin, G. A. (1985) 'Crime and the business cycle', *J. Legal Studies*, 14: 115–28.
Corbett, M. (1981) 'Public support for "law and order"', *Criminology*, 19: 328–43.
Coser, L. A. (1963) *Continuities in Social Conflict* (New York: Free Press).

Coulter, J., Miller, S. and Walker, M. (1984) *State of Siege* (London: Canary Press).

Council of Europe (1986) *Information Bulletin on Prison Statistics* (Paris: Council of Europe).

Crime and Social Justice Collective (1977) *Iron Fist and Velvet Glove* (San Francisco: Centre for Research on Criminal Justice).

Cullen, F. T., Clark, G. A. and Wozniak, J. F. (1985) 'Explaining the get tough movement: can the public be blamed?' *Federal Probation*, 69: 16–24.

Cullen, F. T. and Gilbert, K. T. (1982) *Reaffirming Rehabilitation* (Cincinnatti: Anderson Pubs).

Cunniff, J. (1983) 'Statistics evidence of what?', *Anniston Star*, 9 February.

Curran, D. J. (1983) 'Judicial discretion and the defendant's sex', *Criminology*, 21: 41–58.

Curry, P. M. (1975) 'Probation and individualised dispositions', *Amer. J. Criminal Law*, 4: 31–81.

Czajkosky, E. (1973) 'Exposing the quasi-judicial role of the probation officer', *Federal Probation*, 37: 9–13.

Dannefer, D. and Schutt, R. K. (1982) 'Race and juvenile justice processing in court and police agencies', *Amer. J. Sociology*, 87: 1113–32.

Danser, K. R. and Laub, J. H. (1981) *Juvenile Criminal Behaviour and Its Relation to Economic Conditions* (Washington, D. C.: Dept. of Justice).

Danziger, S. (1976) 'Explaining urban crime rates', *Criminology*, 14: 291–5.

Danziger, S. and Wheeler, D. (1975) 'The economics of crime: punishment or income redistribution?', *Review of Social Economy*, 33: 113–30.

Davies, M. (1974) *Prisoners of Society* (London: Routledge & Kegan Paul).

Davis, D. S. (1985) 'The production of crime policies', *Crime and Social Justice*, 20: 121–37.

Davis, J. (1983) 'Academic and practical aspects of probation', *Federal Probation*, 47: 7–10.

Dean, M. (1983) 'Figures show misuses of part-suspended sentences', *Guardian*, 1 October.

Dean, M. (1984) 'Brittan may move on fine defaulters', *Guardian*, 11 February.

Decker, S. H. and Kohfeld, C. W. (1982) 'Fox re-examined', *J. Research Crime and Delinq.*, 19: 110–22.

DeFronzo, J. (1983) 'Economic assistance to impoverished Americans', *Criminology*, 21: 119–36.

Ditton, J. (1977) *Part-Time Crime* (London: Macmillan).

Dobbins, D. A. and Bass, B. (1958) 'Effects of unemployment on white and negro prison admissions in Louisiana', *J. Criminal Law, Criminology and Police Science*, 48: 522–5.

Doig, A. (1984) *Corruption and Misconduct* (Harmondsworth: Penguin).

Donnelly, P. G. (1982) 'The origins of the Occupational Safety and Health Act, 1970', *Social Problems*, 30: 13–25.

Douglas, J. D. and Johnson, J. M. (eds) (1977) *Official Deviance* (New York: Lippincott).

Dowie, M. (1977) 'Pinto Madness', *Mother Jones*, 2: 18:34.

Downes, D. and Rock, P. (1982) *Understanding Deviance* (Oxford: Clarendon).

Ehrlich, I. (1973) 'Participation in illegitimate activities', *J. Political Economy*, 81: 521–65.

Ehrlich, I. (1975) 'Deterrent effect of capital punishment', *Amer. Econ. Rev.*, 65: 397–417.

Elliott, D. A. and Ageton, S. S. (1980) 'Reconciling race and class differences in self-reported and official estimates of delinquency', *Amer. Sociol. Rev.*, 45: 95–110.

Erickson, M. L., Gibbs, J. P. and Jensen, G. F. (1977) 'The deterrence doctrine and the perceived certainty of legal punishments', *Amer. Sociol. Rev.*, 42: 305–17.

Ermann, M. D. and Lundman, R. L. (1982) *Corporate Deviance* (New York: Holt, Rinehart & Winston).

Fagin, L. and Little, M. (1984) *Forsaken Families* (Harmondsworth: Penguin).

Farrington, D. P. and Morris, A. M. (1983) 'Sex, sentencing and reconviction', *Brit. J. Criminology*, 23: 229–48.

Fine, B. and Millar, R. (1985) Policing the Miners' Strike (London: Lawrence & Wishart).

Fisher, C. J. and Mawby, R. I. (1982) 'Juvenile delinquency and police discretion in an innercity area', *Brit. J. Criminol.*, 22: 63–75.

Fisse, B. and Braithwaite, J. (1983) *The Impact of Publicity on Corporate Crime* (Albany: State Univ. New York Press).

Fitzmaurice, C. and Pease, K. (1982) 'Prison sentences and population: a comparison of some European countries', *Justice of the Peace*, 18 Sept., 575–8.

Fleisher, B. M. (1963) 'The effect of unemployment on juvenile delinquency', *J. Political Economy*, 71: 543–55.

Fludger, N. (1981) *Ethnic Minorities in Borstal* (London: Prison Department, Home Office).

Fogel, D. (1975) *We Are the Living Proof* (Cincinnati: Anderson).

Forst, B. (1976) 'Participation in illegitimate activities', *Policy Analysis*, 2: 477–92.

Fox, J. (1978) *Forecasting Crime Data* (Lexington: D. C. Heath).

Frazier, C. E. and Bock, E. W. (1982) 'Effects of court officials on sentencing severity', *Criminology*, 20: 257–72.

Frazier, C. E., Bock, E. W. and Henretta, J. C. (1983) 'The role of probation officers in determining gender differences in sentencing severity', *Sociological Qrtly.*, 24: 305–18.

Freeman, R. B. (1983) 'Crime and unemployment', in J. Q. Wilson (ed.), *Crime and Public Policy* (San Francisco: Institute of Contemporary Studies).

Funke, A. (1985) 'Costs of alternatives to prison', *Federal Probation*, 69: 56–61.

Galster, G. C. and Scaturo, L. A. (1985) 'The U. S. criminal justice system: unemployment and the severity of punishment', *J. Research Crime and Delinq.*, 22, 163–89.

Garofalo, J. (1979) 'Victimisation and fear of crime', *J. Research Crime and Delinq.*, 16: 80–97.

Geis, G. (1967) 'The heavy electrical equipment anti-trust cases of 1961', in M. B. Clinard, and R. Quinney (eds), *Criminal Behaviour Systems* (New York: Holt, Rinehard & Winston).

Geis, G. and Meier, R. F. (1977) *White Collar Crime* (New York: Free Press).

Geis, G. and Stotland, E. (eds) (1980) *White Collar Crime: Theory and Research* (Beverly Hills: Sage).

Glaser, D. and Rice, K. (1959) 'Crime, age and employment', *Amer. Sociol. Rev.*, 24: 79–86.

Gordon, D. (1971) 'Class and the economics of crime', *Review of Radical Political Economy*, 2: 51–75.

Gordon, M. T., Riger, S., LeBailey, R. K. and Heath, L. (1980) 'Crime, women and the quality of urban life', *Signs*, 5: S144–S160.

Gottfredson, G. (1979) 'Models and muddles', *J. Research Crime Delinq.*, 16: 307–31.

Gottfredson, G. (1984) *Fear of Crime* (London: HMSO).

Grabosky, P. N. (1979) 'Economic conditions and penal severity: testing a neo-Marxian hypothesis' (unpublished paper).

Greenberg, D. F. (1977) 'The dynamics of oscillatory punishment processes', *J. Criminal Law and Criminology*, 68: 643–51.

Greenberg, D. F. (1980) 'Penal sanctions in Poland: a test of alternative models', *Social Problems*, 28: 195–204.

Greenberg, D. F. and Humphries, D. (1980) 'The co-optation of fixed sentencing reform', *Crime and Delinq.*, 26: 206–25.

Greenwood, P. W. (1983) 'Controlling the crime rate through imprisonment', in J. Q. Wilson (ed.), *Crime and Public Policy* (San Francisco: Institute of Contemporary Studies).

Griffiths, J. S. (1977) *The Political of the Judiciary* (London: Fontana).

Gross, E. (1978) 'Organisational sources of crime: a theoretical perspective', in N. K. Denzin (ed.), *Studies in Symbolic Interaction* (Greenwich CT: JAI Press).

Guttentag, M. (1967) 'Relationship of unemployment to crime and delinquency', *J. Social Issues*, 24: 105–14.

Gylys, J. A. (1970) 'Causes of crime and application of regional analysis', *Atlanta Economic Rev.*, 20: 34–37.

Hagan, J. (1975) 'The social and legal construction of criminal justice', *Social Problems*, 22: 620–37.

Hagan, J., Hewitt, J. and Alwin, D. (1979) 'Ceremonial justice', *Social Forces*, 58: 506–27.

Hakim, C. (1982) 'The social consequences of high unemployment', *J. Social Policy*, 11: 433–67.

Hall, S., Critcher, C., Jefferson, T., Clarke, J. and Roberts, B. (1978) *Policing the Crisis* (London: Macmillan).

Hapgood, D. (1974) *Screwing the Average Man* (New York: Banton).

Harrison, P. (1983) *Inside the Inner City* (Harmondsworth: Penguin).

Heineke, J. M. (1978) 'Economic models of criminal behaviour', in J. M. Heineke (ed.), *Economic Models of Criminal Behaviour* (New York: North-Holland).

Hemley, D. D. and McPheters, L. R. (1974) 'Crime as an externality of regional economic growth', *Rev. Regional Studies*, 4: 73–84.

Henry, S. (1978) *Informal Economy* (London: Martin Robertson).

Hewitt, P. (1982) *The Abuse of Power* (London: Martin Robertson).

Hindelang, M. (1978) 'Race and involvement in common law personal crimes', *Amer. Sociol. Rev.*, 43: 93–109.

Hindelang, M. (1981) 'Variations in sex–age–race-specific rates of offending', *Amer. Sociol. Rev.*, 46: 461–74.

Hine, J., McWilliams, D. and Pease, K. (1978) 'Recommendations, social information and sentencing', *Howard J.*, 17:91–100.

Hirschi, T. (1969) *Cause of Delinquency* (California University Press).

Hirschi, T. (1979) 'Separate but equal is better', *J. Research Crime and Delinq.*, 16: 34–8.

Hoch, I. (1974) 'Factors in urban crime', *J. Urban Economics*, 1: 184–229.

Hochstedler, E. (ed.)(1984)*Corporations as Criminals* (Beverly Hills: Sage).

Hogarth, J. (1971) *Sentencing is a Human Process* (University Toronto Press).

Hollinger, R. C. and Clark, J. P. (1983) *Theft By Employees* (Lexington: Heath).

Home Office (1985) *Criminal Statistics 1984* (London: HMSO).

Home Office (1986) *Statistical Bulletin on Ethnic Groups in Prison* (London: HMSO).

Horan, P. M., Myers, M. A. and Farnworth, M. (1983) 'Prior record and court processes; the role of latent theory in criminology research', *Sociology and Social Research*, 67: 40–58.

Hough, M. and Mayhew, P. (1985) *Taking Account of Crime* (London: HMSO).

Hough, M. and Moxon, D. (1985) 'Dealing with offenders: popular opinion and the views of victims', *Howard Journal*, 24: 160–75.

House of Lords (1982) *Report from the Select Committee on Unemployment* (London: HMSO).

Hudson, B. (1985) 'The rising use of imprisonment', *Critical Social Policy*, 11: 46–59.

Hughes, E. (1963) 'Good people and dirty work', *Social Problems*, 10: 3–10.

Hylton, J. (1981) 'The growth of punishment: imprisonment and community corrections in Canada', *Crime and Social Justice*, 15: 18–28.

Jackson, P. I. and Carroll, L. (1981) 'Race and the war on crime', *Amer. Sociol. Rev.*, 46: 290–305.

Jacobs, J. (1978) 'Inequality and the legal order: an ecological test of the conflict view', *Social Problems*, 25:515–25.

Jacobs, J. (1979) 'Inequality and police strength', *Amer. Sociol. Rev.*, 44: 913–25.
Jacobs, J. (1981) 'Inequality and economic crime', *Sociology and Social Research*, 66: 12–28.
Jacobs, J. and Britt, D. (1979) 'Inequality and police use of deadly force', *Social Problems*, 26: 403–12.
Jahoda, M. (1982) *Employment and Unemployment: A Social- Psychological Analysis* (Cambridge University Press).
Jankovic, I. (1977) 'Labour market and imprisonment', *Crime and Social Justice*, 9: 17–31.
Jensen, G. F., Erickson, M. L. and Gibbs, J. P. (1978) 'Perceived risk of punishment and self-reported delinquency', *Social Forces*, 57: 37–58.
Johnson, J. M. and Douglas, J. D. (eds) (1978) *Crime at the Top* (New York: Lippincott).
Johnson, R. E. (1979) *Juvenile Delinquency and its Origins* (Cambridge University Press).
Jordan, B. (1982) *Mass Unemployment and the Future of Britain* (Oxford: Blackwell).
Joubert, P. E., Picou, J. S. and McIntosh, W. A. (1981) 'U.S. social structure, crime and imprisonment', *Criminology*, 19: 344–59.
Katz, J. (1982) 'The attitudes and decision of probation officers', *Criminal Justice and Behaviour*, 9: 455–74.
Kellough, D. G., Brickey, S. L. and Greenaway, W. K. (1980) 'The politics of incarceration: Manitoba, 1918–1939', *Canadian J. Sociol.*, 5: 253–71.
Kingsworth, R. and Rizzo, L. (1979) 'Decision making in the criminal court', *Criminology*, 17: 3–14.
Kinsey, R., Lea, J. and Young, J. (1986) *Losing the Battle Against Crime* (Oxford: Blackwell).
Klein, D. (1981) 'Violence against women: some considerations regarding its causes and its elimination', *Crime and Delinquency*, 27: 64–80.
Kruttschnitt, C. (1984) 'Sex and criminal court dispositions: the unresolved controversy', *J. Research Crime and Delinq.*, 21: 213–32.
Kruttschnitt, C. (1985) 'Legal outcome and legal agents: adding another dimension to the sex-sentencing controversy', *Law and Human Behaviour*, 9: 287–304.
Kvalseth, T. O. (1977) 'A note on the effects of population density and unemployment on urban crime', *Criminology*, 15: 105–10.
LaGrange, R. L. and White, H. R. (1985) 'Age differences in delinquency: a test of theory', *Criminology*, 23: 19–45.
Land, K. C. and Felson, M. (1976) 'A general framework for building dynamic macro indicator models', *Amer. J. Sociol.*, 82: 565–604.
Landau, S. F. (1981) 'Juveniles and the police', *Brit. J. Criminology*, 21: 27–46.
Landau, S. F. and Nathan, G. (1983) 'Selecting delinquents for cautioning in the London Metropolitan area', *Brit. J. Criminology*, 23: 128–49.
Landes, W. M. (1974) 'Legality and reality', *J. Legal Studies*, 3: 281–337.

Laub, J. H. (1983) 'Trends in serious juvenile crime', *Criminal Justice and Behaviour*, 10: 485–506.

Lea, J. and Young, J. (1984) *Law and Order* (Harmondsworth: Penguin).

Leigh, L. H. (1982) *The Control of Commercial Fraud* (London: Heinemann).

Lemert, E. M. (1967) *Human Deviance, Social Problems and Social Control* (New Jersey: Prentice-Hall).

Lemert, E. M. (1981) 'Diversion in juvenile justice: what hath been wrought?' *Research Crime and Delinq.*, 18: 34–45.

Leveson, I. (1976) *The Growth of Crime* (Croton on Hudson: Hudson Institute).

Levi, M. (1981) *The Phantom Capitalists* (London: Heinemann).

Liska, A. E. and Tausig, M. (1979) 'Theoretical interpretations of social class and racial differentials in legal decision-making for juveniles', *Sociol. Qrtly.*, 20: 197–207.

Loftin, C. and Hill, R. H. (1974) 'Regional subculture and homicide', *Amer. Sociol. Rev.*, 39: 714–24.

Long, S. K. and Witte, A. (1981) 'Current economic trends: implications for crime and criminal justice', in Wright, K. N. (ed.), *Crime and Criminal Justice in a Declining Economy* (Mass.: Oelgeschlager, Gunn & Hain).

Lotz, R. and Hewitt, J. D. (1977) 'The influence of legally irrelevant factors on felony sentencing', *Sociological Inquiry*, 50: 65–74.

MacBarnet, D. (1982) *Conviction* (London: Macmillan).

Mack, J. and Lansley (1985) *Poor Britain* (London: Allen & Unwin).

Marenin, O., Pisciotta, A. W. and Juliani, T. J. (1983) 'Economic conditions and social control', *Criminal Justice Rev.*, 8: 43–53.

Mark, R. (1979) *In The Office of Constable* (London: Collins).

Mars, G. (1983) *Cheats At Work* (London: Unwin).

Martinson, R. (1974) 'What works?' – questions and answers about prison reform', *Public Interest*, 35: 22–54.

Marx, K. (1977[1867]) Trans. Ben Fowkes, *Capital*, I (New York: International Publishers).

Mathiesen, T. (1974) *The Politics of Abolition* (London: Martin Robertson).

Matthews, R. and Young, J. (eds) (1986) *Confronting Crime* (London: Sage).

Matza, D. (1964) *Delinquency and Drift* (New York: Wiley).

Matza, D. (1969) *Becoming Deviant* (New Jersey: Prentice-Hall).

Maxfield, M. (1984) *Fear of crime in England and Wales* (London: HMSO).

McGuire, W. J. and Sheehen, R. G. (1983) 'Relationships between crime rates and incarceration rates', *J. Research Crime and Delinq.*, 20: 73–85.

Merton, R. K. (1957) *Social Theory and Social Structure* (New York: Free Press).

Messner, S. (1982) 'Poverty, inequality and the urban homicide rate', *Criminology*, 20: 103–14.

Messner, S. (1984) 'The "dark figure" and composite indices of crime', *J. Criminal Justice*, 12: 434–44.

Mills, C. W. (1956) *The Power Elite* (Oxford University Press).

Minor, W. W. and Harry, J. (1982) 'Deterrent and experiental effects in perceptual deterrence research', *J. Research Crime Delinq.*, 19: 190–203.

Mitford, J. (1977) *The American Prison Business* (Harmondsworth: Penguin).

Morris, N. and Hawkins, G. (1969) *Honest Politician's Guide to Crime Control* (Chicago University Press).

Moxon, D. (1983) 'Fine default: unemployment and the use of imprisonment', *Research Bulletin*, (London: Home Office) 16: 38–42.

Murrah, A. (1963) 'Prison or probation – which and why?', in Kay, B. and Vedder, C. (eds), *Probation and Parole* (Springfield: C. C. Thomas).

Myers, M. (1979) 'Offended parties and official reactions: victims and the sentencing of criminal defendants', *Sociol. Qrtly.*, 20: 529–40.

Nader, R. (1965) *Unsafe at Any Speed* (New York: Grossman).

Nagel, I. H. (1983) 'The legal/extra-legal controversy: judicial decisions in pretrial release', *Law and Society Rev.*, 17: 482–515.

Nagel, W. (1977) 'On behalf of a moratorium on prison construction', *Crime and Delinq.*, 23: 154–72.

NAPO (1984) *Fine Defaulters and Debtor's Prisons* (London: NAPO).

Neubauer, D. (1974) *Criminal Justice in Middle America* (Morristown, NJ.: General Learning Press).

O'Brien, R. M. (1985) *Crime and Victimization Data* (Beverly Hills: Sage).

Orsagh, T. (1979) 'Empirical criminology', *J. Research Crime and Delinq.*, 16: 294–306.

Orsagh, T. (1980) 'Unemployment and crime: an objection to Professor Brenner's view', *J. Criminal Law and Criminology* 71: 181–3.

Orsagh, T. (1981) 'A criminogenic model of the criminal justice system', in Fox, J. A. (ed.), *Models in Quantitative Criminology* (New York: Academic Press).

Papandreou, N., Speed, T. P., McDonald, S. E., Skates, S. and Landauer, A. A. (1982) 'Factors influence the pre-sentence report', *Aust. & New Zealand J. Criminology*, 15: 207–18.

Parkin, F. (1971) *Class, Inequality and Political Order* (London: MacGibbon & Kee).

Paternoster, R., Saltzman, L. S., Chiricos, T. G. and Waldo, G. P. (1983) 'Estimating perceptual stability and deterrent effects', *J. Criminal Law and Criminology*, 74: 270–97.

Pearson, G. (1983) *Hooligan: A History of Respectable Fears* (London: Macmillan).

Petersilia, J. (1985) 'Probation and felony offenders', *Federal Probation*, 69: 4–9.

Phillips, L. (1981) 'Some aspects of the social pathological behavioural effects of unemployment among young people', in Rottenberg, S. (ed.), *Economics of Minimum Wages* (Iowa: American Enterprise Institute). pp. 174–90.

Phillips, L. and Votey, H. L. (1981) 'Crime generation and economic opportunities for youth', in their *The Economics of Crime Control* (Beverly Hills: Sage).

Phillips, L. 'Votey, H. L. and Maxwell, D. (1972) 'Crime, youth, and the labour market', *J. Political Economy*, 80: 491–503.

Piven, F. F. and Cloward, R. A. (1982) *The New Class War* (New York: Pantheon).

Platt, A. (1982) 'Managing the crisis: austerity and the penal system', *Contemporary Marxism*, 4: 29–39.

Pogue, T. F. (1975) 'Effects of police expenditure on crime rates: some evidence', *Public Finance Qrtly.*, 3:14–44.

Pratt, J. (1983) 'Reflections on the approach of 1984', *Inter. J. Sociology of Law*, 11: 339–60.

Pyle, D. J. (1982) *Property Crime in England and Wales* (University of Leicester Economics Dept.).

Quinney, R. (1974) *Critique of Legal Order* (Boston: Little, Brown).

Quinney, R. (1977) *Class, State and Crime* (New York: Longman).

Quinney, R. (1980) *Class, State and Crime*, 2nd edn (London: Longman).

Ramsay, M. (1982) 'Mugging: fears and facts', *New Society*, 25 March: 247–9.

Reasons, C. E. and Kaplan, R. L. (1975) 'Tear down the walls? Some functions of prison', *Crime and Delinq.*, 21: 360–72.

Reasons, C. E., Paterson, C. and Ross, L. (1981) *Assault on the Worker* (Toronto: Butterworth).

Reiman, J. H. (1982) 'Marxist explanations and radical misinterpretations', *Crime and Delinq.*, 28: 610–17.

Reiman, J. H. (1984) *The Rich Get Richer and the Poor Get Prison*, 2nd edn (New York: Wiley).

Reiner, R. (1985) *The Politics of the Police* (Brighton: Wheatsheaf).

Reisman, W. (1979) *Folded Lies* (New York: Free Press).

Roberts, J. and Roberts, C. (1982) 'Social Enquiry Reports and sentencing', *Howard Journal*, 21: 76–93.

Robin, G. D. (1970) 'Corporate and judicial disposition of employee thieves', in Smigel, E. O. and Ross, H. L. (eds), *Crimes Against Bureaucracy* (New York: Van Nostrand).

Robinson, W. H., Smith, P. and Wolf, J. (1974) *Prison Population and Costs* (Washington, D. C.: Library of Congress Congressional Research Service).

Rogowski, E. (1985) 'MSC and YTS', *Youth and Society*, 13: 15–19.

Rosecrance, J. (1985) 'The probation officer's search for credibility', *Crime and Delinq.*, 31: 539–54.

Runciman, W. G. (1966) *Relative Deprivation and Social Justice* (London: Routledge & Kegan Paul).

Rusche, G. and Kirchheimer, O. (1939) *Punishment and Social Structure* (New York: Russell & Russell).

Rutherford, A. (1984) *Prisons and the Process of Justice* (London: Heinemann).

Ryan, M. (1983) *The Politics of Reform* (London: Longman).

Saltzman, L. S., Paternoster, R., Waldo, G. P. and Chiricos, T. G. (1982) 'Deterrent and experimental effects', *J. Research Crime and Delinq.*, 19: 172–89.

Sampson, R. J., Castellano, T. L. and Laub, J. H. (1981) *Juvenile Criminal Behaviour and Its Relationship to Neighbourhood Characteristics* (Albany, N. Y.: Criminal Justice Research Centre).

Savitz, L. D. (1978) 'Official police statistics and their limitations', in Savitz, L. D. and Honston, N. (eds), *Crime in Society* (New York: Wiley).

Scarman, L. G. (1982) *The Scarman Report* (Harmondsworth: Penguin).

Schmid C. F. (1960) 'Urban crime areas', *Amer. Sociol. Rev.*, 25: 527–42, 655–78.

Schuessler, K. F. and Slatin, G. (1964) 'Sources of variation in U.S. city crime', *J. Research Crime and Delinq.*, 1: 127–48.

Schwartz, R. D. and Skolnick, J. H. (1964) 'Two sides of legal stigma', in Becker, H. S. (ed.), *The Other Side* (New York: Free Press).

Scott, R. (1974) *Muscle and Blood: The Massive, Hidden Agony of Industrial Slaughter in America* (New York: Dutton).

Scraton, P. (1985) *The State of the Police* (London: Pluto).

Scull, A. (1977) *Decarceration* (New Jersey: Prentice-Hall).

Shaw, S. (1982) *People's Justice* (London: Prison Reform Trust).

Simon, D. R. and Eitzen, D. S. (1982) *Elite Deviance* (Boston: Allyn & Bacon).

Singell, L. D. (1967) 'Examination of the empirical relationships between unemployment and juvenile delinquency', *Amer. J. Economics and Sociol.*, 26: 377–86.

Singer, R. G. (1979) *Just Deserts* (Mass.: Ballinger).

Sjoquist, D. L. (1973) 'Property crime and economic behaviour', *Amer. Econ. Rev.*, 63: 439–46.

Skogan, W. (1974) 'The validity of official crime statistics: an empirical investigation', *Social Science Qrtly.*, 55: 25–38.

Skogan, W. (1976) 'Crime and crime rates', in Skogan, W. (ed.), *Sample Surveys and the Victims of Crime* (Mass.: Ballinger).

Smith, D. and Gray, L. (1983) *Police and People in London* (London: Policy Studies Unit).

Smith, D. A. and Visher, C. A. (1981) 'Street-level justice: situational determinants of police arrest decisions', *Social Problems*, 29: 167–77.

Smith, M. D. and Bennett, N. (1985) 'Poverty, inequality and theories of forcible rape', *Crime and Delinquency*, 31: 295–305.

Smith, M. D. and Parker, R. N. (1980) 'Deterrence, poverty and type of homicide', *Amer. J. Sociology*, 85: 614–24.

Smith, S. J. (1983) 'Public policy and the effects of crime in the inner city: a British example', *Urban Studies*, 20: 229–40.

Southgate, P. and Field, S. (1982) *Public Disorder* (London: Home Office).

Spector, P. E. (1975) 'Population density and unemployment: the effects on the incidence of violent crime in the American city', *Criminology*, 12: 389–401.

Spencer, S. (1985) *Called to Account* (London: National Council for Civil Liberties).

Spohn, C., Gruhl, J. and Welch, S. (1981) 'The effect of race on sentencing', *Law and Society Rev.*, 16: 71–88.

Spitzer, S. (1975) 'Towards a marxian theory of crime', *Social Problems*, 22: 368–401.

Stack, S. (1984) 'Income inequality and property crime', *Criminology*, 22: 229–58.

Stack, S. and Kanavy, M. J. (1983) 'The effects of religion on forcible rape', *J. Scientific Study Religion*, 22: 67–74.

Stafford, M. C. and Galle, O. R. (1984) 'Victimization rates, exposure to risk and fear of crime', *Criminology*, 22: 173–85.

Stebbins, R. A. (1971) *Commitment to Deviance* (Connecticut: Greenwood).

Stern, L. T. (1940) 'The effects of the depression on prison commitments and sentences', *J. Criminal Law and Criminology*, 31: 696–711.

Stevens, P. (1979) 'Predicting black crime', *Research Bulletin* (London: Home Office) 8: 14–18.

Stevens, P. and Willis, C. F. (1979) *Race, Crime and Arrests* (London: Home Office).

Stevens, P. and Willis, C. F. (1981) *Ethnic Minorities and Complaints Against the Police* (London: Home Office).

Straus, M., Gelles, R. and Steinmetz, S. (1980) *Behind Closed Doors* (New York: Doubleday).

Sutherland, E. (1940) 'White-collar criminality', *Amer. Sociol. Rev.*, 5: 1–12.

Sutherland, E. (1945) 'Is "white-collar crime" crime?', *Amer. Sociol. Rev.*, 10: 132–9.

Sutherland, E. (1949) *White Collar Crime* (New York: Holt, Rinehart & Winston).

Swartz, J. (1975) 'Silent killers at work', *Crime and Social Justice*, 3:15–20.

Swimmer, G. (1974) 'Relationship between police and crime', *Criminology*, 12: 293–314.

Szasz, A. (1984) 'Industrial resistance to Occupational Safety and Health legislation: 1971–1981', *Social Problems*, 32: 103–16.

Tataryn, L. (1979) *Dying For A Living* (Toronto: Deneau & Greenberg).

Taylor, I., Walton, P. and Young, J. (1973) *New Criminology* (London: Routledge & Kegan Paul).

Thomas, J. E. and Pooley, R. (1980) *The Exploding Prison* (London: Junction Books).

Thompson, R. J. and Zingraff, M. T. (1981) 'Detecting sentencing disparity: some problems and evidence', *American Criminal Law Rev.*, 11: 355–72.

Thornberry, T. P. and Christenson, R. (1984) 'Unemployment and criminal involvement', *Amer. Sociol. Rev.*, 49: 398–411.

Thornberry, T. P. and Farnworth, M. (1982) 'Social correlates of criminal involvement', *Amer Sociol. Rev.*, 47: 505–18.

Thornberry, T. P., Moore, M. and Christenson, R. L. (1985) 'The effect of dropping out of high school on subsequent criminal behaviour', *Criminology*, 23: 3–18.

Thornes, B. and Collard, B. (1979) *Who Divorces?* (London: Routledge & Kegan Paul).

Tittle, C. R. (1977) 'Sanctions and the maintenance of social order', *Social Forces*, 55: 579–96.

Tittle, C. R. (1980) *Sanctions and Deviance* (New York: Praeger).

Tulkens H. (1979) *Some Developments in Penal Police and Practice in Holland* (London: Barry Rose).

Turk, A. (1969) *Criminality and Legal Order* (Chicago: Rand-McNally).

Turk, A. (1976) 'Law as a weapon in social conflict', *Social Problems*, 23: 276–91.

Twentieth Century Fund (1976) *Fair and Certain Punishment* (New York: TCF).

Unnever, J. D., Frazier, C. E. and Henretta, J. C. (1980) 'Race differences in criminal sentencing', *Sociological Qrtly.*, 21: 197–205.

Vandaele, W. (1978) 'An econometric model of auto-theft in the U.S.', in Heineke, J. M. (ed.), *Economic Models of Criminal Behaviour* (New York: North-Holland Pubs).

Von Hirsch, A. (1976) *Doing Justice* (New York: Hill & Wang).

Votey, H. L. (1979) 'Detention of heroin addicts, job opportunities and deterrence', *J. Legal Studies*, 8: 585–606.

Votey, H. L. and Phillips, L. (1969) *Economic Crimes: Their Generation, Deterrence, and Control* (Springfield, Va.: U.S. Clearinghouse Federal Scientific and Technical Information).

Wadycki, W. J. and Balkin, S. (1979) 'Participation in illegimate activities', *J. Behavioural Economics*, 8: 151–63.

Waldo, G. P. and Chiricos, T. G. (1972) 'Perceived penal sanction and self-reported criminality', *Social Problems*, 19: 522–40.

Walker, H. and Beaumont, B. (1981) *Probation Work* (Oxford: Blackwell).

Wallace, D. (1980) 'The political economy of incarceration trends in late U.S. capitalism: 1971–1977', *Insurgent Sociologist*, 10: 59–65.

Wallace, D. and Humphries, D. (1980) 'Capitalist accumulation and urban crime, 1950–1971', *Social Problems*, 28: 179–93.

Walsh, A. (1985) 'The role of the probation officers in the sentencing process', *Criminal Justice and Behaviour*, 12: 289–304.

Weicher, J. C. (1971) 'Effect of income and delinquency', *Amer. Econ. Rev.*, 60: 249–56.

Weidenbaum, M. C. (1979) *The Future of Business Regulation* (New York: Amacon).

White, S. (1972) 'The effect of social inquiry reports on sentencing decisions', *Brit. J. Criminology*, 12: 230–49.

Williams, K. R. (1984) 'Economic sources of homicide: reestimating the effects of poverty and inequality', *Amer. Sociol. Rev.*, 49: 283–9.

Williams, K. R. and Drake, S. (1980) 'Social structure, crime and criminalisation: an empirical examination of the conflict perspective', *Sociol. Qrtly.*, 21: 563–75.

Willis, C. F. (1983) *The Use, Effectiveness and Impact of Police Stop and Search Powers* (London: Home Office).

Wilson, J. Q. (1975) *Thinking About Crime* (New York: Basic Books).

Wilson, J. Q. (1982) as quoted in Kristof, D. N., 'Scholars disagree on connection between crime and jobless', *Washington Post*, 7 August: A8 col. 3.

Wolfgang, M. E., Figlio, R. M. and Sellin, T. (1972) *Delinquency in a Birth Cohort* (Chicago University Press).

Wolfgang, M. E., Thornberry, T. P. and Figlio, R. M. (1985) *From Boy to Man – From Delinquency to Crime* (Chicago University Press).

Wolpin, K. I. (1978) 'An economic analysis of crime and punishment in England and Wales, 1894–1967', *J. Political Economy*, 86: 815–40.

Wright, M. (1982) *Making Good* (London: Burnett).

Yeager, M. G. (1979) 'Unemployment and imprisonment', *J. Criminology and Criminal Law*, 70: 586–8.

Yin, P. P. (1980) 'Fear of crime among the elderly', *J. Criminal Law and Criminology*, 70: 585–8.

Yin, P. P. (1982) 'Fear of crime as a problem for the elderly', *Social Problems*, 30: 240–45.

Young, J. (1979) 'Left idealism, reformism and beyond: from new criminology to Marxism', in National Deviancy Conference, *Capitalism and the Rule of Law* (London: Hutchinson).

Young, J. (1986) *Realist Criminology* (forthcoming).

Zedlewski, E. W. (1983) 'Deterrence findings and data sources', *J. Research Crime and Delinq.*, 20: 262–76.

Index